NLP 4 Me!

A Neurolinguistic Course for English Learners

Debrah Roundy

Xinghua Liu

Cranmore Publications

Copyright © 2015 by Debrah Roundy & Xinghua Liu

All rights reserved. This book, or parts thereof, may not be reproduced in any form without permission.

A catalogue record for this book is available from the British Library

ISBN: 978-1-907962-85-1

Published by Cranmore Publications

www.cranmorepublications.co.uk

Meet the Author

Native of Idaho in the USA, **Prof. Debrah Roundy** graduated from the University of Idaho with a M.Ed. and from NLPU as an NLP Master Trainer and Consultant (2009) and a facilitator and transformational entrepreneur (2014). She has been a teacher, special education teacher, a developmental specialist, a school consultant and a Neurolinguist teacher, developer and coach. Her research interest is curriculum development and she created much of the curriculum used in her classroom. She has written a book on Neurolinguistic Programs for special needs and elementary school children called *"NLP 4 Me!"*. Debrah currently works at Tongji University as a Foreign Language Expert with BYU China Teacher's Program in Shanghai, China and as such is titled a professor as an honorary title.

Debrah is the first person as far as we know who has brought NLP to college students in China and the first person who has used NLP as a way to acquire and enhance English Speaking skills.

Meet the Editor

Dr. Xinghua Liu works as a Lecturer in Applied Linguistics at Shanghai Jiao Tong University, China and is the Chief Editor of TESOL International Journal (www.tesol-international.com). His research interests include second language writing, corpus linguistics and systemic functional linguistics.

Preface

A Neurolinguistic Course for English Learners is the first ever book written about Neurolinguistic Programs (NLP) for college students in China and possibly in the world. As an NLP innovator and program developer, I have developed this text book to enhance the skills of English acquisition through the use of NLP programs and skills. The text book and course include reading, writing, listening, comprehending and speaking English skills. Students who complete the course with a certified NLP trainer, will complete the Practitioner Level of certification. Skills presented in the book include but are not limited to the core process, Circle of Excellence, TOTE model, Logical Level Alignment, Eye Accessing Cues, the Meta Model and more.

It is expected that a teacher of NLP on a college level will have been certified by an NLP agency with a certificate higher than an NLP Master. Included would be Master Trainer, Global Trainer, Trainer and Consultancy, and other similar certifications depending on the certifying organization. Generally a Master Certification includes a minimum of 240 hours of training. A weekend workshop is not enough to be qualified to teach this class as a certifiable course in NLP.

Much of the course book was translated into Chinese by students of Debrah Roundy to enhance their translation skills.

Table of Contents

1	Introduction to NLP and the New Name Strategy	9
2	Circle of Excellence	15
3	Stress and the Six Second Stress Buster	21
4	Well-Formed Outcomes	27
5	TOTE Model in Two Sections Beginning and Advanced	33
6	Neurological Level Alignment or NLLA	45
7	Somatic Brain	62
8	Eye Accessing Cues	69
9	Representational Systems and Learning	76
10	Reading Submodalities and Mapping Across	84
11	Building Rapport and the B.A.G.E.L.	90
12	Extemporaneous Speaking and C.O.A.C.H. State	102
13	Para Language	108
14	Perceptual Positions	115
15	Psychogeography and Job Interviews	119
16	Contrastive Analysis	125
17	Presuppositions	130
18	Anchors and the Pentagon of Excellence	134
19	Meta Model and Word Patterns #1	142
20	S.C.O.R.E. Program / Dancing S.C.O.R.E.	152
21	Meta Model and Word Patterns #2	161
22	Disney Creativity Strategy	169
23	Metaphors	176
24	Conflict Integration	180
25	SWISH Program	185
26	VK Dissociation	194
27	Xavier's Strategy	198
28	Reframes	205
29	Six-Step Reframe	212
30	Intervision	218
	Sources	223
	Study Guides for Each Lesson	229

Unit 1: Introduction to Neurolinguistic Programs

Mission Statement: Neurolinguists work on the principle that success and failure are not random. Because they are not random, they can be broken into programs and taught to others.

Lesson 1: What NLP Is and What It Isn't

> The purpose of life is a life of purpose. –Robert Byrne

Neurolinguistic Programs, or NLP as it is called, is the study of excellence. Neurolinguists want to learn how they can do what they do better. Just as biology studies life and living matter, or astronomy studies space, stars and the heavens, so NLP studies our mental and emotional world from a linguistic model. If you want to do something more successfully or be more successful, NLP has programs, models, concepts and techniques to do just that whether you are a businessman, a student, a parent, teacher, healer, into sports or whatever you do.

The core principal of NLP is that success and failure are not random (lacking a pattern or plan). We create success or failure through our environment, behaviors, capabilities, believes, values, thoughts, and feelings. We behave, believe, think and feel as we do because that is what we were taught either directly or indirectly through experiences we have had in life. Our teachers include our environment, our ancestry, families, culture, school, peers, friends, and experiences.

You look at your parents as exemplars (examples) of what a perfect human is and assume that all parents are just like yours. If your parents overeat, then you will tend to overeat also. Growing up my mother always served dessert at lunch and supper. I assumed all families did and that the noon and evening meal required a sweet finish. When I would take lunches to school there was always a cookie or cupcake tucked inside. Imagine my surprise to learn that many families did not eat desserts twice a day and some only ate desserts once a week or even just on a special occasion. Our family's love of sweets was a cultural thing.

One year I had a student I will call Andy. Andy firmly believed he had attention deficit disorder (ADD). One day I taught Andy how to calm his inner self down. Andy and I together discovered Andy did not need to be ADD. Andy had a therapist who worked with him daily. It was important to the therapist that Andy have ADD. He was her paycheck. She would come in and immediately create Andy's ADD for the day. "Andy can't sit still." She would tell me in Andy's earshot. "What would Andy do without me to keep on him and help keep him at his tasks? He is so flighty." There was a funny thing that we noticed. When the therapist did not come in Andy was calm. His ADD appeared when the therapist walked in the door and disappeared when she walked away. She needed his ADD. (Note that some ADD is environmental but other times it is a medical condition caused by a lack of a neurotransmitter in the brain called norepinephrine.) This is one example of countless we accept as natural but in fact has been created in our minds and then manifest in our bodies.

My husband grew up in a middle class family, but his mother had been a single career woman for years before marrying. She enjoyed having the money and time to buy matching outfits with coordinating accessories and having spending money readily available. Even though she married a banker, six children later she no longer could afford the fun trappings of her single life and felt poor in comparison. My husband often told me how poor they were growing up yet they seemed to have everything my family had and more - they had even built a cabin up in the mountains. We compared and our families had very similar incomes growing up, the difference wasn't the income, it was the attitude our mothers had. My mother had gone from home directly to marriage and had never had a job that afforded her a little spending money and matching outfits to wear.

The key point here is that the things that people identify with and believe, i.e.: 'I grew up poor' or 'a meal must have dessert' or 'I have ADD', are usually changeable. Most beliefs are easily changed. You can change your environment, behaviors, capabilities, beliefs and values, identity and even your spiritual purpose.

Lesson 2: History

"Learning is the discovery that something is possible" --- Fritz Perls

It all started back in the 1970's. This was a time of change, the hippy era. People were looking for new ways of doing things and expanding ideas. The actual date of the start of NLP is 1975 but truly it evolved.

Enter Richard Bandler, one of the co-originators of NLP. Richard was a student at the University of California, Santa Cruz. He was invited to a training by Fritz Perls, a psychoanalyst who developed Gestalt therapy, and Virginia Satir, (1916-1988) a psychotherapist world renowned for her skills in Family Therapy. He found it interesting and started running Gestalt therapy workshops to refine his skills. One day he invited Dr.

John Grinder, an assistant professor of linguistics, who used his knowledge of transformation grammar and the two men worked together to produce several works based first on Perls and later on Satir. The resulting linguistic model analyzed how therapeutic recognition and use of language patterns could on its own be used to influence change. This pattern became known as the Meta Model and was the first core model within what eventually became an entire field of study, NLP.

The word Meta in Meta Model takes the English meaning of about or beyond. The Meta Model is about the models and looks beyond the model. It is newer and looks at previous existing models in a more detailed and highly specialized way. We will be studying Meta Model patterns in a later lesson.

Anthropologist Gregory Bateson became interested in the Meta Model and other work coming from early NLP. His interest and influence lead to the addition of logical levels, logical types, the double bind theory as well as others.

These early studies of and resulting models of recognized geniuses formed the bases of workshops and seminars. Essentially they modeled what geniuses did and then broke it down into programs that could be followed. Titled Neurolinguistic Programming, their popularity spread first to psychotherapists and then to business managers, sales professionals, and New Agers. Eventually NLP filtered down to teachers and educators, sports professionals, medical personal and to you.

NLP increased in popularity and a group formed around the founders that included Leslie Cameron-Bandler, Judith DeLozier, Stephen Gilligan, Robert Dilts and David Gordon. Each of these people made significant contributions to the development and growth of NLP.

The 90's became years of unprecedented and uncontrolled growth. Just as many herbal concoctions hit the market and were touted as a cure-all for everything from colds to cancer so was NLP touted as a universal miracle cure to every problem conceivable. Well researched bona fide models existed alongside models and practices of dubious origin. Many practitioners were more interested in marketability and profit than integrity. New Agers embraced it as a new age phenomena losing sight of the tenants upon which NLP was founded. Those with unscrupulous leanings toted programs to get a girl in bed fast, to sell things to people who were not really interested and to control you. This is exaggerated and often used by people to sell a book or get you to buy something by using hyperbole. (Hyperbole is exaggerating ideas to emphasize them.)

Today there are training organizations that tout that they can teach all the skills in a week or over the internet that others are teaching in a three to four week intensive course of 100 to 150 hours. Learning NLP is a Q2 proposition. Quality teaching is needed, and quantity time is also necessary. Quickie courses sacrifice quality.

Research shows clearly that NLP cannot help all people in all situations but it is useful in many areas and can help people be more successful in many areas including business, health, marriage and family and indeed life. It has become a worldwide study. At least one international college offers a degree in NLP with others offering course work. NLP has gone through its infancy stage, hung on through the wild teen age years and is now maturing into a worldwide accepted field of study - the study of excellence.

Lesson 3: New Name Strategy

The one thing I want to leave my children is an honorable name.
~Theodore Roosevelt

Tim Hallbom and Suzi Smith are NLP modelers, presenters and lecturers. Tim met many people in his business of lecturing around the world and wondered how people remember names.

Tim, and another NLP trainer, Suzi Smith, co-developed (developed with another person) the name strategy by studying the thinking processes of people who remembered names well. Franklin D. Roosevelt, a president of the United States, was one of the people they studied. He was a master at recalling names. He continually amazed his staff by remembering someone's name that he had only met once, months before. Asked how he did it, he said he saw the person's name written out on their forehead. The strategy is based on the way people learn and recall information, which is through the three primary senses of sight, sound and touch.

Let us look at hearing first. The place in your brain that processes where you hear others is
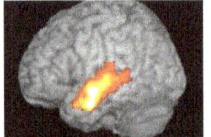
the same place that processes where you talk to yourself. You cannot clearly hear what another person is saying if you are talking to yourself inside. You need to concentrate on what they are saying giving the person your full and undivided attention as you say their name three times to yourself. The visual part is to imagine the person's name written on their forehead. You can even imagine it in a color.

The last way is touch. Write the name with your finger on your hand or leg. Even imagining you are writing it will work. This puts the name deeper into your neurology to help you remember it.If you tell people you like to know how to spell their names correctly they will appreciate you. Practice doing this every time you meet someone new and it will soon be automatic. You will not have to think about it. Last of all, use the name several times in the conversation. This helps imbed the name deeper into your neurology so it will stay longer. A pretty good strategy for a new school year!

Imagine yourself using the New Name Strategy next time you meet someone new. We call this future pacing, imagining yourself doing something in the future. See yourself in your mind's eye giving the person your full attention and writing the name, putting it on the forehead, and using it. This will help you make it automatic.

Give the person all of your attention, do not multi task. (do two or more things at once,)	Pretend their name is on their forehead	Imagine you are writing the name with your finger.	Use the person's name several (more than once or twice) times in the conversation.

Who was a model for this process? In the USA there was a president, Franklin D. Roosevelt, often known as FDR. FDR was the 32nd president of the USA (1933-19450 and was president during World War II. He was well known for being able to recall the name of almost everyone he ever met.

Maybe like Tim Halbom, you, too will be able to remember seventy to eighty new names in a day. Maybe, like FDR, you will be able to recall the name of almost everyone you ever met!

Lesson 4: Hints and tips on using Names

Regard your good name as the richest jewel you can possibly be possessed of - for credit is like fire; when once you have kindled it you may easily preserve it, but if you once extinguish it, you will find it an arduous task to rekindle it again. The way to gain a good reputation is to endeavor to be what you desire to appear. ---Socrates

It is often said that nothing is sweeter than the sound of your name. Knowing a person's name shows you care. It is also important to know a bit about the culture you are in. In some cultures it is best to use last names, others first names. .Know your culture. In American usually last names for elders, first names for peers. An elder would be a person significantly older than you. For a child, an elder would be anyone over 18, a grown up. Some cultures have special titles like auntie (Hawaii) or ayi (China). Showing respect for another person's culture will win you friends and motivate them to want to learn more about your culture also.

Unit 2: Circle of Excellence

"Do not sit down and try to attract the thing you want to you; but begin to move toward the thing you want, and you will find it coming to meet you." --Wallace D. Wattles

Lesson 1: What is a state?

We go through life in states, or conditions of being. Our state of being might be happy, sad, glad, mad or angry. My daughter Alyssa has a darling little baby. When Alyssa leaves, little Chloe works herself up into a big state of anger with crying, kicking and screaming. But as soon as her mommy is gone for a few minutes she calms right down. She works herself up to tell her mommy she wants her to stay. Or she might do it to see if she can make her mommy stay.

People used to think, and many still think, that we have no control over our state of being. Feelings are, by nature, fleeting. We cannot hold on to feelings for very long. We have a built in set point of normal. Studies have been done that show that even when something wonderful or something very terrible happens, within a short time we have gone back to our status quo feelings. As an NLP Practitioner you will learn to manage your own state to be more effective. This will help you in your school work, in speech and debate, and in your future career.

What if we could reach the feelings we wanted to, even if only briefly. NLP has learned a way. By hooking with an anchor a feeling we want to re-access we can recall the feeling for a short time to help us in other situations. We can control feelings and utilize them for our good. This program is just such a program as we learn to bring up powerful feelings, hold them and anchor them to a color. Join now in the exploration.

As an example, let us imagine you are going to give a short speech, like next week for class.
Would it make a difference if you could manage your state and come to class happy? It might make a big difference so look forward to seeing that difference.

Lesson 2: About the Circle of Excellence

The Circle of Excellence is a fundamental (important, original or basic) program of NLP. It is used to help people find a state of optimal performance (the best or most favorable performance) and then to re-access (return to) it when desired. In other words the Circle of Excellence gives people a tool to use to self-manage their own state of being.

In class you likely created (make, bring into existence) your Circle of Excellence on a time you were excellent. You can create it around any state of being you would like such as happy, calm, excited, intense, and so on. Without knowing it, Tai Chi experts create their own state of being similar to a Circle of Excellence for a state of calm and peace as they step into their Tai Chi stance (position or posture) of feet hip distance apart and arms beginning to rise. If you do Tai Chi you know how it happens. I practiced Tai Chi in the USA some years ago. Then my teacher had to quit and I was not able to do it again until I came to China. The very first time I did it and step out into the beginning stance I felt the calm and peace that I had known before return to me.

Runners and other people involved in sports often do the same thing. They have a state of optimal performance and when they take a certain stance it becomes like an anchor (something, often a metal device attached to a boat or ship, that serves to hold something firmly in place) holding them in the state. Your anchor is an imaginary circle. Later in the course you will learn more about anchors.

Let's go over the steps to creating your own circle of Excellence. You may practice the one you did making it even stronger or you may create a new one for something else. Michael Colgrass, a Pulitzer Prize winner and one of my teachers and friends, has a Circle of Excellence he adds to every day. It is just a feeling of good. Each day he looks for something that makes him feel good and he adds it in to his Circle. It might be a nice word someone says to him or a beautiful sunset. He just continues to add things. Then when he steps onto the stage he uses it to access quickly the good feeling he needs to be an effective performer, lecturer and artist. Later you will learn how he holds that feeling with something called an anchor so that you can replicate it yourself.

Lesson 3: Creating Your Circle of Excellence

1.	Choose a state you would like to have more often. A state where your resources (things you have as a supply or source of support) are available to you. Here are some examples: Learning, sports, courage, gentleness, in control, happy, strong, self-assured, creative, or peaceful.
2.	Choose a place on the floor for your imaginary circle. Give your circle a color representing the state you choose. You may wish to add texture and other things to your circle.
3.	Think of a time you were in this state. Relive it as if you were really there. What did you see, hear and feel? You may even add taste and smell. When you feel it strongly step into your circle. Enjoy reliving it.
4.	Step out and talk for a minute or so with your guide. If you are doing it alone just think about something else. We call this breaking state, or taking yourself completely out of that state and into another one.
5.	Test it out. Step back into your imaginary circle. Notice how quickly just stepping back in to an imaginary circle takes you back into the state you created for your circle. When you step back in you should immediately re-access the same feelings. If you want, you may add more resources to it to make it even better. If so, repeat the steps above adding more resources, more times when you had this state of being.
6.	Future pace: Think of a time in the future where you will want to access this state. Imagine yourself stepping into your circle and having immediate access.
7.	Later when you learn anchoring you can learn many ways to anchor this. For now your anchor is your imaginary circle. Some people are very particular about their circle and like to imagine they are picking it up, folding it and putting it in their pocket. Others just imagine it disappearing and reappearing when they need it. It does not matter how you do it. This is your circle and you own it.

People think that everyone does things the same way as they do. This is not true and you will be in for a wonderful exploration of how we are all different as we study

Neurolinguistic Programs this year. Everyone, every person on this earth, is different and it is the differences that make the world interesting.

As you do this program over several times you may begin to notice that there are things that you do every time. Maybe you hold your hands or body in a certain way. You might find your breathing speeds up or slows down. Maybe you notice a lift or a dip of your chin or your shoulders shift. Each person has things that are idiosyncratic or unique to that person. You can become aware of your own personal strategies. Other strategies might be cultural strategies unique (the only one) to your culture. An example would be the Chinese "zh" sound. It is unique to Chinese culture. There is an African tribe that speaks by clicking their tongues. That is an example of the use of a sound that is unique to their culture.

The assignment for this lesson included giving a short speech telling about the experience you put in our Circle of Excellence. Below is a sample speech. Enjoy your exploration as you learn more about----YOU!

Sample Circle of Excellence Speech

Before your speech	Imagine you put your Circle of Excellence in front of you. Take a breath before you start.
Name	Professor Roundy
What event did you put in your Circle of Excellence? This should be something new that you have done since class. What did you see, hear and feel?	I remembered a time when I lead a group of Special Olympics Athletes signing in American Sign Language (ASL) a song called "God Bless America." I could see the audience quietly listening to us. We did very well and I could hear as everyone clapped and cheered afterwards. People reached out to touch us afterward because they wanted to feel our energy. We could feel their joy! I made my circle red and blue with a white star in it to symbolize my country.
Closing statement	Each time I step into my circle I feel like a stand a bit taller because I love my country and the people I was working with. My breathing seems to be deeper and slower as I feel the depth of peace that comes with a job well done.
Finish	Pause before you sit down. Look at your audience and smile.

It can make your talk more interesting if you have a picture to share. For a short talk one picture is just enough. If you choose to share a picture bring it on paper or share it on an iPad.

Sentence content samples for homework:

points	Sample sentences
1-2	I chose a time when I signed a song with my team.
3-4	I signed a song with my team and every one clapped.
5-6	I chose a time when I signed a song in American Sign Language with my special Olympics team and people clapped afterward.
7-8	For my Circle of Excellence I chose a time when I signed a song in American Sign Language with my special Olympics team for a competition and people clapped afterward cheering us as they felt our energy and we felt their joy.
9-10	Several years ago I was with my Special Olympics team, the Spuds. We were asked to sign a song for an opening ceremony and chose to do "God Bless America." After we were done the whole audience clapped and cheered. They reached out to touch us as we returned to our seats because they wanted to share in our energy. It felt really good. Each time I think of that day I remember how good it felt to bring joy into the lives of those special people and so I chose to use it for a time I was excellent as I created my own Circle of Excellence.

As you look at each sample can you tell that each one fills the requirements but the answer to the one that would get 10 points is much richer and more interesting than the one that would only get 1 or 2 points?

Your teacher may or may not allow you to read your talk or may take off points if you read it. Make certain you know what the requirements are.

Unit 3: Six Second Stress Buster

"The world we have created is a product of our thinking. It cannot be changed without changing our thinking" -- Albert Einstein

Lesson 1: What NLP is and what it isn't

At the core or center of NLP is the technology for modeling how people do what they do successfully. Richard Bandler, one of the pioneers in the field, explained how a new process is developed. He wanted to develop a process go help people let go of phobias (irrational fears). He went out and recruited two people who had a phobia (irrational fear) in the past and then got over it. He then found out what they did that worked and broke it down into steps. He then took those steps and created a program (plan to be followed) that others with phobias could follow.

When I first started NLP I found this fascinating because I used the same process as a developmental specialist. I would take a skill that most people could do well and break it down into steps that my developmentally disabled students could follow. During a training I attended the leader presented a contest. The challenge was to break down opening a piece of candy into as many steps as possible. I won with 43 steps.

This made sense to me. Just as I could break down simple things like opening candy or tying a shoe into smaller steps that my students could follow, so more complex things like creativity, goal setting and even parenting and leadership could be broken down into a process that could be replicated.

After modeling how a successful person does something the other part of the NLP core is then transferring that knowledge to other people. That is where the "P" in NLP comes in. We model someone, then create a program that can be taught to others.

How very simple. Little children do it all the time. My little granddaughter Chloe is learning how to talk. She does not talk yet, but she watches other people. Right now she is fascinated with tongues and if you will stick out your tongue and move it she will stick out her tongue and follow what you do. Children have specialized neurons called mirror neurons. Those mirror neurons help a person copy or mirror what others are doing and also what they are feeling (empathy). We have them also as adults but babies have many more. In the growing up process the mirror neurons are trimmed and the unused ones are trimmed out while the well-used ones are encouraged to grow.

You are asking now, how does this modeling process work? The creativity program is a good example. Almost the entire world knows and has admired the creative genius of Walter Disney, the person modeled for creativity. An NLP modeler started by finding people who are very uncreative, then looked for the structure of the lack of creativity. How does that person manage to stay uncreative? What does he do when he is trying to be creative but just isn't? Then they modeled Walt Disney. How did Walt manage to be creative? What did he do when he was most creative? Then came the next step, compare and contrast. What is the difference that makes the difference? Then the program Walt Disney used was broken down into steps. Finally the steps were taught to people who wanted to be more creative. Using Walt's strategy, they were more creative. People that are already creative also tried the program. They often found that they were doing some of the things that Walt Disney did, but not others. When they added other steps they found that they could enhance their creativity also. That is NLP. It is that simple.

And truly it is simple. I had my special needs students use the Disney Strategy of Creativity to create little skits and plays. Everyone said they could not because special needs people are not creative. They may not naturally be creative but I learned and they learned that creativity can be taught as a skill. So let me share a picture. They could learn creativity and I am one proud teacher.

Lesson 2: Five Fingers of NLP

Now NLP practitioners all over the world are using modeling to create programs for excellence in many fields including business, education, international affairs, sports, health, family, and counseling. The illustration (picture) below shows the various areas of study for NLP today. As you take this course you will be surprised to find that you will use it in many aspects of your daily life. My first thought was that I would be using my skills only in education. I soon learned to use those skills in negotiation, leadership, management, creativity, training and presenting, and most important to me, in health where I have learned new skills to become and maintain my personal health through the words I use and through modeling others who maintain good health and overcome major health obstacles.

Lesson 3: Stress Buster

This week you learned a program called the Six Second Stress Buster. This is a brief review of the program. Stress (pressure or tension that constrains or holds us back) is found in our daily lives. We cannot escape it. We have traffic, tests, jobs that need to be done and even little things like misplacing our room key. A recent Stanford University study concluded that more than 95% of all disease is created by stress.

Dr. Charles Stroebel, MD, a psychiatrist from Connecticut in the United States, was very stressed. For seven years he had chronic headaches so severe he thought he had a brain tumor. He consulted with twenty doctors from all over the United States and all gave him the same advice, relax. He was the kind who, when he was driving in traffic, would yell at people driving other cars. He did not like this aspect of himself and knew that it was not good for his health. As a doctor he knew that stress would cause high blood pressure, headaches and sleep disturbances. He determined that he was going to change. He knew that meditation would work, but he knew he would not take the time to do a long meditation. That would be more stress.

He looked for a way to undo stress quickly. He studied people under stress and what happened to their bodies and their thoughts, their internal dialogue. He learned that people go into a stress state the same way no matter what the stressor is. He discovered it took six seconds to go into a state of stress. Since it takes six seconds to build he wanted a program that took six seconds to bust (break up) the stress.

This is part of the up to 1700 physiological reactions that happens to us within six seconds when we go into a stress state. These reactions, often called fight, flight or freeze, were necessary to keep our ancestors alive when life was pretty wild. Our bodies still use this reaction and it gets applied to all stresses. The body is just doing what it has been programed over thousands of years to keep you alive.

- First the eyes get tense. The vision periphery (the outward bounds) widens, the pupils of the eyes go wider.
- Next the shoulders and jaw get tight. There is a frown and the jaw may set.
- Negative words are often said inside the head (internal dialogue).
- The breath is stopped.

This entire process takes 6 seconds. He thought, if I can develop something that will take six seconds to counteract this stress process I could stop stress, so he did. This is his program, The Six Second Stress Buster.

1. Sparkle eyes and twinkle smile. Let your eyes relax with a smile on your face. Turn the lights on in your eyes.
2. Say a positive self-statement such as "mind alert-body calm," or another one a person makes up like "I'm relaxed" or "I'm in control," or "I can handle it." This counters the negative internal dialogue.
3. Breathe deeply down through the belly. Imagine you have holes in the bottom of your feet and imagine you are breathing through those holes. You can put hands on abdomen and make your tummy move out.

4. Exhale and relax. Just relax your tongue, jaw and shoulders.

Try the Six Second Stress Buster and notice how it makes you feel. Now think of times you could use it such as just before a test, when you are in traffic, or most important, just before you give a speech in your speech class. Imagine you doing it at those times and your imagination will help you remember to do it when you need it.

Imagining something that you will do in the future is called future pacing. NLP'ers discovered through research that you can imagine something and your brain will accept it as really being done. When a similar situation occurs, your brain then says, "Oh, I've done this before" and does what was practiced in the imagination.

This phenomena was first explored in basketball. Three groups of students were used for the experiment. First the group was tested for a baseline and divided into three equal groups depending on their scores. Then one group practiced every day on the ball court shooting baskets. The second group did not practice at all but did sit for a few minutes each day and imagined making the perfect shot. The last group did nothing. In two weeks they were tested again. The students who practiced in their minds did very well, in fact almost as well as did the ones who actually practiced. Those who did not practice at all made no improvement. Why did mind practice work so well? In your mind you never have to miss or make a mistake. It is those mirror neurons. They are firing and get about a 30% advantage over not practicing.

Sample Presentation: Break down a simple task into smaller steps. You might try tying a shoe or putting on a shirt. Plan on presenting to the class or to your group. Your presentation should be 1-3 minutes.

How to Dig an Idaho Potato
Look for a potato plant that has/had blossoms.
Put your fingers in the dirt about 20cm from the stem.
Dig around slightly until you feel something hard.
Carefully pull it out of the ground
Snap the potato from the root.
Wash off the dirt and cook it for supper

Extra information: Here is a great video on mirror neurons:

http://www.pbs.org/wgbh/nova/body/mirror-neurons.html

Unit 4: Well-Formed Outcomes

Lesson 1: More History

As the study of Neurolinguistic Programming has developed it has branched out into several subspecialties. These include:

- Training and presenting skills. This sub area is used by people who present workshops, trainings and lectures.
- Leadership and management. Teaching people skills to be more effective leaders is what this subtopic is about.
- Health. NLP programs have been created to maximize health and often to empower a person with the programs needed to overcome life threatening illness. NO promises are made but tools are shared that others have used and very often optimal health can be achieved.
- Creativity and innovation is a fourth area of exploration and programs. Businesses use programs to help their staff work more creatively and innovatively as they develop new products, programs, and advertisement to target the needs of their consumers. People use creativity to enhance their skills at creating everything from looking at a simple thing in a new way to creating a new and better life.
- Learning and education. NLP modelers have created many programs for both more effective learning and teaching. The first breakthrough was the NLP Spelling Strategy. Eight hundred spellers were modeled, both good spellers and poor spellers. How each of the people spelled was broken down into little bits of information and compared. What do good spellers do that bad spellers do not do. Then a program was developed to teach people to spell better and it really works.
- Sports. A new area of focus is sports. NLP'ers began to realize that they had a good thing and could help in the sports world. As an example, what makes a good golf swing as compared to a poor one? Is it more than just technique?

Lesson 2: Story of the Dolphins

Early in the development of NLP, a group of NLP'ers went to a place where dolphins were trained to explore what they could learn there to enhance the development of programs. Dolphins are such wonderful animals with a high energy and intelligence. When a young dolphin started its training the trainer would catch it doing something the trainer wanted it to do, then would make a sign such as a hand clap or whistle toot, and give the dolphin a fish. He would pair the actions with the reward. It is common training procedure developed by Pavlov and used by developmental therapists such as myself and called Antecedent-behavior-consequence or ABC training.

When the dolphin had learned to match the action to the sign a new action was paired. Eventually many actions were grouped together for a fish. Much to the trainer's amazement, eventually the dolphins would begin to come up with their own tricks and come to the trainers for a fish. Now the trainers were also being trained. After talking with the trainers for a while the NLPer's wandered off to enjoy the other displays.

In the evening near closing time the NLP'ers drifted towards the gates and thought they would take one last peek at the wonderful dolphins. There, much to their surprise, were the trainers just feeding the dolphins fish but the dolphins were not doing tricks at all. They were puzzled. Shouldn't the dolphin always do a trick to get a fish?

The trainers explained that the fish during training were called training fish and these fish were called relational fish. It was important to take some time to create a good relationship with the dolphins, to be their friends. That was the purpose of relational fish.

It is the same with good school classes. Students need training fish to help them learn more quickly. If students get positive feedback on what they are doing well they will learn quicker and better. Soon, like the dolphins, they will be creating even better work. Relational fish are important too. I, Professor Roundy, will often ask the students to pass along a positive note to others in the class. This is a relational fish. You tell the person a positive thing (positive affirmation) that they were able to do and it will encourage them to do better. Some people could think that lifting another up will push you down but this is not true. When you lift another up they reach to lift you up and soon the entire class rises higher than expected because they synergistically grow together.

I have been training for many years. I treasure the fish people give me and I think I have almost all of the little papers that people what given me for all of the years I have been studying and learning NLP.

Lesson 3: Well Formed Goals

In this lesson we will explore goals and learn more about creating a good goal. Creating well-formed goals will benefit you for the rest of your life.

This tells the entire story. In 1953 a study was done at Yale University. Interviewers asked the graduating class how many of them had clearly defined a set of goals with a written plan to achieve them. 3% had a clear written plan for their lives with specific goals. Twenty years later the surviving class members were interviewed and it was found that the 3% with the clearly written goals were worth more financially that the other 97% together. And money wasn't all. They also seemed happier, better adjusted, and more excited about their lives. The researchers soon realized that good goal setting skills was critical for future success.

So what makes a good goal? You might guess that NLP modelers have been at work. The program and tools they used is called well-formed conditions for outcomes. The outcome you want is your goal.

A good goal must be both effective and ecological. Effective means it will get you where you want to go. Ecological means that that the outcome must fit the environment that it will be used in. For example, if your goal is to make highest scores in all of your classes and take all difficult classes, but you work so hard that you are ill much of the time, it is not ecological for the school environment of the student.

To be a well-formed outcome there are certain criteria it should meet:

- ➢ The goal should be positive.
- ➢ The goal should be sensory based.
- ➢ The person who wants the goal should be able to initiate or start the progress towards the outcome and also able to maintain the progress.
- ➢ The goal should be able to retain the positive products of the present state
- ➢ The goal should fit gracefully into the surrounding environment, it should be ecological.

Lesson 4: More about the Four Criteria for Well-formedness

Let's look at each of these criteria separately. The goal should be positive. Researchers have learned that people's brains only look at things one at a time and only in a forward motion. If you say to someone, think of a blue rabbit, their brain must first think of a rabbit, then think of the color of rabbits they have known before, and last turn the rabbit blue in the imagination.

Similarly if you tell a child "do not run in the house," first the child must think of running in the house, then it must think of what to do next. If the child is small it may not have an idea of what to put in place of running so the child continues to run in the house, much to the consternation of its parent. Knowing this information, we know that our goal must move in a positive direction for example, not "I don't want to be sick," but, "I want to be healthy." Not "I don't want to fail my class," but "I want to pass my class with a good grade."

The goal should be sensory based. The outcomes should be testable and demonstrable in sensory experience. What is an explicit way of knowing that the goal is reached? For instance if a person says " I want to lose weight" there is no sensory based outcome. A well-formed goal might say, I want to remove 12 unneeded pounds from my body in the next three months. The goal is testable and the person can see the goal as it is reached on a scale. A good goal is one that the person can start by themselves. If the person has to rely on someone else it may not get done. The other person may not want to, there may not be "buy in."

The well-formed goal should also be one that the person can continue to work on without outside help. As an example, if the goal was "The teacher will give me a good grade in class," the goal requires the teacher to "buy in" to the goal. If the work is good it might happen, but if the work is not good the teacher is not going to give the good grade. A well-formed goal might be, I will complete the assignment doing the work well so that I get a good grade in glass. The student then initiates and maintains the goal him or herself.

The goal retains any positive products of the present. This is an example of the criteria. There was a man named Carl who got up every morning and ate breakfast with his wife Tina. While they ate they would talk about what was to go on that day. They would talk about their child and her progress at the university. It was a nice, quiet time together.

Then Carl got worried. The doctor told him he was overweight and needed to work out so Carl decided to get up each morning, skip breakfast and run around the nearby track. After her ran he would rush in the house, shower quickly, grab a breakfast bar and run out the door to work. He was feeling better yet something was happening at home. It caused him to feel uneasy inside. His wife seemed to be unhappy with him. She did not say much but he knew her well and she was just quiet. Then one day his daughter had an important concert at school. He did not know about it. He came home late from work and Tina was angry. She had missed the concert because he was late and it was important to her to be there for their daughter. She was furious and yelled at him. He was baffled. What had happened to his happy wife and his happy life? Couldn't they see that he was working out to stay healthy for them?

He and Tina sat down that very night. She cried and said that she was unhappy with their marriage. Maybe they should get a divorce. They started to talk about why things were not good now. Do you understand what the problem was? He had not retained the positive product of the present, which was time every morning with his wife, when he made the goal to exercise. He began to realize that the time was important to both him and his Tina. They made a new, well-formed goal. Now he gets home from work each night and runs the track while she is fixing dinner. Their marriage is happy again and both Carl and Tina were happily supporting their daughter at her last concert.

The goal should fit the surrounding environment and be ecological. Sometimes people will state their goal as an absolute, it must happen. It will happen every time and everywhere, in every context and situation. Joe, a student, says "I will get 100% on all of my papers." It appears to be a great goal, but then Joe gets a bad cold in his nose. He is very tired and needs to sleep a bit more than usual. Joe cannot sleep as his goal is to get 100% all of the time. Joe then pushes himself and puts his body under stress. His body rebels and he gets pneumonia. The doctor then puts Joe in the hospital and now Joe is way behind on his studies. Joe would have made a better choice of a goal if he had said, "I will strive to get great grades." Then he could say, "I am not feeling well this week. I will put a little less time in on this assignment so I can get more sleep and recover quickly. Joe will have more flexibility if he can create goal that will allow him to be flexible.

Lesson 5: SMART

Businesses often talk about having SMART goals. This acronym will help you remember what a good goal is:

S - specific (what will you see, hear and feel when you get your goal); M – measurable; A – achievable
R – realistic; T - timed.

Sample: Here is my Well-formed Outcome for the 2012-13 school year.

1	Positively stated	The mind works in one direction, lead it to the positive.	I will provide my students with the opportunities to learn to speak good English by using NLP skills,
2	Sensory based	What will you see, hear and feel when you get your outcome?	I will see their body language flow more freely and see them using their 6 –Second Stress Buster and Circle of Excellence often to maintain a positive state. I will hear a gentle easy flow to their speech. I will feel in myself their excitement at learning and presenting.
3	Initiated and maintained by yourself	You can start it yourself and keep the goal going to completion	I will use a variety of teaching ideas to make speaking English interesting and fun and help them. I will write their text and include a lot of examples so that the reading will be both applicable to most of the students and fun to learn.
4	Maintain positive present state	Will it work in all areas of your life	I know that it is important for my students and me to get adequate sleep and to also have a social life so I will be concise for my students also so they will have plenty of time for other assignments and a social life for themselves.
5	Ecological	What will you lose or gain when you achieve your positive outcome	I will gain a sense of happiness at bringing tools for success to my students at Jiao Tong University. When I hear from my students later in life I will know that I had a part in helping them be successful in whatever they chose to do with their lives. I lose the opportunity to be at home in Idaho with my family.

Make this a well formed outcome:
I do not want to get behind in my teaching during the Autumn Festival.

I will spend one hour or more grading papers each day until they are all graded before I go out and explore Shanghai.

Unit 5: TOTE Model

> Imitate until you emulate; match and surpass those who launched you.
> It's the highest form of thankfulness. -- Mark Victor Hansen

Lesson 1: What is an NLP Program?

"The whole world steps aside for the man who knows where he is going."--Anonymous

Neurolinguistics provides us with tools to take major steps towards overcoming limitations. The field of NLP was developed from modeling human thinking skills. Neuro is the part of finding out how the brain and nervous system work and Linguistics is the analysis of the language patterns as well as the non-verbal communication. The results of the study became the creation of a step-by-step strategy or program that may be used to transfer a skill to other people.

Now that you have a bit of a background in NLP, learned to chunk something down into small steps, and you have learned to make a well formed outcome or goal, you are ready to create a program for yourself. So what is a program? A program is a set of steps you can follow to achieve the thing the program is about. For instance in school it might be in a reading program to learn specific reading skills or a math program to learn math skills.

Our NLP program for this lesson is called the T.O.T.E. model, which stands for test, operate, test, and exit. It was developed by George Miller, Eugene Galanter and Karl Pribram and presented in their book *Plans and the Structures of Behavior* (1961). The concept of the T.O.T.E. is that most mental strategies are organized around a feedback loop. This program has a fixed goal and an assortment of ways to get that goal. It is a self-correcting feedback loop. NLP has taken this basic program and enhanced it. These are the steps of the program:

Test		The test is the goal we want to achieve, your well-formed outcome. It includes what you will see, hear and feel when you achieve the goal.
Operate		Operate can mean to do or to work. To operate a car is to work a car. It is the things you will do to get your goal.
Test		The test of the goal is to ascertain that you have achieved it. This is much like a math test will check to see if you know the math work.

| Exit | EXIT | When your goal is done you are ready to move on, to exit your program. Part of the exit may be deciding where you will go next. Another part may be to have a reward in place for achieving your goal to help motivate you. |

The program works like this.
- We first set a goal that we want to achieve. We have learned about setting a well-formed goal. The test is the criteria we set to show that the goal is reached.
- Next we operate or do something to get us closer to the goal. I think of this like operating a car. As you drive or operate a car you are getting closer to your destination.
- Then we test our criteria to decide whether we have reached it or not. If we have reached it we move on to the next step, exit. If we have not, it is time to get back in our car and operate it again choosing, and evaluating why we did not reach our destination. Did we choose the wrong exit or road, make a wrong turn, hit a detour or have a breakdown? If so we can redo our program using the information gained to help us reset the goal or the operations as needed so that we can---
- Exit. We can leave the program with our goal achieved. Part of the exit strategy may include setting up a reward for ourselves to help motivate us, or to choose a new goal we want to achieve.

It works like this:

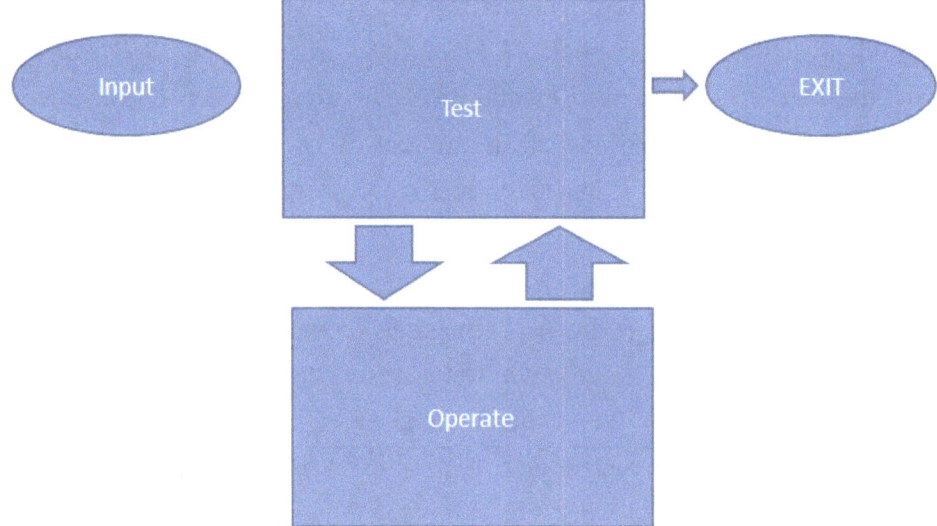

What is the purpose of all this goal setting? How many times have you said that you were going to do something, and then not done it? In many places people make a resolution (a firm decision to do something) at the New Year. It is a goal they will work on for the entire year. Businesses make goals for productivity or for customer service. A doctor might make a goal to be attentive to his patients. A mother might make a goal to spend time exercising so she can be a healthy mother.

A well-formed goal provides purpose and commitment. It directs our focus and is an energizer. One day I was talking with a girlfriend. She said, "What is the importance of NLP? I do some of this stuff all the time." You may be really good at goal setting, but you will likely have observed, maybe with frustration, that you have friends who are not. You may be one of those persons that a modeler would have chosen to model. Statistically it is proven that only a small portion of the population sets, writes down, and achieves their goals. Learning the T.O.T.E program increases the probability that you will achieve your goals.

Lesson 2: Creating a Goal

"Unless you try to do something beyond what you have already mastered, you will never grow"
-- Ralph Waldo Emerson

To create a goal you will want a well-formed outcome. As you have surely guessed by now, NLP modelers have modeled people who form good goals and achieve them. Lesson Four covered Well-formed goals. As a review, your goal should be:

1. Goal or test is stated in positive terms
2. The goal is sensory based
3. The person or group that makes the goal also maintains it
4. The goal keeps the positive by-products of the present state
5. The goal is appropriate

Something you might want to consider is this, if your goal is to be the top in something you will by nature have to push down everyone else. This is not usually the best choice as pushing others down makes you unpopular. We love to be top dog but it is an empty victory as we realize that the price for needing to be top is to make everyone else below you. Of course in a race this must be as there can only be one winner. In the game of life there can be many winners. Make your outcome to be with the other top students, or chose an outcome where you best yourself. Go to raise your overall score by a certain number of points. Then the person you are competing with is only yourself.

I would like to share what one of my friends and a fellow author said, "I am becoming the creator of my own reality." (And Then a Miracle Happens. page 209) Her well-formed outcome was to be healthy and leave Multiple Sclerosis behind. She did.

Lesson 3: Operating Your Program

"It is not because it is difficult that we do not dare, it is because we do not dare that it is difficult." – Seneca

Now we are ready to explore the spot where the rubber meets the road, operating your program. This is where the chunking down of your goal starts. What small steps or chunks do you need to get where you want to go?

In NLP we learn that we want to broaden our choices. Having only one operation can become a problem if, for some reason, it doesn't work out as then you have no other options. As you create your TOTE you will want to generate as many choices as possible. You can then create a feedback loop. You have a choice, it leads you closer to the goal, then you continue that choice. You have another choice, it does not take you where you want so you go to the next choice. There is an NLP saying that goes, "If you have only one choice there is no choice. Having two choices is a dilemma. There is magic in having three choices. "

A good example of this would be a road trip. My children and I one year piled in the family car and headed out on an 1800 mile trip to a Scout camp in New Mexico. We had a basic idea of where we wanted to go, Philmont, New Mexico. As we went along there were things that got in our way. Some were  delightful, we spent more time than we expected at Mesa Verde, but we had options of other sites we could drop to keep our schedule and arrive on time. We also got lost. Again having choices gave us other options to keep that schedule. Latter we were driving along and were nearing a less exciting but planned for site. The children were peacefully sleeping. i skipped it and let them sleep leaving again flexibility to spend more time at the next major attraction, Arches National Park. Last but not least, there were obstacles in our way. One of the roads we had to take was barricaded off and we had to take a detour in unfamiliar territory. I got lost on the detour, too. It went for miles in the middle of no-where with no one to ask for directions. We made it, obviously, for I am here today to laugh about it. Again it called for flexibility to arrive on time.

Some TOTE programs can be quite large. For that you might create TOTEs within a TOTE. There will be more about that later.

Lesson 4: Test Your Goal

"It is in the moments of decision that our destiny is shaped" - Anthony Robbins

Now we arrive at a decision point. How will we know we have achieved our goal? This is truly the test. What are the feelings, the inspirations and the ah-ha's that let you know that you are on the right track? Let's take for instance, purchasing a pair of shoes. Mary has set as her test to find a pair of shoes in the right size to match the new red outfit she has purchased to wear to work. She has set a price of $75 maximum and wants them to be comfortable for a full day on her feet. She likes leather because it breathes and her work requires that she choose a closed toe shoe.

Next she sets up her operation. She will go to her favorite shoe store. Then she considers what she will do if they don't have the perfect shoe. She could settle for another. She could check out other stores in comparable ranges. She could check out the bargain bins at more expensive stores.

Armed with a good set of operators, Mary heads out to shop, excited with the thrill of the hunt. Mary goes to her favorite shoe store and they do have a red shoe, but it just isn't the right one. She now considers her options. She already has them in place and she reflects that at one time she would have just grabbed the shoes and been done with it. Then she wouldn't have been happy with the shoes and they would have inhabited the lower level of her closet until the next big pitch fork cleaning day. She is prepared and goes to a couple of stores in comparable ranges. Still nothing seems right so she heads into an upper crust store, a bit intimidated by its luxury. She walks past rows of beautiful expensive shoes, but she does not stop. She is a woman with a mission, to find the right shoes at the right price. She heads down to the bargain basement and there they are, the perfect shoes. She tries them on and they are a lovely fit. She walks around to check them out and feels that ah-ha feeling she is familiar with, the feeling inside that tells her the choice is right.

She thinks to herself as she feels that ah-ha, before she had used the TOTE model, she might have grabbed the more expensive shoes upstairs because she did not have the same focus. The TOTE provided focus. She would have purchased the more expensive shoes then felt disappointed every time she wore them knowing that they were too expensive for her budget. It was the focus that made the difference now, she thought, the focus and the choices. It seemed to free her up inside. That ah-ha was a good one.

So how do we know we have achieved our goal? All of the requirements we have set up are met, and the goal holds or is generalized across settings. The choice feels right. There is a feeling of completion that holds firm in other settings. That is what Mary in the example above felt.

Lesson 5: Redo or Exit

"Every exit is an entry somewhere" --Tom Stoppard

Part of the fun of setting a goal is the feeling we get when we achieve the goal. There is that bit of exhilaration when we have achieved what we set out to do. Often for us, especially as adults, the intrinsic reward of feeling triumphant or exhilarated is enough. Other times the completion of the TOTE itself may be the reward, for instance the TOTE could be getting ready for a family vacation and the exit is the vacation itself. Other times we may want to set a reward. One year my students set a goal to drink more water at school and keep hydrated. They set a goal of so many bottles of water, and then they set up a reward, suitably a juice box when they achieved their goal. I still recall their happy faces as they sipped on the juices, a sweet ending to that TOTE program.

We know ourselves and know what we need to self-motivate. If it is a group project, a suitable reward may pull the group together whether it is a bonus from the factory or a lunch out with the girls who all lost a certain amount of weight, a reward can provide the extra stick to it power to achieve the TOTE.

It would be wonderful if we always got every goal we set, but life is real and things get in our way. One year I had a student in school I will call John. I taught my students the TOTE model the first week of school and his goal was to make it through the year without getting a detention. He did well for eleven weeks. Then we went on a field trip. He had not yet generalized his good behavior across settings. In other words he had not yet considered how to act in unfamiliar territory, in this case the school bus. He sat beside a pal who immediately got him to use inappropriate language. Pretty soon he had his first detention for the year. He was disappointed. I was disappointed, not only in him, but also in myself. I realized that he did not generalize across settings yet and I had not taken this into account. Still some good came of it as we tackled it as a class. We talked about what to do when you do not get your goal. Do you give up? No! We decided that the goal covered too much time and we needed to cut it down because it was important to feel the success of getting the goal. He redid his goal making it a shorter period of time to help insure success.

An important part of the exit is to decide where to go next. When we are finished, are we truly done? If the TOTE was a family vacation, then we may leave it. For other TOTES it may be a jumping off point for a new TOTE model. My students wanted to participate in a service opportunity, to decorate a Christmas tree to be sold to raise money for our local hospital. Here they are beside the tree they decorated. It was sold for $200 and the money given to the local hospital.

Lesson 6: TOTES can be Wonderfully Complicated

"If you don't know where you are going, you might wind up someplace else." --**Yogi Berra**

Now you have learned the basic TOTE model. The TOTE model can get complicated. Remember we are working with the human brain and modeling how those who achieve their goals do it best. Not all goals are simply create a test, operate, test, and exit.

A second type of TOTE is a parallel TOTE where two things are done simultaneously. An example would be balancing both a relationship and task in a training situation.

The third form of a TOTE model is the sequential TOTE. One small TOTE must be carried out completely before the next is started. Washing dishes would be an excellent example. In the operations stage of the TOTE to get the dishes washed could be clear the table, wash dishes and put dishes away. Each one follows the other in sequence. One doesn't start putting the dishes away first. The dishes must be removed to the sink and washed before. A sequence is necessary.

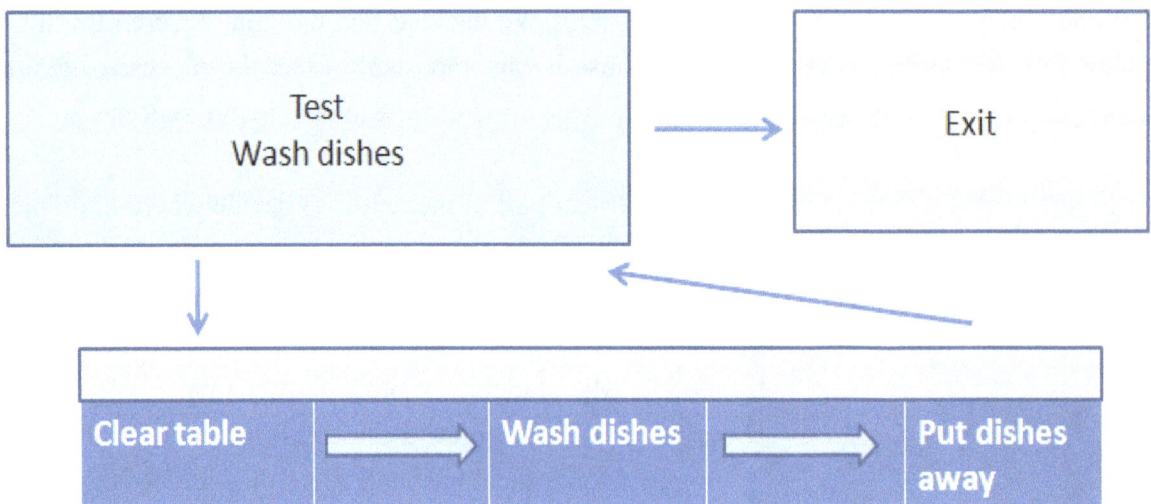

A core feature of the TOTE model is nested TOTES. A nested TOTE is a number of sub TOTES nested into a larger large TOTE. An example of this would be cooking a big meal for a dinner party. Erika has invited several friends over for her husband's birthday. She wants to create for them a beautiful meal. There is her TOTE goal, a beautiful dinner in honor of her husband. Within that large TOTE is the operate phase and within it are several smaller TOTES, each unique with tests and operations nested inside. Mary wants to make a pot roast with potatoes and vegetables. She plans on homemade rolls and a salad. Mary wants to finish the meal with a favorite dessert of her husbands, a cherry pie. Her TOTE may appear like this, with five sub TOTES to accomplish the task.

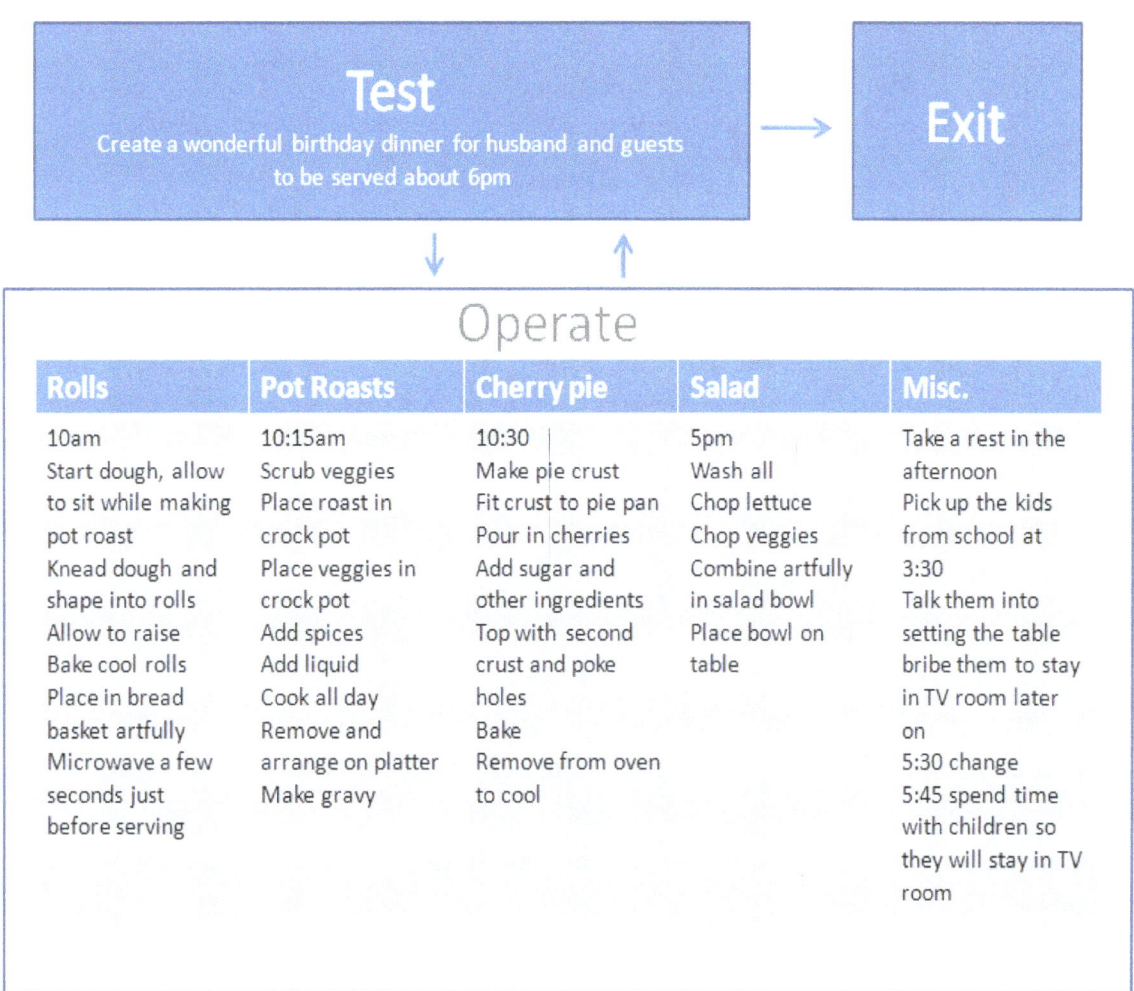

Each of the nested TOTEs has its own test and operation. The pot roast has a separate operation from the rolls or cherry pie. A nested TOTE has a hierarchal structure where one thing must be done before the next. In other words sub routines or TOTES are nested in the larger operate step for the test.

Now we have a program but what does this mean neurologically? Our nervous system is wired to continually check the current state of what we experience and compare it with what we want to maintain or achieve. Depending on the results we adjust our behaviors accordingly. These aspects range from maintaining our balance to riding a bike; from focusing our eyes to reading a book; from picking up a pencil to painting a masterpiece. Our neurology does this continually on both unconscious and conscious levels. This is the natural way the brain operates and by following the natural operations of the neural circuitry we can make our own programs more effective. Our neurophysiology naturally sets up tests; it then has built in natural operations with feedback loops that will adjust to the information given to the neurology and exits.

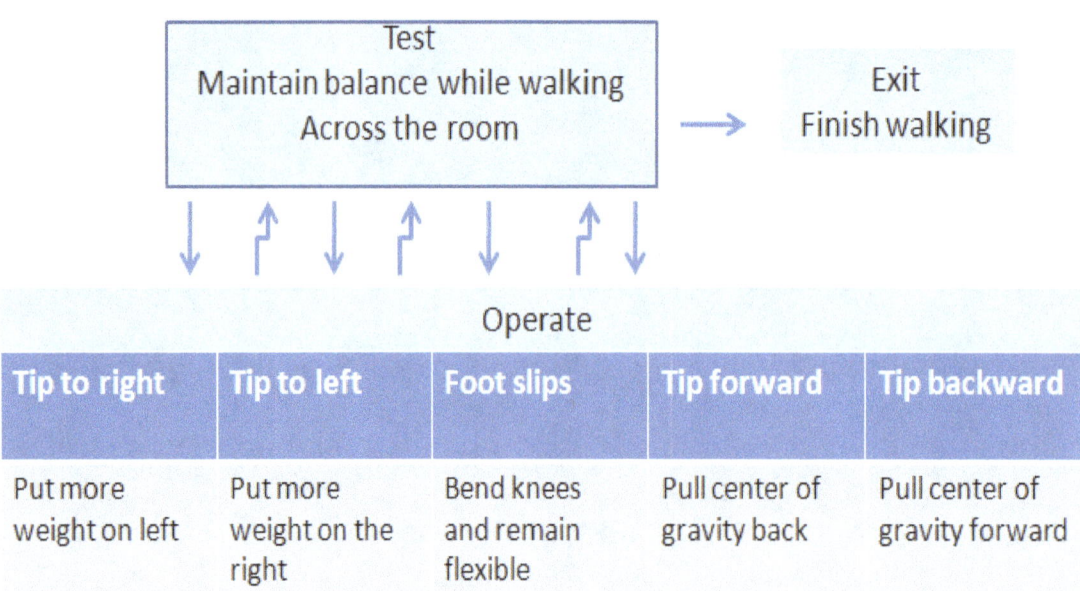

All of this is going on subconsciously in your brain and body as you go across the room. Your brain has already created its program with built in feedback loops that you access without it being in your conscious awareness. The TOTE program utilizes this natural program that resonates well with your circuitry and leads you into creating great programs where you no longer feel like you are wondering around, but now are reaching your goals.

Chloe learning to walk

Sample

1. Test: What is your well-formed outcome?
I will assist my students in learning to speak and write good English.

2. Operate: What are some steps to getting this outcome? List at least four.
Prepare lessons well in advance.
Choose material that will be interesting to the students and motivate them to learn.
Find pictures to illustrate what is being taught to help increase student vocabulary
Create slide shows to make lecture more interesting
3. Test: What is your test for your goal?
Hear? I will hear my students asking questions that relate to the subject matter so that I know they understand.
I will see them talking English with each other during practice sessions
See? I will see them engaged with each other during practice sessions
Feel? I will feel the energy of the students as they incorporate NLP programs and become more successful students.

4. Exit: What will you do if you get your goal?
I see myself sitting with my husband eating a dinner in Shanghai before we leave and sharing the successes we have had during our time here. I hear myself expressing pleasure at the motivation of the Chinese, Korean and Japanese students. I hear myself telling my husband about the students who will visit English speaking countries on exchange and I will feel a feeling of satisfaction knowing that they will be more successful because of the year of study they spent with me. Maybe they will be like the Chinese family I met from Shanghai last summer that helped me learn some Chinese while we stood in line waiting for a trolley car in San Francisco, California.

5. What can you do if you do not get your goal?
I will evaluate myself during the year and ask my students what helps them learn best so that I can modify my teaching to best meet their learning styles.

A new Chinese friend on the bus   and a family from Shanghai at the trolley

And a note in 2013. I had forgotten I had done this TOTE for you students and I went back over the material for this year. I did indeed sit down to dinner in Shanghai and discuss exactly as I had set my goal for without even remembering. It had worked on a subconscious level. I wonder what goal you will achieve.

Unit 6: Neurological Level Alignment

Lesson 1: Introduction to Logical Levels

> "It's not hard to make decisions when you know what your values are."
> --- Roy Disney

Have you ever had a friend who said, "I know you!" to which you thought, you hardly know me at all? I am so much more than the person you know. The person you know is just the tip of the iceberg compared to the real me.

This chapter will introduce you to a favorite model of Neurolinguistic programs (NLP), Logical Level Alignment (LLA). LLA helps you achieve the ideal of understanding the outcome that you want. My teacher, NLP developer and Trainer Robert Dilts developed this model, known as logical levels developing it from the previous work of Gregory Bateson. It helps you understand what makes you tick, an idiom that means how something works, in this case how you work. LLA also helps you understand what makes other people tick and what makes an organization tick. It helps you break down experiences into manageable parts and helps you confidently adjust your goals and outcomes to make them well formed in your future and with your purpose in life.

You may see Logical Level Alignment referred to in NLP literature as Neurological Level Alignment (NLLA) as each level goes deeper into your neurology. They are all basically referring to the same model but called different things by different authors. In this simple model below you can see them as a simple hierarchy:

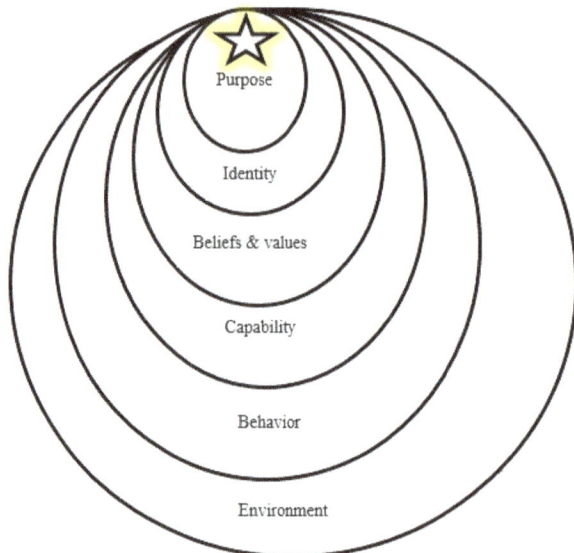

However the levels tend to be intertwined and related to each other. The French have an expression, 'elle va birn dans sap eau' which means that you feel comfortable with yourself and the world. When I was a college student, we called it 'feeing groovy.' We use the word *congruence* when we describe ourselves as feeling truly ourselves, on track and consistent.

Lesson 2: Logical Levels

Some processes are created by the relationships between other processes. As an example, take the rate of change (speed) of a car. The speed is the function of how much ground the car v=covers in a given amount of time such as 10 km per hour, especially in Shanghai traffic! Speed is a relationship between the distance covered and the time that it takes to cover that distance. The car's velocity in moving from the roadway to a parking space can be said to be different than the parking space, the road way, or the clock that tracks the time. It is the property of the relationship between them.

On the same vein (still staying with the same subject) the academic success of a university is at a different level than the teachers, students, administrators and the many workers who create that academic success. Likewise an idea is at a different level that the neurons, synapses and synovial fluid that produce the idea.

The idea of logical levels of learning, behavior and change was initially put together by  Gregory Bateson and based on the work of Bertrand Russell. He was working with logics and mathematics. Bateson's work was adapted and expanded for NLP by the creative genius Robert Dilts in the mid 1980's. It can be adapted for levels in a person or within a group or organization. Have you ever Googled "Powers of Ten?" If you do there are many programs taken something from itself up to universe size or reverses to the smallest of fractals and then on to photons of light.(try this one at http://micro.magnet.fsu.edu/primer/java/scienceopticsu/powersof10/).

Likewise, any activity is a subsystem embedded with in another activity and can be expanded into a greater activity within which it resides. An example of different levels occurred to me today. My computer crashed. On one level it was negative, I have to find a repair man and get it fixed. But at a higher level it became a positive thing as I had needed to back up files and I only had one hour left of power so I got the files I had needed to back up for days all backed up quickly. My environment was negative but at a higher behavioral level it led to a positive behavior.

Bateson identified four levels of change. These are:

A.	Who am I	Identity -	Mission, Purpose	Who?
B.	My Belief system	Values and Meanings	Permission and Motivation	Why?
C.	My Capabilities	Strategies and States	Maps and Plans	How?
D.	What I do or have done	Specific Behaviors	Actions and reactions	What?
E.	My Environment	Things that externally hold us back or constrain us and opportunities	Constraints and opportunities	Where and When?

Lesson 3: Taking the Levels Step by Step

Let's look at each level individually and see if we can "get a handle" on them. (Understand them more deeply and fully)

Environment

Environment is about the place, time and people, the place where you "hang out." It includes what you can see, hear, feel, taste and smell. Much of your environment comes from your senses. You want to learn English and the best way to do that is to change your environment. Make friends with people who speak English and hang out with them, visit an English speaking country and immerse yourself in English and English culture and you will learn it most rapidly. Soon English will be a "piece of cake" (easy to do) for you. In a similar note (related to what was being talked about), if you want to learn a new video game on your computer the best way is to change your environment, go to the computer lab and work with someone who knows the game. Soon you will be playing it easily.

The environment concerns your external world and what you are allowed externally as well as what stops or constrains you. It answers the questions of when and where in your life. In a greater model it answers the when and where of the activity, business or organization which it is being applied to.

Behavior

Behavior is about what you consciously say and do. It refers to your thinking as well as your actions. Interestingly, everything you do has a positive intention. An example of this would be found in the excellent book and movie, Les Miserable, a French novel written in 1862 by author Victor Hugo. In the story Jean Val jean steals a bit of bread for his starving sister and her family. Of course stealing is wrong, but if we look at the stealing and watch for the positive intention we find that he wanted to feed those he loved.

Developing behaviors and habits that serve you well is a good idea. As an example, I used to always misplace my keys and would forever be hunting for them. I would say, "I am scatter-brained.' Then I created a habit of always putting my keys on the banister as soon as I entered my house. Now I always know where the keys are.

As humans we are able to sense and coordinate our body's behavior as we move through different environments. This week end I went to the Fabric Market to buy a coat. I tried on a beautiful coat. It was warm, too warm for the nice Mid-Autumn Festival day. My body immediately detected the heat and started to perspire. Soon I took off the coat to change my environment. It was a lovely day and I got a coat to wear when the Shanghai weather turns cold.

Behavior goes from neurology and often comes from a level deeper than your sense organs, your psychomotor system. Other behavior is simply reflexive. For instance when I hit a crack on the sidewalk my reflex system kicks in and keeps me from falling down. Behavior level things answer n the question "what?" are your actions and reactions to the environment.

Capabilities

On a personal level, capabilities are the talents and skills we have within ourselves. On a larger scale, such as a company, they are the talents and skills of the many people that make up the organization. Often they are skills you have learned in life like walking or hitting a soccer ball, and now need no conscious effort to do. I, Debrah, love to dance; some of my students have seen me dancing at the school... I am older now and not as good as when I was young, but I still love to dance. Last week I found an aerobics dance group at my park on campus. I quickly learned a new dance, much more quickly than some of the other ladies because I have taken and taught dance for more than forty years. It has become an easy capability for me.

Many behaviors come from mental maps that we make. As an example, when you first made your Circle of Excellence you were asked to think of a color. You now have a mental map of a Circle of Excellence for yourself and you can come up with it in your head whereas before you had to construct it by first thinking of what excellence looks like to you and then coloring it. Now you have a mental image or construct of it. Your magnificent brain has the capability to create a new mental image for you, file it away and then bring it forward into your memory when it is needed.

As you acquire more capabilities in your life, the "world is your oyster", or opens up to you greater opportunities. You are able to take on more challenges and to cope better with the challenges life brings you. Capabilities are your strategies and your state. Capabilities answer the how question in the person or organization they are applied to.

Beliefs and Values

Often we are not aware of our beliefs and values and yet they direct our life. Our perceptions are deep and often at a subconscious level. Our beliefs and values change over time as our perspective of life broadens. In this area is where older people gain their greatest value to society because they have great experience and their beliefs and values are rooted in that life experience.

Our capabilities are shaped by our beliefs and values. Take this example; I was accidently poisoned many years back. The American medical doctors told me I would die of liver disease and there were no medications to cure it. They tested me and showed me the test results. They sent me home to die, or if I was "lucky," to have a liver transplant. I believed them. I was very sick. Sometimes I even wanted to die.

Then I met a doctor, Dr. Charles Wilcher, D.C., N.M.D., C.Ac., D.N.B.H.E., D.I.A.M.A. who specialized in Chinese medicine. (http://drwilcher.com/index.html) He studied in Shanghai and other parts of China and the Asian world. He did not believe the other medical doctors. He believed that he could help me get well. I was not sure. The American Medical doctors had told me I could not. I had a strong belief that I could not get better and that someday I would die of liver disease. I had seen the tests that showed what they said to be true. From him I began my exploration of Eastern medicine. I learned about herbs, teas and acupuncture. I learned about another kind of medicine called Homeopathy. I learned about chiropractic, too. He was able to make me much better. I was so much better that now I no longer wanted to die. Still he was not able to bring up to where I should be. Something was still needed. You see I had what we in NLP call a thought virus. I had been told by people I had been taught to believe and trust with my life that I would someday die of liver disease. Like a virus that causes disease, this virus still lurked quietly in my system reminding me at a subconscious level that I would die of liver disease. I had only bought more time.

 Then one day I found an NLP counselor. She worked on my beliefs and values. We found that I still believed deep at a subconscious level that I would die of liver disease. We worked to change my beliefs and values at the subconscious level. I am so glad that I did.
Now I can dance in the park in Shanghai, China, and I can teach English and speech. I now have a new belief. I believe I can teach NLP and speech and open more opportunities for my Chinese students to be successful and make the world a better place somewhere and somehow. I will be excited to read and

hear about what my students do and I want to be here for many more years. I have changed my beliefs and values.

Beliefs and values are what make you get up in the morning; they govern how you treat yourself and how you treat others. The Beliefs and Values level tells the values and meanings a person or organization puts on things in life. It answers the why question.

Identity

Identity level describes your sense of who you are. It is the answer to "I am_____." Whether it is a person or an organization you express yourself through your beliefs and values, capabilities, behaviors, and environments yet you are more than these levels. NLP assumes that your identity is separate from your behavior. You are more than what you do.

You may have seen the Chinese dancers, the girl without an arm and the boy without a leg. They dance beautifully together. Others would say that they are not capable of being dancers, that they are handicapped and would not believe they could dance, but they surpassed that level of belief and said, "We are so much more than handicapped people. At the identity level we are dancers and they became what they believed their identity was.

Identity level separates the intention of an action from an action itself. For instance in Les Miserable's the action was stealing bread but at the identity level Jean Val jean was acting not as a thief, but as a desperate and caring brother.

The identity level consolidates (puts together) the beliefs and values, capabilities and behaviors into a sense of self. The dancers were dancers, Jean Val jean was a loving brother, I became a person who was so much more than liver disease, I became a conqueror. It is our experience of who we are.

I have had a large family of four children. Even before they were born they had an identity. Seresa was active and my tummy was always moving when I carried her. She became an active child and now an active adult. Joshua was slow to turn and when he would move it was like a giant whale turning over. He is always slow and careful and thinks things out. He is a thinker. Sam was so active I could hardly believe it. People would see my tummy get kicked from the inside and say, "You sure have an active baby. It is true. Now he is a biker who bikes miles and miles and wins races. His muscles are well developed and strong. Alyssa was a just right mover. She did not turn a lot or a little, just medium. Now she is a just medium person who gets things done and is a good little mama, too. They each had an identity of their own that was obvious and undeniable. They were not blank slates with nothing on them. They were born with a personality and an identity that would flourish and grow until they are what they are today and will become what they will be in the future, and I am excited to find out what that will be!

This identity changes through life yet it is much the same. When I first went to visit my exchange student, Hajime, in Japan even though he was much older he was still the same identity and I knew him immediately. Now he is such a loving husband and father and I am so proud of him. He has a solid identity of a man who is caring and tender yet has a "good nose" (detects well) for medical inventions and "bird dogs" (when he looks for something he keeps going until he finds it)them out.

"Who am I?" is answered at the identity level whether it is who am I as an individual or as a group of organization.

Purpose
The purpose level, also known as spiritual level, is that level that is beyond us, it reaches beyond our body and into the greater field of time and space. It is about more than us. It looks at the greater vision whether it is an individual, a group or an organization. NLP Developer, Robert Dilts, was the creator of this level which goes beyond and expands the work of Gregory Bateson. He is also the one who coined (made up) the term "Neuro-Logical Levels."

As my husband and I got older we wanted a higher purpose. We had the purpose to raise good children who would become assets to the community by doing good works, supporting themselves and having the skills needed to be good parents. This purpose was reached. We wanted a new purpose. We wanted to make the world a better place. We remembered our exchange students and how when they learned English they were able to go farther in the area they chose to work in. Could we give this gift to more people? We could again have exchange students, but that would be one person at a time. We will not live forever. Then we learned that some universities in China wanted American professors who were retired to come and teach English. We thought about it, we contacted BYU China Teachers and then they contacted us in late June. Soon we were here with a new purpose, to make the world a better place by sharing English. I have another purpose also; it is to share my NLP skills with you so that you can be even more effective in the area you go into.

I love this poem by Will Allen Dromgoole called, "The Bridge Builder" It illustrates a man with a purpose. Will you know what it is?

An old man, going a lone highway,
Came, at the evening, cold and gray,
To a chasm, vast, and deep, and wide,
Through which was Flowing a sullen tide.
The old man crossed in the twilight dim;
The sullen stream had no fears for him;
But he turned, when safe on the other side,
And built a Bridge to span the tide.
"Old man," said a fellow pilgrim, near,
"You are wasting strength with building here;
Your journey will end with the ending day;
You never again must pass this way;
You have crossed the chasm, deep and wide—
Why build you the bridge at the eventide?"

The builder lifted his old gray head:
"Good friend, in the path I have come," he said,
"There followeth after me today
A youth, whose feet must pass this way.
This chasm, that has been naught to me,
To that fair-haired youth may a pitfall be.
He, too, must cross in the twilight dim;
Good friend, I am building the bridge for him."

Purpose is a higher level and recognizes that we are so much more than even an identity. We, whether it is an organization or a person, have more value to give to the world. There is a vision or a greater mission to fill in life. There is something to pass onto posterity. That is the vision. There is a saying, the greater the vision, the greater the mission. Can you think of famous leaders in your own country who had a great vision and achieved a great mission?

Purpose is the greater level beyond you and can stretch through time and space. It answers the questions "For Whom" or "For what?"

Lesson 4: Finding the Right Level for Change

> What lies behind us and what lies before us are tiny matters compared to what lies within us. --- Ralph Waldo Emerson

Logical Level Alignment can be compared to a tree. Underneath are the roots. They provide the nourishing scaffolding that holds the tree up. Above are the branches. They also nourish the tree with the air and the water they need from the atmosphere. They are also like scaffolding. The tree must have both to survive.

Our identities are like the roots that for the neural networks of our personalities. The branches are our external identity where we participate as families, communities, groups, organizations and indeed the global community. Attributes such as healing, joy, love, compassion, honesty, integrity and commitment are fruits of the tree, of the purpose of our being. These fruits will be more luscious if the root system and the branch system are fully developed and nourished both by the unseen neurology of our body and the leaves and branches of our family, organizations and the world community.

Let us look at an example from the plant world. I grow grapes at home in Idaho. I planted my vines about 30 years ago. When the roots are fertilized and keep weeded the branches will grow strong. The roots will send nutrients through the xylem up to the branches. As the branches grow strong and make many leaves, through the miracle of photosynthesis they make the glucose that will then flow through the phloem back to nourish the root system through the winter. In addition they will produce fat grapes that will nourish the greater system, my family and friends. It is a natural cycle.

Asking questions will help identify the level you are at. You might recall that each level had a question it answered. Let's review these and look at some actual questions you could use.

Environment	Where and When?	Where do you study best? If you could go anywhere, where would you like to visit? What time of day is best for you to study/
Behavior	What?	What do you do that makes your life fun? How do you act when you have had plenty of time to study? What do you do to get ready for English class?
Capabilities	How?	What skills have you learned in life that you are proud of? What can you learn from your teacher that will make you a better worker in the future What have you learned from your father?
Beliefs and values	Why?	What do you believe you must have in order to study well? What character trait do you most value? What do you believe is important to you?
Identity	Who?	How do you describe yourself? How would other people describe you? What kind of a person are you?
Purpose	For whom or for what?	What would you like to contribute to the future? How would you like to be remembered when you die? What is the reason you are here?

You may be asking what Logical Level Alignment is used for. Often it is used to create change. We all have some aspect of our life that we would like to change. In order to change we must identify that thing that we want to change. Carl Jung, a leading thinker in psychology in the 20th century said: "We cannot change anything until we accept it. Condemnation does not liberate, it oppresses." He is right. Your first step to change is to have a need. An example of this could be a girl, Chloe, who is thin and she likes to be thin. Her clothes fit nicely on her and flow as she moves. Her friend Danna is fat, and calls Chloe skinny. This does not liberate Chloe, it oppresses her. However if Danna accepts that she is too fat then she is ready to make a change and become thin like Jessica. This will only happen if Danna accepts that she is overweight.

How can you use this for yourself? Notice what you are thinking. Next find out what level it is at. Then think about the next level. What can you do to move your thinking up to the next level? Here is an example.

I believe that I am bad at studying.
I identify the level, it is behavior. The next level up is capabilities.
I ask myself, Am I capable of studying? Do I have the skills I need to study effectively?
I answer yes I do. Now I look at what I need to be better. I want to study two hour each night. I am capable to studying two hours each night. I have enough time, I can start and maintain it myself, it will still leave me time to be with my friends and it is a reasonable amount of time to still allow me to get enough sleep. It is well formed. I am capable of studying two hours each night. Then I might even do a Circle of Excellence for studying that I can pull out of my imagination when it is study time to put me in a state of learning. Do you think my grades will be good?

Lesson 5: Figuring out Other's Levels

Love builds bridges where there are none."--R. H. Delaney

When I started my NLP training and learning about the Logical Levels, at NLPU my teacher Robert Dilts told us, "You will never be bored in conversations again. He was so right. When you chat with someone, find out the level the person is at then ask questions that will move them to the next level. It is always interesting and often you will hear afterwards, "Thanks, you really helped me out. I am so glad I chatted with you today."

When we want to make a change in our lives, we can find out the level we are at and then go up a level to make a more effective change. If we want to help another change, we can do that by finding their level and then giving them a suggestion that will move them up to the next level. Here is a classic example of a poor speller.

Level	What might be said?	Moving up a level
Environment	"The classroom is too noisy so I can't learn my spelling words."	Behavior – I could cover my ears so I can think better
Behaviors	"I don't know how to learn my spelling words."	Capabilities – I can find someone who spells well to help me.
Capability	"Should I write my spelling words five or ten times?"	Beliefs and values- I believe that if I learn to spell better I will be more successful at school
Beliefs and Values	"Learning spelling words is dumb."	Identity – I am smart, it is just spelling words that "trip me up." (slow progress) If I could study them like I do math I will be more successful.
Identity	"I am dumb"	Purpose – if I learn to spell well I can help my future child in spelling so that child can be more successful.
Purpose/spiritual/ Vision/Greater System	"The school is dumb for making us learn spelling words."	An even greater purpose – I will learn the NLP spelling strategy and teach it to others so that they will be good spellers.

Here is a conversation between me and a friend showing a way to use the NLLA in conversation.

Huang-Fu is my friend and we are chatting. He tells me he smokes and wants to stop.
Huang-Fu says, "I need to have a cigarette when I am stressed."
That is a belief. The next level would be identity so we want to make a change at identity level.
I might ask, "Who are you that is greater than a cigarette?"
Huang-Fu replies, "I am a father."
Notice he says, "I am." That is identity level. Then I might ask him why it would be valuable for him as a father not to smoke.
Huang-Fu might then say, I want to live a long and healthy life so I can watch my child and my grandchild grow up.

I could reply, "You want to be a healthy father?"

"Yes!"

"A healthy father who handles stress independently?" I query.

"That is what I want to be," replies Huang-Fu confidently.

Now Huang-Fu is ready to expand his identity to a person who can handle stress without a cigarette. Now we can go back and talk about what environment, behaviors, capabilities, beliefs and values he needs to modify or change in order to create a new and healthier identity.

Here is an important conversation tip. If you start a conversation at the lower level of environment or behavior you will usually get a good answer. Start a conversation on the identity level and you may not get the conversation going. You could get a blank stare or even anger and hostility such as "Why do you want to know?" or "that is none of your business." People want to know you are interested in them truly before they want to trust you and explore the higher levels.

When you want to start a great conversation work up the logical levels. Always start at or near the bottom and work up. When you get to the top levels you will find that you can have some very deep and intense conversations and learn a lot about a person or subject.

Using NLLA you will have a skill in conversation and in change that will help you for the rest of your life. My wish for all of you is no more dull conversations. Let each conversation you have be interesting and make your life richer.

The assignment for Logical Level Alignment is a two week one. Next week you will all get to present a NLLA exercise, however you will not do it on your own. You will have a partner. One will ask questions and the other one will answer them. Below is a form to help you. You will not know what the topic will be nor who your partner will be.

Below is the form you can use to help you. You will be assigned a topic and then take your partner through the levels. At the end you go back down through the levels and experience what has changed, It is always interesting to do LLA. Experiential learning is when we do something in the learning process. We go beyond rote learning into experiential learning. NLP is all about experiential learning. We call it "Getting the learning in your muscle." That means your whole body is engaged in the learning process. Let's dive into (start) some experiential learning.

Start	Take a minute to say hi and to help each other be as ease. This is called establishing rapport and we will learn more about it in a later lesson. This is a good time for you to do the Six Second Stress-buster together and take out your Circles of Excellence.
Environment	Ask where and when questions.
Behavior	Ask what questions about the environment questions.
Capabilities	Ask how they will get what they need, what skills and inner resources will be needed from the behavior level.
Beliefs and Values	Ask why do you do what you do, why do you have the capabilities you have.
Identity	Why do you have those beliefs and values? Who are you? Who are you going to become or become more of when you come back?
Purpose	Who or for whom will you do what you do are questions for the purpose level?
Reverse	Then move backward into the environment one step at a time. And notice if there has been change and what that change is.

Lesson 6: Further Explanation

I had a student ask for further clarification on the levels. His question was on representation systems but needed to be answered at the NLLA level. I have added this chapter to provide that clarification.

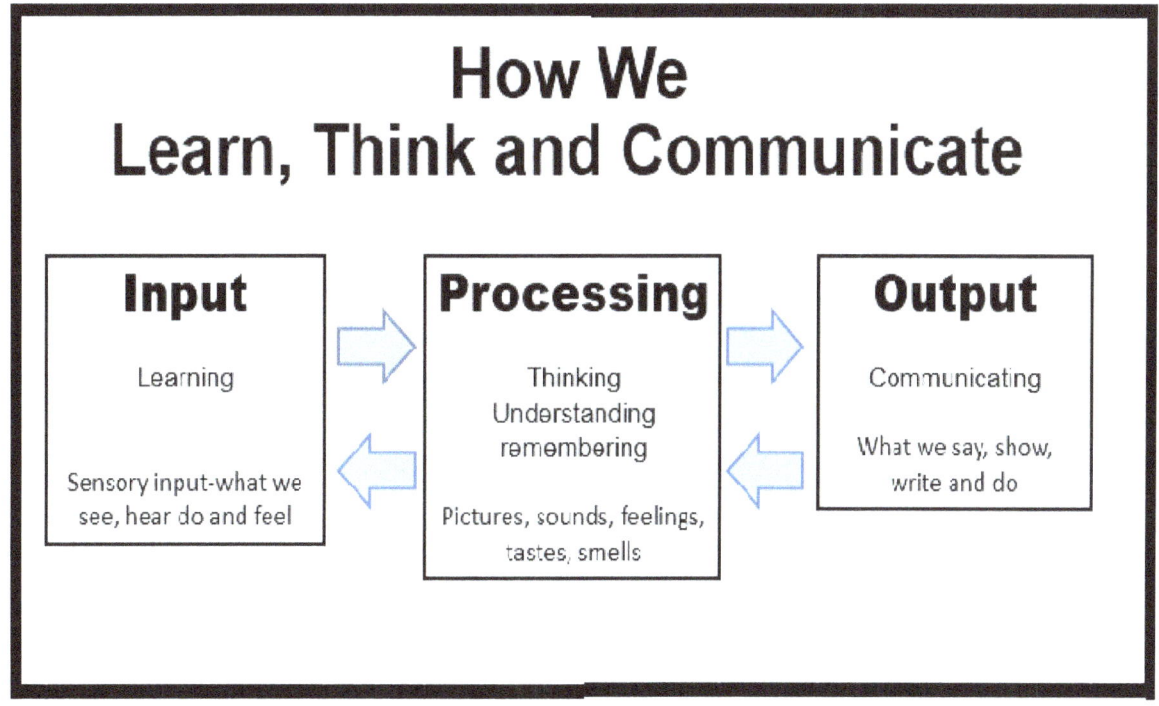

The modalities or senses are information gatherers. The brain then takes this information the senses have gathered and processes it, we call that thinking. It is at a higher level. From there we communicate with the information we have processed.

Here you will see the neurological level alignment chart. It was first developed by Gregory Bateson, then expanded from four to six levels by Robert Dilts. Each level moving up from the bottom is more complex by nature. If you choose to continue with your NLP studies You will learn that this is only the bottom and there is a second part of the chart that expands even further upward. The environment level includes the senses.

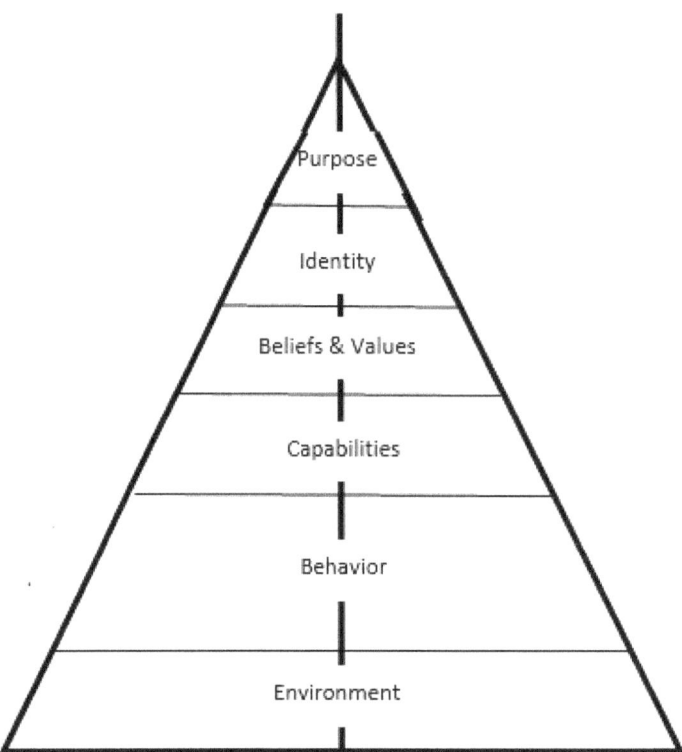

Behaviors are at the next level and include reflexes and simple thinking. Continuing up to capability is there we get complex thinking. What are we capable of doing with our sensory input and our reflexes and simple actions that is even greater? Having those capabilities leads us to creating beliefs and values, the why we do things we do.

As we understand our beliefs and values we know who we are. This is much more complex, and answers, "I am……"From here there is one more personal level that of our purpose, vision and mission. I spent three weeks at UCSC the summer of 2014 at a workshop exploring my own personal mission, vision and purpose of life. This level can get really intense, deep and interesting. If a whole room of fifty people can spend 3 weeks on it, well it must be capable of being a very deep subject and it is. We are wonderfully complex and capable human beings and when we learn who we are and where we want to go, well, we are amazing and can be a gift to the world!

Sharing my mission, vision and purpose in life

Some good videos that deal with Logical Level Alignment:

Avatar
Ratatouille
Dancing with Wolves

Unit 7: The Somatic Mind

If you change the way you look at things, the things you look at change.
Dr. Wayne Dyer

Lesson 1: Introduction

- Take a minute to notice how you are sitting. Do not change the way you are sitting, just notice. Notice how you are feeling, note your energy levels. Note how alert you are feeling.
- Now change the way you are sitting. Change your back, the way you hold your head, where your feet and hand are. Note again the way you feel, your energy level and your alertness level.
- Next put a pencil or pen sideways in your mouth to hold it. This makes your lips turn up slightly as if in a smile.
- Your body posture dictates a lot of other things. Today's lesson is an exploration of the field of the heart and gut mind, the somatic mind.

Here is a TED talk you may want to watch to enhance your understanding.
http://www.ted.com/talks/amy_cuddy_your_body_language_shapes_who_you_are.html

Lesson 2: Brain Development

In the tiny embryo of the human nestled within its mother's womb, a brain begins to develop. First cells divide then they begin to differentiate and some cells become the neural crest. The neural tube forms. This happens before the mother usually even knows she is pregnant yet drugs, cigarettes, alcohol and even emotions and life events can all critically affect the development of this vital piece of the human body. A brain stem begins to emerge in the center of this little being of potential. This bundle of nerves begins to grow and move or migrate. Part of it becomes the central nervous system with a part that migrates into the area that will become the skull and offered protection through the life of the individual it will become. It will form the brain. Many people think of the brain as a single organ but truly it is not. The brain has three main parts, the reptilian brain or limbic system, the cortex and the neocortex.

The limbic system controls automatic responses. It operates by influencing the endocrine system and the autonomic nervous system. For instance, if something tickles your nose, you sneeze and the limbic system again protected you from things that tickle your nose.

The cortex is the part of your brain that gathers information from your senses. It is the most developed section of the brain and plays a critical role in memory, attention, perceptual awareness (being conscious at some level of impulses one or more of your senses sending a message to your brain), thought, language, and consciousness. It controls motor responses such as walking and running. It is often referred to as the mammalian brain.

The neocortex is involved in higher functions such as sensory perception, generation of motor commands, spatial reasoning, conscious thought and language. Man is the only animal with a neocortex. This is what differentiates man from animals. It is sometimes referred to as the thinking brain. The neocortex is grey and wrinkled or convoluted like a walnut. Indeed it looks like a walnut. It is the outer layers of the cortex. Ninety percent of the human brain is neocortex.

Most people think that the brain stops here, but that is not true. Dr. Gershon teaches us that when the beautiful embryo is developing another set of nerves develops from that brain stem and moves into the torso. Only later are the two systems connected via a cable called the vagus nerve. It is often called the second brain. It is made of two parts, the heart brain and the enteric or gut brain. Scientists are just beginning to study and understand this brain however Traditional Chinese Medicine Doctors have been aware of it for thousands of years. They now ascertain that this brain has at least the intelligence of a cat. We often refer to it in NLP terms as the somatic mind or the somatic brain. It is a brain of feelings, hormones and automatic actions and reactions. Let's learn more about these newly re-discovered brains.

Lesson 3: The Heart Mind

...our hearts may actually be the 'intelligent force' behind the intuitive thoughts and feelings we all experience.

Throughout time, the heart has been called a source of not only virtue and love, but also of intelligence. One of the most common themes in ancient traditions and inspirational writing is the heart as a flowing spring of intelligence.

Many ancient cultures, including the Mesopotamian, Egyptian, Babylonian, and Greek, assert that the heart is the organ responsible for influencing and directing our emotions and our decision-making ability. Similar perspectives of the heart as a source of intelligence are found in Hebrew, Christian, Chinese, Hindu, and Islamic traditions. For example, the ancient Hebrews saying in the ancient book of Proverbs, "For as a man thinks in his heart, so is he,"

Balance and the attainment of bodily equilibrium are recognized as the essence of Yoga traditions. Yoga identifies the heart as the seat of individual consciousness and the center of life. In traditional Chinese medicine, the heart forms a bridge between the mind and the body.

Even with all these traditions and colorful heart metaphors, most of us have been taught that the heart is just a ten-ounce muscle that pumps blood until we die. Modern medical science claims that the brain rules all of the body's organs, including the heart. However, it is interesting to note that the heart starts beating in the unborn fetus even before the brain has been formed.

Neuroscientists have recently discovered exciting new information about the heart. It is far more complex than we'd ever imagined. Instead of simply pumping blood, it appears that it directs and aligns many systems in the body so that they can function in harmony with one another.

These scientists have found that the heart has its own independent nervous system – a complex system referred to as "the brain in the heart." There are at least forty thousand nerve cells (neurons) in the heart. That is as many as are found in various subcortical centers of the brain.

The heart communicates with the brain and the rest of the body in three ways documented by solid scientific evidence. These are:

- neurologically (through transmissions of nerve impulses),
- biochemically (through hormones and neurotransmitters),
- biophysically (through pressure waves).

Growing scientific evidence suggests that the heart may communicate in a fourth way, energetically (through electromagnetic field interactions). The heart, then, has a significant influence on the function of our brains and all our Systems.

Scientists are discovering that our hearts may truly be the "intelligent force" behind the intuitive thoughts and feelings we all experience. New scientific evidence shows that the heart uses the above methods to send our brain extensive emotional and intuitive signals. Scientist now know that the heart is in constant communication with the brain.

Thanks to the discovery of heart intelligence, with its premise of the heart as a primary source of emotions, we have a new paradigm for understanding our emotions. With the strong scientific tie established between our wellness factors through emotional management. As we learn to listen to and follow our heart intelligence, we become more educated, balanced, and coherent our own emotions. The more balanced and congruent our emotions become, the less likely we will be to experience sickness and disease.

Some of the most interesting research coming out now arises from heart transplants. When a person dies his heart may be transplanted into someone who needs a new heart to live. It appears that memories of things a person loved are also transplanted as if the heart is a memory storage system. Often when a person had a heart transplant s/he would talk with the doctor afterward and report that s/he suddenly likes music, food and places he had not before.

As transplant abilities by the medical profession improved it was found that children with cystic fibrosis who needed a new set of lungs did better if given new lungs and the heart that went with the lungs. Their original heart was still in good shape and could then be given to someone in need of a heart. These people were able to talk to each other and found that it was true, the heart carried with it memories.

The most interesting story that I have read is of a young girl who was given the heart of another girl who was murdered. Soon after the transplant she had nightmares (bad dreams) of someone killing her and was able to identify the murderer of the heart donor though the memories stored in the heart she had received.

Sometimes we think we know so much about the human body but we are beginning to discover that our bodies are a vast and barely charted wilderness waiting to be explored. Because of the ever growing body of scientific research on the heart as intelligence, it may be time we developed a new personal attitude about following our hearts.

Lesson 4: The Enteric or Gut Mind

You do not know something until it is in the muscle. --- Hawaiian Huna saying

The gut has a mind of its own. It is called, the **"enteric nervous system".** It is literally the brain in your gut. Researchers tell us that just like the larger brain in the head, this system sends and receives impulses, records experiences and respond to emotions. Its nerve cells are bathed and influenced by the same neurotransmitters. The gut can upset the brain just as the brain can upset the gut.

The gut's brain or the "enteric nervous system" is located in the sheaths of tissue lining the esophagus, stomach, small intestine and colon. Considered a single unit, it is a network of neurons, neurotransmitters and proteins that pass messages between neurons, support cells like those found in the brain proper and has a complex circuitry that enables it to act independently, on its own, learn, remember and, as the saying goes, produce gut feelings.

The gut's brain is reported to play a major role in human happiness and misery. Many gastrointestinal disorders like colitis and irritable bowel syndrome originate from problems within the gut's brain.

Dr. Michael Gershon, professor of anatomy and cell biology at Columbia-Presbyterian Medical Center in New York, is one of the founders of a new field of medicine called "neurogastroenterology." He shares how the enteric nervous system is very similar to the central nervous system. He shares that the gut contains more neurons than the spinal cord and included neurotransmitters and other parts of the nervous system. Between the brain and the gut our bodies have command neurons that send signals to gut and interneurons that carry messages back to the brain..

Dr. Gershon and other researchers are now beginning to understand why people act and feel the way they do. When the central brain encounters a frightening situation, it releases stress hormones that prepare the body to freeze, fight or flee. The stomach receives these chemicals and we feel "butterflies" in our tummies (stomachs.) Other reactions are controlled by these. People sometimes "choke" with emotion and have difficulty swallowing or may get diarrhea when over stimulated. Heartburn is caused by altered nerve function between the stomach and the esophagus.

Drugs cause an interaction between the gut brain and drugs. According to Dr. Gershon, "when you make a drug to have psychic effects on the brain, it's very likely to have an effect on the gut that you didn't think about." One fourth of the people taking Prozac and similar antidepressants have gastrointestinal problems like nausea, diarrhea and constipation.

Diseases often affect both the gut and the brain. People with Alzheimer's and Parkinson's diseases generally have constipation. The nerves in their guts are as sick as the nerve cells in their brains. Many autoimmune diseases like Krohn's disease and ulcerative colitis may also involve the gut's brain.

You may ask, "Can the gut's brain learn? Does it "think" for itself?" Dr. Gershon tells a story about an old Army sergeant who was a male nurse in charge of a group of paraplegics (people who are paralyzed from their lower back down and cannot move their legs). With their lower spinal cords destroyed, the patients would get impacted bowels. They could not move their bowels and defecate normally. "At 10 a.m. every morning, the patients got enemas. Then the sergeant was rotated off the ward. His replacement decided to give enemas only after compactions occurred. But at 10 the next morning everyone on the ward had a bowel movement at the same time, without enemas." Had the sergeant trained those colons? What do you think? Can the gut learn?

The human gut has long been seen as a repository or storage place of good and bad feelings. Perhaps emotional states from the head's brain are mirrored in the gut's brain, where they are felt by those who pay attention to them.

Lesson 5: The Somatic Brain and NLP

Neurolinguists ascertain that the heart and gut brain, the somatic brain, is a very important part of our learning system. If we can learn to become more aware of this brain and the way it communicates, we will enhance our learning just as we can enhance out learning by understanding how the right and left hemispheres of our brain influence our learning.

Remember the activity at the first of the lesson where you noted how you felt, then changed your positioning and noted again how you felt? NLP modelers started noticing something. When people changed their physiology they also changed the way they looked at things and the way they interacted in the world.

I first became aware of this long before I entered the study of NLP. I was taking courses towards my master's degree. Each person in the class would share with the others in the class a little about their specialty. Everyone was already a specialist in some area of the field of special education. One lady was an expert at positioning of people in wheel chairs. Scientists, she told us, have discovered that how a person sits in the wheel chair affects how well they learn at school. Try this to understand. Sit up with your back straight and tall, then tip just a bit forward. Lift your eyes. Note the changes you feel.Now contrast it by sitting with your back crooked and slouched. Tip your chin down. Let your hands and feet dangle (hang). Note the feelings inside. Where do you feel most like learning? Using your somatic brain wisely you can increase your learning potential. Grandma knew what she was doing when she told you to sit up straight when you study!

Throughout our study of NLP Practitioner level we will be doing exercises to become more aware of the somatic brain. As you become more aware it will help you in your studies, your relationships with others and even with your health. Enjoy your studies!

Unit 8: Eye Accessing Cues

Lesson 1: Eyes

"All action is of the mind, and the mirror of the mind is the face, its index the eyes." --
Cicero

What is the eye? The human eye is a hollow, liquid filled orb about one inch in diameter. It is suspended in its orbit and cradled in a cushion of fat and blood vessels laced with both motor and sensory nerves including the optic nerves. There are six muscles attached to each eye that allow the eyes to work together.

The eyes are connected to the brain by the optic nerve. The right eye is connected to the left brain and the left eye is connected to the right brain. If someone gets an injury to their brain on the left side, it may affect their sight on the right side. This is because the optic nerves cross sides to reach the brain. Let's learn more about our eyes as a communication system. Remember only about 8% of our communication is the words we speak. We learned about our heart brain and somatic system that communicate with feelings. Eyes give us many communication cues also. They are a part of that other 92% of our communication.

Lesson 2: Eye Accessing Cues

Before you start this unit, find a pal and run through the Eye Movements Exploration Activity. Remember to have fun. There is no right or wrong answers, it is an exploration and through that exploration you will learn.

As you did the game, what did you notice?
Do people always look the same place when they answer a question?
What are their eyes doing?
Do you always look the same place when you answer a question?
What are your eyes doing?

You may have noticed how people's eyes seem focused when they are paying close attention to something. Then you noted the difference when the same person is in a dream world. You can detect the lack of focus in the eyes. After asking the eye accessing questions you may have noted something different. People's eyes go different places when they answer different questions.

You will remember that John Grinder and Richard Bandler started the NLP movement on the University of California Santa Cruz campus in the 1970's. They gathered a group of interested students together. The groups were sent out to explore then return and report what they had discovered and two of those students are now world renowned NLP trainers, Robert Dilts and Judith DeLozier.   Robert tells this story:

"I have a very clear memory of a key moment in early 1976 when I was in John Grinder's Syntax 100 class at UC Santa Cruz. We had been discussing the generative power of language. John gave us the assignment to notice something that we had not paid much attention to before, give it a name and notice how our experience of it changed. After class I was talking with John to get a little clarification about the kinds of things he meant. At a certain moment, he said, "What about that? Your eyes just moved to the side."

As soon as I became aware of the movement, I remember being cognizant that I had "gone inside" and had been thinking about something that was just below my conscious awareness. I gave this phenomenon the name of something like "unconscious cuing." From that moment it was as if scales fell from my eyes and I suddenly became aware of all the things people did unconsciously to cue themselves: blinking their eyes, touching their faces, looking to different locations, making little gestures, noises and facial expressions, etc.

John seemed pleased with these observations and gave me more specific assignments with respect to observing various cues, including eye movements. I vividly remember sitting with Judith DeLozier during one of Bandler and Grinder's weekly evening group meetings and looking into each other's eyes as we asked each other questions and noticing the spontaneous movements in different directions.

My early work with eye movements culminated with a research study at the Langley Porter Institute in San Francisco in 1977 correlating EEG recordings of brain waves with eye movements and representational systems. This study was written up in Roots of NLP (1983) and also appears in the Encyclopedia of Systemic NLP (2000) - which can be browsed for free at www.nlpuniversitypress.com"

What Robert found we now call eye accessing cues. Eyes do most of their seeing automatically and are run by the brain. We can often get a picture of how a person is thinking internally by watching their eyes and where they go. Paying attention to eye accessing cues gives us clues to whether a person is thinking in image, sound, feeling, or movement terms. They serve as specific indicators of cognitive processes.

Do all people's eyes look in the same directions to the same questions? People are different, and people's brains are organized differently. As you learn about eye accessing cues you will want to keep this in mind. Eye accessing became a deep interest to Robert Dilts and in 1977 Dilts conducted research at the Langley Porter Institute in San Francisco on a variety of people of different cultures and racial backgrounds from all over the world. He found that not all people are the same. Notably, right hand people tend to be the same. We call them "normally organized." Left-handed people as a group vary more. Some are normally  organized, others are the opposite or mirror organized. Their accessing cues are a mirror image of "normally organized" people. Basques, as a group, have the most variety with "exceptions to the rule" being common. A small number of people, both ambidextrous and a few right handed people will be reversed in their some of their eye accessing cues, but not the others. Suzi Smith, a world renowned NLP presenter, is one example of the 12-15% of the world that is mirror imaged on top. Her visual remembered is on the top right and her visual create is on the left. Her other eye accessing cues follow the normal patterns. Each person tends to be stable and consistent in their own eye accessing cues. The picture is of Suzi Smith at Qibao, Shanghai China in 2013.

Has this research been supported by other research? Research should be questioned and proven in a variety of studies. Eye accessing research done by Loiselle in 1985 and Buckner, Reese and Reese in 1987 have supported Grinder, Dilts and thousands of NLP practitioners around the world who claim that eye movements both reflect and influence key cognitive components of cerebral thought. Take some time in conversations, lectures, talks and chatting to notice eyes and where they access.

Lesson 3: Eye Accessing

Could a greater miracle take place than for us to look through each other's eyes for an instant?
--Henry David Thoreau

Now you will want to know what the accessing cues are. Below is a chart to guide you. Remember that people are not all "standard models." These are guides for you to spring from.

Here is a breakdown of what the words mean.

Vr : Visual remembered – to remember something as you saw it, remembering a picture or "movie"

Vc: Visual Constructed – to create a picture or movie in your mind's eye.

Ar: auditory remembered - Remembering a sound or conversation

Ac: Auditory Constructed - Imagining what a sound will sound like

K: Kinesthetic - accessing emotions and feelings

Ad: Auditory Digital - having a conversation with themselves, mind chatter, hearing voices inside of your head. Digital refers to words.

VKS visual kinesthetic synesthesia – when a person sees something they also have a feeling that goes with what they see.

KVS kinesthetic/visual synesthesia – when feeling, having a picture come to mind. One new word is synesthesia. This is when a two senses are stimulated together, for instance some people, when they hear beautiful music also see a lovely picture.

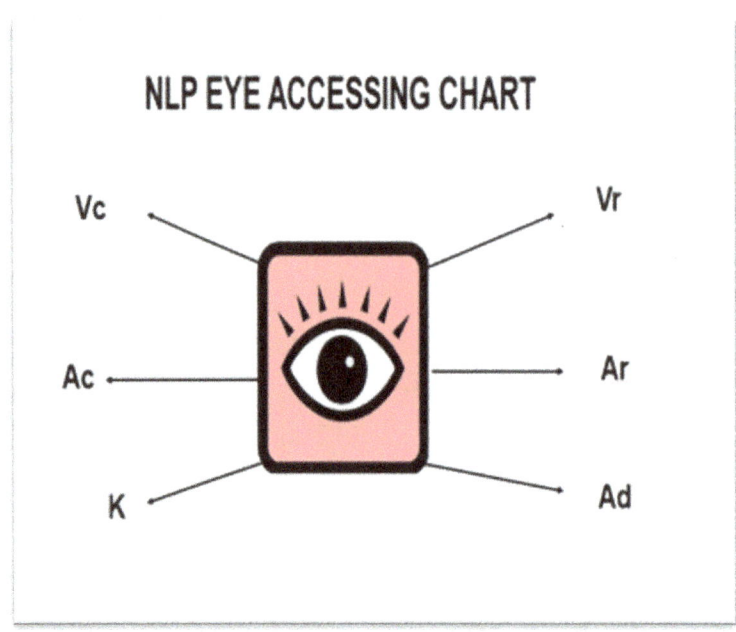

When someone is doing this	The eyes usually are doing this
Vr - Remembering a picture or movie	Moving to their top left
Vc - Creating a picture or movie	Moving to their top right
Ar - Remembering a sound or conversation	Moving to their horizontal left
Ac - Imagining what a sound will sound like	Moving to their horizontal right
K - accessing emotions	Look down and to their right
Ad - having a conversation with themselves, mind chatter	Look down and to their left
Quick access to all sensory information, but usually visual	Eyes straight ahead but defocused or dilated
VKS - visual kinesthetic synesthesia	Top Center
KVS - kinesthetic/visual synesthesia	Bottom center

Note that the auditory area is sounds and tones, not words. Digital is words. Note that not everyone is organized this way. About 85% of the population is normally organized.

In the first chapter the concept of integration of eye movements with the brain was introduced. The chart below expands on this subject. Again remember that we are not all the same, and "normally organized." However the research of Dilts and others shows that this pattern is most common.

Eye movement Patterns and the Brain		
Eye accessing	Left Brain	Right Brain
	dominant Logical verbal oriented	Non-dominate Memory artistic and spatially oriented
Vr Eyes up and left		Non-dominate hemisphere visualization, remembered imagery
Vc Eyes up and right	Dominant hemisphere visualization. Visual fantasy Where day dreams take place	
Ar Eyes lateral left		Non-dominant hemisphere auditory processing. Remembered sounds, words, tape loops, and tonal discrimination
Ac Eyes lateral right	Dominate hemisphere auditory processing Constructed sounds and words	

Ad Eyes down and left		Internal dialogue or inner self-talk
K Eyes down and right	Feelings, both tactile and visceral	
People tend to look in the opposite direction of the part of the brain they are using to complete a cognitive task. This is true for all of the senses. Again it is not "set in stone" (always the same).		

The challenge, to practice your new found skills and knowledge in conversations, lecture and classes. Maybe this will even keep you awake in the next boring lecture you attend that you really didn't want to go to.

Lesson 4: Not Set in Stone

When you ask a person the questions on the chart they may not respond as you expect because of their primary representation system. For instance, you ask a very visual person to think of his or her favorite song. The person looks up and to the right. You wonder what is going on. The person may be visualizing the cover of the CD, or where it is on his Mp3 or smart phone. He or she may then look at two or three songs before choosing a favorite and listening to it in their head.

Ask instead a kinesthetic oriented person and he or she may look down and check out his or her feelings for several songs before choosing a favorite. This is where a conversation can get interesting as you ask the person what they did in their mind as they were answering the question. By asking you will get a more accurate sense of what their eye movements signify.

As you practice you will get more confidence in "reading" the cues and the many ways they can be used.

Lesson 5: A Life Long Exploration!

How are you going to use this new skill and knowledge? Does it have a purpose? Will it be applicable in your life for anything other than keeping you awake in a boring lecture hall?

Eye accessing cues have many uses. A most important use is to gain rapport with another person. If that person is looking up as you discuss a problem, you might ask how they see the solution because you know they are making a picture in their mind. If you are looking down and to the right, how they feel about the problem. If they are looking in the auditory area, you might ask what sounds like a good solution to them. They will feel you understand them better and you do. That is part of the NLP magic.

Eye accessing cues can be used in family, business and everywhere you work with people. Are you a parent or a spouse? Watch the family members. If the family member is saying, "I don't know how to do this problem" and looking up you might ask him or her to picture the problem and ask what is needed to make the picture complete. If the person is looking right or left you might suggest they use you as a sounding board to figure out the answer. Say the family member is looking down in a kinesthetic area, ask how s/he is feeling about the problem and what they need to do the change that feeling. How about down in the auditory digital area? Ask s/he what that little voice inside is saying. It might be saying, "You are so stupid." Tell him "you are smart and you will get the right answer soon."

Then ask that voice what it needs to get the right answer.

Students sometimes ask if there is a difference in intelligence with eye accessing cues. There is no difference in intelligence. IT is the way your brain wired itself when you were small. You should not try to change them either. They are an important part of your neurology.

It will be interesting for you to explore eye accessing cues for the rest of your life.

Unit 9: Representation Systems and Learning Styles

Mission Statement: NLP practitioners discover the representation system they themselves use and then use this information to better their learning and their relationships with others. They also learn to detect representational systems in other people and use that information to gain rapport, and to assist others in learning.

Lesson 1: Representation System

"Sometimes a glance, a few casual words, fragments of a melody floating through the quiet air of a summer evening, a book that accidentally comes into hands, a poem or memory-laden fragrance may bring about the impulse which changes and determines our whole life."
—Lama Govinda

The first thing you as a student may ask is, "What is a representation system?" Our brain takes information in through our senses. We then use our thought processes to recreate our sensory experiences internally. For example, think of a fun family vacation you took as a child. You are probably smiling right now. Think of a time you got a really good grade on a paper and the teacher praised you. Now contrast that with a time you accidently ate some rotten food. Your senses remember that one well; it is a form of protection for you.

We represent our experiences internally to ourselves using our senses. In NLP we refer to that as our representational systems. We utilize the five senses plus speaking. We call these modalities. A modality is one of the main avenues of sensation (as vision).

NLP Representational Systems COMMUNICATION & SENSORY EXPERIENCE		
sense	Communication Channel	Abbreviation
sight	Visual	V
Hearing	Auditory	A
Feeling	Kinesthetic	K
Smell	Olfactory	O
taste	Gustatory	G

It is helpful to see each sensory system as part of a network.

- Input – gathering in information to the body. The information comes both from in the body and from outside of the body
- Thinking and processing – the way we use the information we bring in. Learning, mapping, motivation strategies, storing information, picturing the future, storing memories and making decisions.
- Output – the ways we express ourselves to others, body language, speech, language, voice and our physiology.

Lesson 2: Verbs

"The best and most beautiful things in the world cannot be seen or even touched--they must be felt with the heart." ---Helen Keller

People often tell you with words what representation system they are using. Watch for the verb in each sentence. If someone says to you:

"I *see* red dresses are popular this year." that tells you they are using their sight channel.
"I *hear* red dresses are popular this year." tells you that they are using their auditory channel.
"I *feel* red dresses are popular this year." tells us they are using the kinesthetic channel.

Later this year we will learn about rapport. Being able to tell what sensory channel a person is using can help you build rapport.

Some verbs do not refer to an auditory channel. The person may not be using a specific channel or they may be using more than one. We call this unspecified because the verb does not specify which channel is being used. For example,

I *understand* that red dresses are popular this year.

Most people have one channel that they use more than the others to represent their world. However, most people also use all five channels at one time or another.

Finding out your primary (first) representation system can be useful.

REPRESENTATIONAL SYSTEMS

VISUAL	AUDITORY	KINESTHETIC	UNSPECIFIED
see	Listen	Bite	Seem
view	Hear	Burst	Be
observe	Overhear	Bend	Aware
Witness	Sound	Bind	Have
Sight	Order	Break	Think
Spot	Ask	Fall	Believe
Look	Beg	Hit	Allow
Glance	Ring	Climb	Become
Eye	Sing	Feel	Know
Examine	Speak	Touch	Understand
etc.	etc.	etc.	etc.

Lesson 3: What is your preferred Representation System?

You are probably wondering what your preferred representation system is. Print out the quiz below. Fold up the side that tells what each question is looking for so you can do it without bias. As you read through the quiz put an X beside the ones that are most "you." Do not ask others, ask yourself.

1	K		You enjoy touching and handling things.
2	V		You were a good speller in school.
3	A		You enjoy listening to books on audio.
4	V		You love to read.
5	V		If you just have spoken directions you get confused. You want a map or diagram.
6	V		When you are working on something you enjoy a little background music.
7	A		You enjoy getting with a group and discussing things more than reading about it.
8	V		You use colors and colored paper for handouts and notes.
9	A		You enjoy writing and journaling.
10	A		When you work, you often talk to yourself.

11	V		You like to do things with your hands.
12	V		You are into athletics, sports, and/or working out.
13	V		You could spend many happy hours doing jigsaw puzzles.
14	V		You tend to tap a pencil, jiggle your foot or otherwise have a lot of nervous energy.
15	A		You remember jokes, stories and conversations.
16	V		You are a collector.
17	A		If you need to really understand something you will often read it out loud.
18	V		You find maps easy to use and you understand them.
19	V		You like to doodle or draw pictures.
20	A		When you read you like to follow along with your finger or a marker.
21	V		You enjoy games, role playing and simulation activities.
22	A		You use rhymes and jingles to remember things.
23	V		Much of your understanding of a conversation comes from reading body language and facial expressions.
24	V		You have a natural sense of direction and can locate places easily.
25	V		You almost always take notes at lectures.
26	A		If someone tells you what to do, you understand quickly.
27	V		You follow written directions well.
28	V		You talk rapidly and use your hands a lot when you speak.
29	V		You like to take things apart to understand how they work and then put them together again.
30	A		You enjoy talking with others on the phone

A_____   V_____   K_____

The highest number is your learning style or modality. The second highest is your secondary preference. If you are about equal you tend to shift from one to the other depending on the activity.

When this first came out, some teachers put a lot of effort into teaching the child in his preferred style only. However most people now agree that using all three styles helps the student gain greater flexibility. Knowing your own style will help you maximize your learning when the learning is important to you.

You can boost your learning potential when working to learn more. For instance, the following suggestions can help you get more from your study.

If your primary learning style is **visual**, draw pictures in the margins, look at the graphics, and read the text that explains the graphics. Envision the topic or play a movie in your thoughts of how you'll act out the subject matter. If your primary learning style is **auditory**, listen to the words you read. Try to develop an internal conversation between you and the text. Don't be embarrassed to read aloud or talk through the information. If your primary learning style is **tactile/kinesthetic**, use a pencil or highlighter pen to mark passages that are meaningful to you. Take notes, transferring the information you learn to the margins of the book, into your journal, or onto a computer. Doodle whatever comes to mind as you read. Hold the book in your hands instead of placing it on a table. Walk around as you read. Feel the words and ideas. Get busy—both mentally and physically.

Lesson 4: Using Modalities with Learning

How can representation systems be used in learning? A group of Neurolinguists wanted to find out what makes good spellers. They interviewed 800 spellers, some good and some not so good at spelling. They then looked for what was the difference that made the difference. They learned that visual people were the best spellers. They would make an imaginary picture of the word out in the air in front of them. They would then spell the word that they saw it in the imaginary picture. Sometimes they would check to find out if it felt right. The researchers could watch their eyes. Those that just visualized looked just at the word. Those that checked for feeling would have their eyes go up, then down to kinesthetic and back up again. So now the researchers asked, "If we could teach the poor spellers to visualize, would it make them better spellers? Indeed it did. Anyone can be a better speller by using and strengthening their visual representation system.

If you do not already visualize spelling words, try it. Make an imaginary chalkboard or whiteboard out in front of you. It will be in the visual area of your sight. Put the word up there on that chalkboard then spell it. This will help you get better grades on your vocabulary tests. Some people even like to add a picture of what it is to help them. Others will visualize a definition right with the word. When it is test time they just look up to their imaginary board and find the answers. Once the word and the definition are connected in your brain they will be easy to access.

You can make your ability to visualize stronger. Some people say the more vivid they make their imagery, the better they see in reality. One visual representation development exercise is to:

> ➤ Take an onion and place it in front of you.
> ➤ Close your eyes and imagine exactly the same onion.
> ➤ Open your eyes and take another good look at the onion.
> ➤ Close your eyes again and make the onion bigger in your mind.
> ➤ Now return the onion to normal size and change the color.

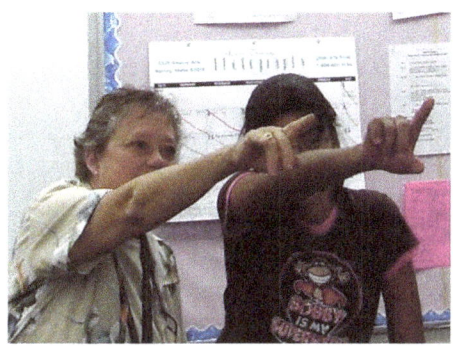

It is good imagery practice. In fact, if you bring in your other senses maybe you can make your eyes water. This might be a fun one to try imagining your girl or boy friend.

A truly amazing thing is when I used this as a developmental specialist teaching students who had low IQ's (intelligence quotients). People said they would never spell, but after they learned to visualize they could even spell big words. They could see the letters so clearly that we could erase letters on their imaginary boards and change them, then spell the new word. (write cat. C-A-T. Erase the C and put a B. Now what word is it? B-A-T Bat).

The picture is of one of my students using the spelling strategy. She was one of the best and could spell Albuquerque easily. I was very proud of her. She was already visual and it just took teaching her to put up the words and then she could spell well. You can use your preferred learning modality to boost your learning, too.

Sample

Modalities EXPLORATION

1.	Pick something you are thankful for.	*rain*
2.	Picture it in your mind. Now make the picture brighter. What happens	*the rain appears closer and brighter, I do not see the grey of the day, I see the raindrops instead*
3.	Now make the picture grey. What happens?	*rain is drizzly and the day is grey and mellow*
4.	Put a frame around the picture. What happens?	*It looks more like it is in the past of future to me.*
5.	Now make the picture all in tones of red? What happens?	*Lipstick rain, It looks shiny and bright. Not at all gloomy.*

MODALITIES PRESENTATION FOR NEXT WEEK

1.	Ground and center Circle of Excellence, COACH or 6 Second Stress Buster	*Circle of Excellence*
2	Pick something you are thankful for.	*Thanksgiving holiday*
2.	Share one visual characteristic	*I can see my family gathering at our house to share friendship.*
3.	Share one auditory characteristic	*I hear them all chattering away like a swarm of bees*
4.	Share one kinesthetic characteristic	*I feel happy to be a mother and enjoy my children who are so special tl me.*
5.	Have a closing statement	*I hope you have a loving family also. It is the greatest blessing of all, Thank you.*
6	Reconnect with the audience	*1 second smile at the audience*

NLP Spelling Strategy
(Tune: The Old Grey Mare)
Lyrics by Debrah Roundy

I just use the NLP Strategy,
NLP Strategy, NLP Strategy.
I just use the NLP Strategy,
When I spell a word.

Write the word on imaginary chalkboard,
Imaginary chalkboard, imaginary chalkboard
Write the word on imaginary chalkboard,
When I spell a word.

Chorus
When I spell a word. When I spell a word.
I just use the NLP strategy when I spell a word.

Unit 10: Modalities and Sub-modalities

Mission Statement: NLP practitioners discover a richer speech through the use of sub-modality words. They learn that people's words often reflect the modality they are using at that time to know the world around them.

Lesson 1: Modalities

Last week you learned that the way we represent the world internally is through our senses. We call this our representational system. Often people think that everyone knows the world in the same way but this is not true. Some people see the world while others hear the world and still others feel the world. There is no one way that is better than the other but the more we can magnify and amplify our sensory system the more effective we can be in communication. Research by Truner and Frost complete in 2005 showed "on average studies have shown rough 29% have a visual preference, 34% auditory and 37 kinaesthetic" SMITH (IN TRUNER,T & FROST, T. 2005, 146)

NLP Representational Systems COMMUNICATION & SENSORY EXPERIENCE		
Sense	Communication Channel	Abbreviation
Sight	Visual	V
Hearing	Auditory	A
Feeling	Kinesthetic	K
Smell	Olfactory	O
taste	Gustatory	G

Within each of the representational systems there are subdivisions or sub-modalities. These are parts or small chunks of the modalities. Here is a list to give you an idea.

visual	auditory	kinesthetic	smell	gustatory
Bright / dim	High / low pitch	Soft / hard	fruity	salt
Swirly / smooth	Loud /soft	Hot / cold	Sweet	sweet
Sparkly / dull	Harmony/dissonance	Rough / smooth	floral	bitter
Smooth / rough	Near / far	Slick / sandy	Sharp	sour
Fuzzy / clear	One side / stereo	Enveloping	pungent	spicy
Large / small	Fast / slow	Intense	foresty	burnt
Still / moving	Rhythm / free	Edgy / fuzzy	salty	rotten
Close / far	Bass / treble	pressure	sweet	smooth
Head on /above	Clear / muffled	location	sour	robust
Flat / 3-D	Flowing / jolting	Strong / weak	decomposing	fruity
Frame/unframed	Rhythmic/ arrhythmic	Heavy / light	burnt	acidic
Tilt /straight	Driving / forceful	Light / heavy	fresh	moldy
Black & white/ color	Compelling/ non-compelling	pebbly	stale	fresh

We often use sub-modalities in NLP to enhance a goal or a dream. We want to create a full and rich experience so we explore the sub-modalities to make it richer and fuller. Try it on your own.

1. Think of a dream you have. With my students I have them dream of graduating
2. If you haven't already, create a picture of your dream. With my American students I help them paint a mental picture of the chairs, the caps and gowns, and seeing family there. Add colors and other sub-modalities to your picture.
3. Now add to your dream auditory sounds. In the USA, we listen to a famous song called "Pomp and Circumstance," and imagine parents and friends cheering.
4. Kinesthetic is fun. Add some feelings, both internal and external. I ask my students to imagine the soft gown on their skin. Then I ask them how they feel inside, that bubbly feeling that we feel when we are excited. By now they are all smiling. The dream is becoming richer.
5. Next add smells that would fit the dream. Our graduation is outside so we can add the smell of freshly mowed grass.

6. And now the final enrichment, gustatory. Allow yourself to taste what you will taste. Our graduates are treated to pop and pizza so I add that to their dream.
7. Now contrast your dream with what is was at first. Does it feel fuller, richer and more real? Do you feel like you are more likely to make your dream now that it is fuller and richer?

Some of my students express the desire to be rich. Everyone can be rich in sensory experiences. Make yourself sensory rich. It has been found that the more fully you can develop your goal or dream using the sub-modalities, the more likely you are to achieve that goal or dream. Take your time and make your goals and dreams rich.

You can also use it when you are stuck with something. Change the sub-modalities and experiment. Will a change of sub-modalities get you "out of a rut?" A rut is a place where you are stuck. Let's try it:

1.	Pick a pleasant experience to play with.
2.	Select a submodality to play with. Use the list above for an idea.
3.	As each person takes a turn they tell what submodality they chose and each person in the group tries it with their pleasant experience.
4.	Share with the group each time
5.	Do other submodalities change with the change you made?
6.	Do your feelings change?
7.	Is there a place in your life that this change might be useful, for instance making a good memory better or a bad memory less intense and impactful?
8.	Do auditory and kinesthetic as well as visual
9.	What are the effects of adding, the effects of taking away?
10.	There is often a threshold. What happens when you cross it? For instance if you speed up the sound of a voice it will start sounding like the chipmunks. How does that affect you?
11.	Is there a point on some of these that you feel like you pop into the picture? This is associating into the picture.

Lesson 2: Mapping Across

"When we tire of well-worn ways, we seek for new. This restless craving in the souls of men spurs them to climb, and to seek the mountain view." -- Ella Wheeler Wilcox

How can you use sub-modalities? One way is an NLP exercise called Mapping Across. First you think of a stuck state and a state where you are not stuck. Then you find the sub-modalities of each one. Lastly you take some of the sub-modalities from the open state into the stuck state and see what you need to becomes free of the stuck state. This is similar to the Circle of Excellence you learned. You find a Circle of Excellence in what you want and then do the stuck state. Last you add sub-modalities from your Circle of Excellence into your stuck state and see what you need to get out of the rut.

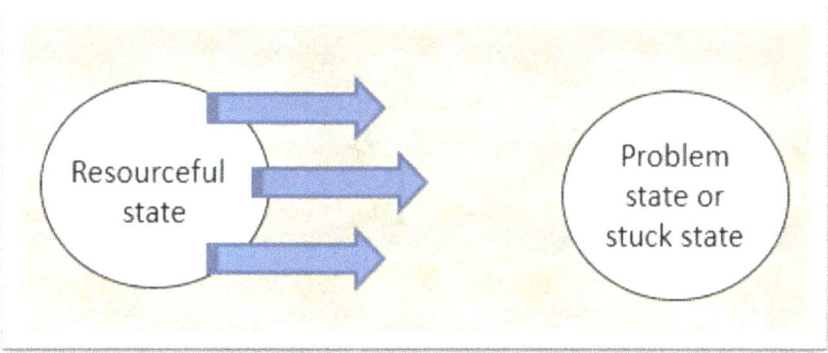

Often just by changing sub-modalities you can free yourself from a stuck state. What ruts do you get stuck in? A "do your homework rut? How about an "I'm tired" rut? Maybe your roommate is stuck in a rut and you n help your roommate out.

Lesson 3: Sub-modalities

You have learned that people use different representation systems. How do you know which one they are using? There are two ways we have learned so far. First you can watch their eyes. The eyes tell you what part of the brain is being accessed and how the person is representing the world.

There are other clues also, the words people use. This is where it is good to have made a list of sub-modality words so you can know how a person is representing their world. Here are different ways a person can tell you he understands:

I see what you mean.　　　　I <u>see</u> it <u>clearly</u>.
I hear you.　　　　　　　　I <u>hear</u> you <u>loud</u> and <u>clear</u>.
I feel it is right.　　　　　　It is not <u>hard</u> to figure out that answer.
I understand, it is a <u>piece of cake</u>.　　　That new car is SWEET!
<u>Smells</u> good to me.　　That idea stinks.

The words tell you a lot that the person does not know he or she is telling you. The words tell the representational system being used. Often if you can answer a person in the same representational system it helps them understand themselves and their own thoughts better.

You have now learned several ways you can use sub-modalities. You can use them to make a goal or dream more clear and inviting. Sub-modalities can be used when you are in a stuck state and want to get out by mapping across. You can use them to gain rapport with someone else. (You will learn more about that in a later lesson.) You can use them to tell what representational system a person is using. Lastly, you can use them to make your own speech richer.

Sample of Assignment:

For your homework assignment, choose two states and mark the chart of each. Here is a real life example I did with a young woman who had a big problem in China. What you are seeing below is the real thing. For her it made a huge difference.

Mapping Across Sub-modalities Work Sheet

resourceful state	stuck state
I have a powerful purpose in life	Incarcerated because a friend she was with had an expired VISA

Visual				Visual			
BrightX			dim	bright	X		Dim
ColorfulX			Black/white	colorful	X		Black/white
CloseX			far	CloseX			far
ClearX			hazy	ClearX			hazy
large			Xsmall	large			Xsmall
InX			out	InX			out
flat			X3-D	FlatX			3-D

Auditory				Auditory			
loud		X	soft	loud		X	soft
high		X	low	high	X		low
left	X		right	left			Xright
fast		X	slow	fast			Xslow
CloseX			far	close			Xfar
words			Xtones	words			Xtones
ClearX			muffled	ClearX			muffled

Kinesthetic				Kinesthetic			
StrongX			weak	StrongX			weak
LargeX			small	LargeX			small
heavy			Xlight	HeavyX			light
SmoothX			rough	smooth			Xrough
ConstantX			jolting	constant			Xjolting
HotX			cold	hot			Xcold
IntenseX			Xgentle	IntenseX			Xgentle

Change and what you noted when you mapped across
As she looked at it in 3-D she was able to see the entire experience more clearly. She could tell the only way was to go through it.
Left sound made a big change. It was easier.
She was able to link the sounds to people she knew.
Change you noted that did not make a change.
For her everything that contrasted made a change. Usually only some of them will cause change but it is likely her experience was so strong that every change was noted.
We did not test for her representation system. You know yours. Do you think it affects the ones that cause change for you?

Unit 11: Rapport and the BAGEL

Lesson 1: What is Rapport?

"All action is of the mind, and the mirror of the mind is the face, its index the eyes." –
Cicero

Have you ever been with someone that you seemed a natural match to? Last weekend at a Shanghai Speech Contest I met a fellow judge named Fred. We immediately" hit it off." We liked the same things and even though he was French and I was American, we "talked the same language." We had good rapport. That is when you and another person have a good understanding of each other. It sometimes feels almost magical, as if you have known each other for a very long time. When you talk it feels like you are being listened to and when the other person talks you want to listen. That is the magic of rapport.

The world is filled with an amazing variety of people. Each person in the world is unique, different from anyone else. Being able to establish rapport with all of the wonderful variety of people you met will lead you to success in your personal and professional life. It is about appreciating and working with differences. Rapport means that if you are a doctor you are able to help your patient open up and even read subtle clues that the person has missed that may lead to a diagnosis. As a spouse, a husband or wife, it means that you can communicate your feelings and needs more accurately. In a business those who can establish quick rapport have more effective meetings and get more business. Rapport allows the salesman to provide good customer service. Rapport even saves you time as when you have rapport with your clients it takes less time to understand their needs. Rapport will help you when you speak English. You will learn how to communicate in more than just words to get your point across.

Rapport happens naturally with some people, yet with others it needs to be created. Rapport is an art that can be learned. Rapport building is a very broad art and you have learned many skills in your NLP classes to help you. Rapport uses your words, eye accessing cues, modalities work, and body language, too.

7% Words
7% 词语
VERBAL 言语
38% Tone, pitch, volume, etc.
38% 音调、音高、音量等
VOCAL 声音
55% Face & body expressions
55% 面部表情、肢体语言
VISUAL 视觉

Professor Mehrabian of the University of California in Los Angeles (UCLA) researched the topic how people receive and respond to live communication. His study showed that only 7% of your message is conveyed (passed, transferred or given to) through the words you say. Most of your communication is delivered through the tone of your voice and your body language, gestures, posture and facial expressions and more. Clearly, words are not the major way we communicate even when we are having a conversation. Our linguistic communication extends far beyond words.

Other researchers have found slightly different percentages but they all agree that words are not the major conveyance of communication. The impact of what you see influences you more than the words that are spoken.

One day I was helping a young man from Jiao Tong University get his speech prepared for the Shanghai Speech Contest. He was working on his extemporaneous speech. After a speech his teacher, Ms. Dai turned to talk with her colleague. They spoke in Chinese so I could not understand the words they were saying. I decided to  watch their other cues so I paid attention to the body language, eye accessing cues, and gestures. After they were done talking I asked them if I could tell them what they were talking about. I then said what I had read. They were so surprised. I think they think I can understand Chinese but I can't, however body language is much the same in many ways all over the world. This will be especially important to you as students who likely will travel in many places throughout the world and use your English skills. As you learn to read body language cues you will be able to communicate better with others whether those others are your clients, your patients, your spouse, your family or just people walking down the street, even people you do not share a common language with.

In some places in the world there are people who tell fortunes. They always seem to know more about you than they have been told. Often people think they can see into the past or into the future. Truly, most or even all of these people do have a special ability, but the ability is not to see the unseen but to read the body language cues that people naturally do and are not aware of. As they begin to make a statement they will watch the client. If his body language is positive they continue, if it is negative they will back away and say, "no, no, I did not see that clearly, let me look again." With careful questions and answers they can quickly tell a great deal about a person because of their special talent to read body language.

Lesson 2: Eye Accessing Cues and Rapport

The best and most beautiful things in the world cannot be seen or even touched --they must be felt with the heart." ---Helen Keller

Now that you have learned about the somatic and intellectual minds, the eye accessing cues and about modalities and sub-modalities, you are ready to put this knowledge to work in learning new tools to build rapport. Having rapport with others is especially important in a speech class. When you speak to an audience and you have good rapport with them they will respond well to your speech. You can influence them in the topic you are talking about. If you have good rapport you speech will likely be a success.

It is the same way if you are working with clients or patients. If you have good rapport you will be effective. Even if you do not make the sale or cure the illness or whatever you are working on, you will still have a person who supports you and trusts you.

Let's go into greater depth with eye accessing cues now. As you are observing eye movements remember that people already have habitual eye movements that are related to their primary representation system. The representation system, you recall, is the way you represent the world. Some people primarily see the world in a visual capacity - they remember and store their memories in pictures or movies. Other people hear their world - their memories are likely to be stored in a way similar to audio tapes or songs. Still others feel the world around them and most often store their memories in feelings. Occasionally you may even meet a person who tastes or smells the world and stores many of their memories in gustatory or olfactory ways. You might also recall that no one representation system is more or less than another, and those who expand their representation system to include others more fully and completely get a more rounded and full view of the world. CEO's tend to represent the world in multiple modalities. This helps them understand and communicate effectively with more people and may well be why they are CEO's.

When you ask a person the questions on the exploration chart they may not respond as you expect because of their primary representation system. For instance, you ask a very auditory person to think of his or her favorite song. The person looks up and to the right. You wonder what is going on. The person may be visualizing the cover of the CD, or where it is on his Mp3. He or she may then look at two or three songs before choosing a favorite and listening to it in their head.

As you practice you will get more confidence in "reading" the cues and the many ways they can be used. Habitual eye movements will reflect a person's preferred modality. You will learn to separate the habitual modality cues from the eye accessing cues. Ask someone, "What is something really important to you?" Watch the placement of the person's eyes as they answer and you will likely get a lot about the person's most preferred representation system.

Lesson 3: How can You Use Eye Accessing Cues for Rapport

How are you going to use this new skill and knowledge? Does it have a purpose? Will it be applicable in your life for anything other than keeping you awake in a boring lecture hall?

Eye accessing cues have many uses. Are you a parent or a spouse? Watch the family member. If the family member is saying, "I don't know how to do this problem" and looking up you might ask him or her to picture the problem and ask what is needed to make the picture complete. If the person is looking right or left you might suggest they use you as a sounding board to figure out the answer. Say the family member is looking down in a kinesthetic area; ask how s/he is feeling about the problem and what they need to do the change that feeling. How about down in the auditory digital area? Ask s/he what that little voice inside is saying. It might be saying, "You are so slow." Tell him or her "You are a good thinker who looks at all the possibilities and you will get the right answer soon. Ask yourself what you need to get the right answer.'

How about in the work place? You look at your coworker, Burt. You note that Burt's eyes are staying at mid-line and his voice has a lot of variety and there is a rhythm to it. He tilts his head to the side almost as if he is on the phone. You think he most likely is auditory.

You note that Burt likes to talk things through. It's as if he needs to have a sounding board and hear the problems out loud. You recall that he tends to take a lot of notes in meetings. Knowing what you know now, and wanting Burt to be effective, you plan to give Burt some time at the start of the day for a chat and then leave him alone so he can get notes written. You understand now why he doesn't use maps. You laugh now as you recall riding in his car and hearing him talk with his GPS that he treasures. Sometimes it used to irritate you but now it delights you as you understand that this is how his brain is structured and it is this auditory communication going on inside his head that makes him effective in the work place, just as your own skills and talents, though very different, also make you effective. It is both of your unique talents that make your business profitable and able to flourish in the business world.

How about the teacher? You have a student, Susi, who is a treasure. She has the brightest smile and is always eager to please. During a spelling bee one day you notice that Susi always looks down before she spells a word, and that she often missed the spelling. Now you know that she is looking in her kinesthetic area to find the spelling of the word, not a very effective place to store words, especially since she misses words often and has created for herself a kinesthetic "feel bad" for spelling.

You take a couple of minutes the next week and teach her to write her words on an imaginary display board in her visual remembered area. You help her put each of her spelling words there for the week. Next week you give a word to Susi and she immediately looks down. You coach her to look up and find the word. As her eyes go up and you see that she is feeling lighter already. She finds the word in space and spells it accurately. You quietly celebrate knowing that the success will be an attractor for her and soon she will store all of her words in her visual field.

Eye movements can also help you determine how truthful or congruent a person is being. If a person is describing an event s/he has witnessed or been a part of the eyes will likely go to his or her left or Vr field indicating s/he is accessing the memory of the event. If instead the person keeps going up to the right, he or she may be uncertain, or being untruthful. One important caution. This is not foolproof. The person may be trying to reconstruct what he does not remember, or s/he may be cognitively organized in a different way. It could also be a part of this or her cognitive strategy. If this were consistent all of the time police, lawyers and courts would be using it consistently and criminals would be trying to figure out ways to rewire their eyes to their brains.

In NLP the most common application is to determine the representational strategies a person used in thinking and making a decision. Thinking processes are usually unconscious and spontaneous. The person is unaware of what they are doing. A good NLP guide can help a person by guiding the person's inner strategies. An NLP modeler will elicit from the client their own effective inner strategies for decision making, learning, motivation or memory. The pattern the eyes follow is often called the eye scanning pattern. Then the NLP practitioner will guide them in the way that is most effective for that person to accomplish what the client wants to accomplish using the person's own eye scanning pattern.

An example of this would be a child who spells well. The teacher notices that Tommy is a good speller. She also notes that when Tommy spells he follows this eye scanning pattern, first he looks up then down and the up again before he puts the word on paper. He does this so quickly she almost didn't catch it. One day she asked Tommy how he spells. Tommy answered. "I see the word hanging in the air. I then check to see if it feels right. If it does I look back in the air and then write it on paper. If it doesn't feel right I go back in the air and change a letter and then see if it feels right.

You have likely guessed by now that Tommy's primary representation system is visual- he uses the kinesthetic to check it out. Tommy is having a lot of trouble in math. He keeps saying the numbers over and over out loud but he is stuck. His teacher now can direct Tommy to look up in the air where he sees his spelling words and see the problem, put the answer up in the air and check to see if it feels right then tweak it in the air if he needs to. This is an effective strategy for Tommy - he had just not learned to apply it to math. Tommy may find his grades going up and Tommy just knows he is getting smarter every day. You know he is too, because he is learning to use his own brain and cognitive skills for success.

Mrs. Jones is a coworker. She has been assigned to put together the specs (specific details) for a big account. You know her well and she is so auditory it makes you laugh inside sometimes. How often you have seen her talk about a problem then when she has all the facts out, her eyes go up to see them organized. You know her eye scanning pattern well. The eyes may even go from Ar to Vc back and forth several times in a conversation if there is a lot of material to sort. Next her eyes go down to feel if is right and last she will say a finishing "this sounds good," as she puts the finishing touches on the document.

As she walks past on the way to the bathroom she mentions that she is stuck and does not know what to do. You haven't heard her quiet, almost musical chattering for a while. When she returns you invite her to talk about it for a minute to give you a break. Soon you see her eyes fluttering Ar to Vc and back again. She is starting to relax and you ask, "How do you feel now?" She replies that it is starting to come together and maybe what she needed was a bathroom break. You chuckle inside knowing that soon you will hear a finishing "this sounds good," as she finishes the specs document and passes your cubicle on the way to see the boss.

And what about you? You give yourself an NLP pat on the back knowing you contributed to the success of your workplace and made the workplace a place where people want to belong.

Lesson 4: Physiology and Gestures

Eye accessing cues are only one tool we have for gaining and keeping rapport with others. Social psychologist Amy Cuddy in the TED Talks *Body Language Shapes Who You Are* said,

> "… social scientists have spent a lot of time looking at the effects of our body language, or other people's body language, on judgments. And we make sweeping judgments and inferences from body language. And those judgments can predict really meaningful life outcomes like who we hire or promote, who we ask out on a date. For example, Nalini Ambady, a researcher at Tufts University, shows that when people watch 30-second soundless clips of real physician-patient interactions, their judgments of the physician's niceness predict whether or not that physician will be sued. So it doesn't have to do so much with whether or not that physician was incompetent, but do we like that person and how they interacted?
>
> Even more dramatic, Alex Todorov at Princeton has shown us that judgments of political candidates' faces in just one second predict 70 percent of U.S. Senate and gubernatorial race outcomes, and even, let's go digital, emoticons used well in online negotiations can lead to you claim more value from that negotiation. If you use them poorly, bad idea, right? So when we think of nonverbals, we think of how we judge others, how they judge us and what the outcomes are."

Our body language influences rapport. Often our body language also tells what representational system we are using.

As we talk with people we can use their eye accessing cues to tell us what representational system they are using. We can also use their physiology to gain rapport. We do this by matching or mirroring their body language. To match a person is to choose something they are doing and match it. For instance if they are tilting their head to the side you also tilt your head to the side. Mirroring is doing just the opposite of what a person is doing so if the person raises his right hand you raise your left. This shows a person you are paying attention to them and helps them feel that you are connecting with the person mentally as well as physically. Try it. Talk with a friend and purposely match what they are doing. Do not match everything as that will make them uncomfortable, just match their gestures or their head tilt; only one thing. Then when it feels comfortable purposely mismatch. It will be interesting to experience what happens. Often the other person will look baffled. They thought they were having a good conversation and suddenly it changed but they do not know why. Note to if you feel a difference in your somatic mind.

Have you ever talked with someone who is sitting down and you are standing? Often it feels very uncomfortable and you find yourself leaning over to get to their level. That is another area of interest. If you can get at or near the same level as another person it helps you maintain rapport. If a person is very tall or very small, sitting down may be a better choice for a conversation. In America we say it "evens out the playing field." It makes the people more equal.

Below is a summary chart of Accessing Cues and what also often is going on in the person's physiology.

Summary of Accessing Cues and VAK				
VAK	*Eyes*	*Voice*	*Body*	*Breathing*
Visual	Looking up right or left	Rapid, high, and clear	Tense, upright posture	Breathing in the top part of the chest
Auditory	In the middle Side to side	Medium paced and often rhythmic and varied in tone and pitch	Head tilts to the side in a "telephone position"	Even breathing from the mid chest
Kinesthetic	Usually down Usually right	Slow, soft and deep often with frequent pauses	Tends to be a slumped posture	Deep breathing from the abdomen
Auditory Digital	Down To left	Internal dialogue May take a bit to respond	Often intent and spacey or distant	Depends on the conversation going on inside
Gustatory	Down and center			
Olfactory	Up and center			

Did you notice voice, posture and breathing? They are also a part of gaining and maintaining rapport. As you talk with a person if you can also join them in the way they hold their body it will help you gain rapport. For instance if you become a doctor and a patient comes in all slouched and you stay very tall and straight, you may find that they do not communicate well with you. You will feel intimidating to the patient. If you can soften your posture a bit, get on their eye level and match their voice tones you will find they are more able to open up to you.

Breathing is also important. Have you ever come into class late and breathing very rapidly? ou sit down and you are finally there but you still do not feel as if you are a part of the class. As you slow down you begin to feel you belong. A good speaker who is going to give a long speech often will get the audience to breath together. One quick way is to tell a joke. As everyone laughs their breathing tends to come together.

I, the author Debrah, used to lead groups of children called Scouts. We would go in the mountains and camp overnight. In the evening we would have a campfire. All of the Scouts would gather around the fire and there would be stories, skits and usually a special message. My job was often to get the group working together at the start of the campfire so we were all in rapport with each other. Starting with a song can do that, so I would usually start with a song even before anyone had talked. We would sing a few songs together and then the skits and speakers would come in. The group now had rapport with each other and was willing to sit and enjoy each other's performances.

A story is told of a lady who was very ill and in the hospital. Her doctors thought she would die. To everyone's surprise she started to get better and someone asked what made the difference. She said, "It was the nurse who sat with me at night. She made me want to get better." What did she say? "She didn't say anything yet she just seemed to care and it made me feel like I wanted to continue in the struggle to get better." The doctors started to ask around. Which nurse was the wonderful nurse that made the woman desire to live? Surely she was special. They checked with all of the nurses yet none had sat with her.

Then they discovered who it was. It was the cleaning lady. She was an older lady and when she got to the room of the woman who was fighting death, she would sit down for a few minutes to rest her feet and as she did she would just breathe with the woman. She would sit and match the breathing pace of the woman who was too sick to even talk. Matching her breaths was a simple thing yet it was enough to let the woman know that someone cared about her and gave her the will to live. Establishing rapport can be especially important to the medical community. It can literally mean life or death.

Matching voice tones is another important part of gaining rapport. One day a woman lost all of her credit cards. This can be a very serious problem. She had to call many people to stop payment on cards and to explain what had happened. She was scared because someone could take all of her money and she did not know what to do. When people answered the phone they would talk to her in a calm voice to try to calm her down. Then she called a secretary who let her voice rise and almost match her own. "Finally," she said, "Someone understands me." As she calmed down the secretary also calmed her voice just a bit ahead of hers.

This is called pacing and leading. First the secretary nearly matched her voice tones, pacing her. Then instead of immediately making her voice calm, she would calm just a little bit at a time leading the woman who lost her money into a calmer state.

A doctor can use this also. Let us imagine that a patient comes in with a broken leg. He is all upset. The doctor can pace by acting upset also. Then he can calm his voice just a bit as at a time and as he does his patient will calm down also.

"Oh, this is awful; I see you broke your leg. We have to do something NOW." Then a bit quieter, "Let me help you on the table so I can see it better." (The doctor can also match the breathing then as he looks at the broken leg, the doctor slows his breathing a bit and watches that the patient does also. Then calmer still, "Let's both of us take a deep breath together to calm down. I can see that this is a break of your tarsal bone. It has snapped in the middle. We are going to need an x-ray. I am so surprised at how calm you are. You are doing great."

In this conversation can you tell how the doctor is pacing and then leading? He acknowledges the break, and matches the tone. The he matches the breathing and slows his own down leading the patient to slow down also. Finally at the end the doctor tells the patient what he wants the patient to be, calm, and praises him for it. A good Doctor with good rapport can make a big difference at a scary time in the patient's life.

It can even work with emails, we chat and other social network groups. When someone appears to be upset, or extremely happy or whatever, match them with words and emoticons. You will be delighted at how much people appreciate it.

People also give clues to what is going on with their physiology accessing cues. If a person gestures towards the ear they are likely to be telling you about something they have heard. If they point up towards their eyes it is likely something they have seen and so on.

Lesson 5: Matching Modalities in Conversation

The last area we will address in this lesson is matching modalities in conversation. You have learned to identify what modality a person is working in with their eye accessing cues. Often their words will also give you a clue. If the person says, "I see what you mean," he is using the visual modality and if you can match him with a visual answer you will create better rapport. "Let's take a look at what is next."

If a patient says, "Do you hear what I mean when I say my stomach hurts?" The doctor might answer, I'm hearing you. Let's see if this medicine will be harmonious to your healing." The doctor has matched the patient and the patient is likely to feel that he is being understood. If a patient feels understood and comfortable with the doctor he is likely to tell the doctor more and actually do what is asked more quickly as he will not feel afraid. That fear feeling often comes when a person does not feel like they are understood.

When you work with others you will always be more effective if you can gain rapport. NLP has a little mnemonic device to help you remember. When you want to gain rapport, or even want to find out more about a person look for the BAGEL.

B – body posture
A – accessing cues
G – gestures
E – eye movements
L – language patterns.

(a real bagel is a type of bread. It is simple and chewy.)

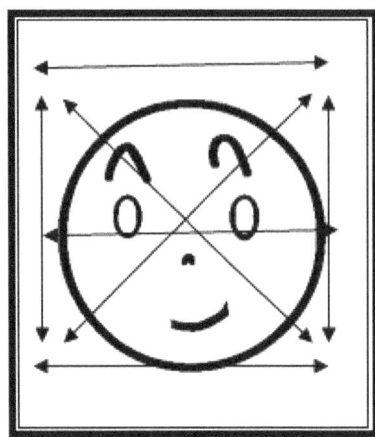

Exploring Representational Systems through Eye Positions

Keeping your head straight in front of you and nicely balanced on your neck, go through each of the eye position areas and hold for 30 seconds.
Were some easier than others?
Were some more natural and comfortable feeling than others?
Did some seem to take longer for 30 seconds to go by than others?
Did some change what you were thinking about?
Did some draw a blank?

Exploring the effects of Eye Positions on Problems Solving

Take a problem or idea you are working on and take it though each of the eye positions as above.
Notice how different eye positions affect your thought processes.
How did the problem change in each position?
Do any of the positions bring out a sound, feeling or an image?

Exploring Patterns of Eye Movement and Synesthesia

Synesthesia is linking sensory representation systems together. Sometimes it results in a Eureka moment. Other times you may feel a neat, nifty feeling as the synesthesia occurs. Maybe you will hear a bell ring its pleasure.

Move your eyes back and forth through the various combinations. There are a total of 45 different combinations you can try. Go back and forth between the two you choose six times. This is something you can do when you are board in class or riding a bus somewhere with nothing to do but explore you!

Unit 12: Extemporaneous Speech and COACH State

"You have to leave the city of your comfort and go into the wilderness of your intuition. What you'll discover will be wonderful. What you'll discover will be yourself." --Alan Alda

Lesson 1: Extemporaneous

We are asked to speak on the spur of the moment (extemporaneously) in many situations. As a student the teacher calls on you. In business the boss calls on you. Some people answer easily or get up in class and are eloquent (vivid, moving, persuasive or powerful) as they deliver their message. Other people feel a rush of butterflies in their bellies and hit the panic button.

Speaking on the spur of the moment means spontaneous, improvised, extemporaneous or impromptu. You do not have time to prepare. Here are some examples of uses of the idiom spur of the moment.

- The choir director fell off the podium and the second violinist was asked to lead the orchestra on the *spur of the moment*.
- The driver saw a crash ahead and on the *spur of the moment* decided to turn at the next corner to avoid the crash.
- One day in Hawaii I was visiting my son and waiting on the street while he went into a store. I saw a street vendor selling music. I purchased the CD's on the *spur of the moment* and they are some of the best music I have to listen to. (true story)

Surveys have been done of what is the most common fear in people. You may think it is spiders or snakes, but it is not. It is the fear of speaking in public, especially extemporaneously. Because this is such a common fear it was a good one for Neurolinguists to create programs for. There are several good programs and some you may already know. These include the Circle of Excellence, Six Second Stress Buster, Pentagon of Excellence and the COACH state.

Lesson 2: COACH State

A useful strategy to know is the COACH state. COACH is an acronym for

- Centered
- Open
- Attending with awareness
- Connected
- Holding

The COACH state uses somatic syntax, or the wisdom of the body. The words come from the Greek word *soma* which means "body" and *Syntax* another Greek word meaning "to put in order" or "arrange".

Somatic Syntax is based on these concepts:

- The order or arrangement of the body deep in us comes out of the deep structure of the body
- Meta model are the words that emerge
- 92% of what is going on in the deep structure emerges as body language
- There is wisdom in the body
- There is knowledge in the muscles

Somatic syntax includes gestures, eye movements, posture, and movements. It says that once you learn something at a surface level it goes deeper into your neurology. The knowledge is stored all over your body. For example, you can take you can take your fingers and walk them across your page, or make your arms move like they are walking. You can move your toes as if they were walking or your knees. But you never learned to do that. The ability to move your limbs or digits in an opposable manner as you do when you walk exists in the deeper structure of what is you. Once you have the movement in the deep structure, you can move it to various parts of your surface structure or generalize across settings. This learning came from the work of Noam Chomsky. Sensory and Emotional experiences (deep structure) are expressed through linguistic experiences (surface structure).

Your body works differently than your cognitive mind. It stores bits of learning all over your body. That is why you can walk your fingers across a page. It works like an old computer. I used to have to defrag mine often. Information was stored all over the system.

We can understand everything in two ways, literally and figuratively. For instance I can say your brain and literally mean your brain or I can say the computer you have upstairs in your body and it is a figurative metaphor for your brain.

Lesson 3: The Landscape

Certain things in the world trigger a memory in the body. They can be comfortable or not comfortable. The memory becomes an attractor. The more we stay in the attractor the stronger it becomes. If the attractor is good that works great. I have beautiful memories of NLPU and that has become an attractor to me. Maybe you also have a memory of a vacation that is so wonderful you want to return again.

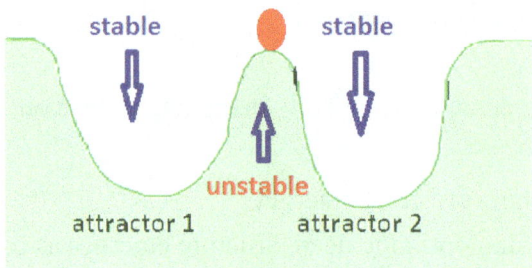

As long as both attractors are equal the emotional state ball will stay balanced. But if one of the attractors is larger than the other it soon erodes the stability of the middle ground and the emotional ball rolls in. What if it rolls into a stuck state? The person tends to keep going back and re-accessing the stuck state. One teacher I had called this a "Feel Bad," another called it a CRASH State. CRASH is an acronym for

    C - contracted
    R - reactive
    A - analysis-paralysis
    S - separating
    H - hurt/hateful

To put it simply, you do not feel in control and you chase the problems around in circles like a dog chasing its tail.

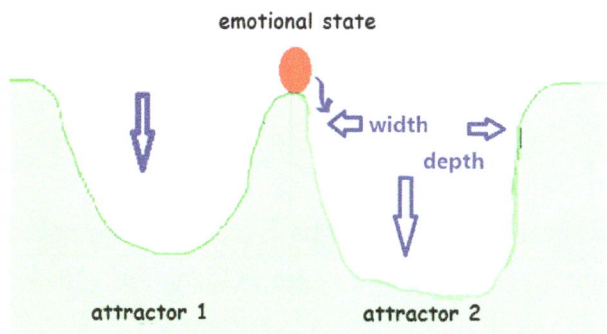

So the trick is to widen and deepen or enrich the basin of the places you want to be so that the Feel Bad's, the CRASH States are not as deep and rich as the places you want to be. Creating a COACH state will help you have an easily accessible rich, wide, deep basin you can access often to keep you out of those Feel Bads, those CRASH states that happen in life.

Now take a present state you might want to work with and chunk or break it down.

> Symptom (Your problem)
> Cause (Something from the past holds the symptom)
> Outcome (What you want in the near future)
> Effect (What kind of an effect will the outcome have in your life)

Then ask what stops me? Go wisely. Sometimes we are stuck for a good reason. I wanted to get a master's degree when my children were young. Then I realized that to get that degree I would have to make sacrifices that would affect my young family. I waited until all of my children were in school and then it was a better option.

Lesson 4: the COACH State Exploration

Now create a COACH State. Like a Tai Chi practitioner take a relaxed posture. Begin to breathe from clear down to your toes, maybe even beyond as you let your energy go down to the earth and bring up energy from the earth into your feet, your legs and up into your abdomen. There let it settle as you think of being centered and congruent with yourself. Now allow the energy to move up into your belly and be open there. As you feel that sense of openness allow the energy to rise up to your solar plexus and be aware of what is around you. Allow the energy to move beyond your being and into the area around you, attending with awareness. Next allow the energy to find your heart and connect with others around you. Finally move that energy to your head and allow it to be a part of the environment as you hold the space for yourself and then come back to reality refreshed and with heightened awareness.

This COACH State can be a new basin you have created that can be richer and deeper than the CRASH state beside it. But maybe it is not rich enough. Now the exploration begins. Each person is a bit different so it is a personal exploration.

As you take on your COACH State notice there are movements that naturally occur. For each person these are a bit different. They are unique to you. Explore---

- What happens if you do that movement faster?
- What happens if you move more gently?
- What happens if I do it more staccato?
- I widen the space I use?
- Deepen and intensify the space?

What can I change to make my COACH state more effective? This is where it is good to have a coach. The coach can watch for subtle little micro movements that you are not even aware of. Then s/he can guide you with ideas like these-

- Make it bigger. Note what happens to your coach state.
- Change you balance point, shift to one foot or the other. Note what happens to your coach state.
- Note if there is a rhythm inside of you. Then slow it down. Be aware of it and note what happens to your coach state.
- Where can you hold your coach state in the body?
- What movement best strengthens your coach state?
- What movement best enriches your coach state?
- What are the Neurolinguistic elements that make up your coach state?
- Who or what do you know that has the element that you would like to add or strengthen in your coach state?
- Step into that person or thing and notice how that strengthens your COACH state

Finally future pace your exploration. Where will you want to use it?

- with your family,
- riding on the metro,
- driving a car and focusing on the road,
- with your client, fellow workers, boss or professor
- At the computer

And
- Go fully into the state and – Walk, sit, carry something and write or play on your electronic gadget while you hold your personal COACH state.

Remember the beginning of the unit. It was about people's greatest fear, public speaking, especially impromptu. Now that you have a COACH State that is well formed, you have another tool to assist you in maintaining good composure as you answer eloquently. Enjoy your COACH State.

Lesson 5: Reflection

NLP was started in California, as you know, but has covered the world. The COACH state takes much of its effectiveness from Tai Chi and Yoga practitioners. COACH state may not have the same depth as Tai Chi but NLP modelers used Tai Chi and Yoga to build the program.

As you have all likely watched a Tai Chi practitioner, they start in a state of stillness. That is the COACH state. I took a class in 2013-14 from a Tai Chi expert and we would often do the ground and centering part for 30 minutes, just standing there breathing, grounding and connecting with mother earth and attending with awareness to our environment. We would feel our connection to each other and to our inner self, then hold the feeling. After we learn it well we can go into the soft, open state. If you are a practitioner of Tai chi or another similar art, you may already know this state with a different name. Use this state as it is already yours, just widen the basin with any pieces you have not used and have it even better for that is a lot of what NLP is about, taking something you already have and making it even better.

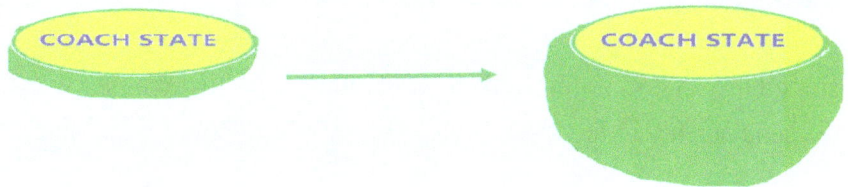

Unit 13: Non Verbal Communication

Lesson 1: What is Paralanguage?

All of us know that the meaning of what we say is contained, in part, in the words, or what we say. HOW we say things also contains powerful messages. This is the area of nonverbal communication. It includes touch, distance, appearance, time, and eye contact. Not only does eye accessing cues but also the time a person looks or glances at another, pupil dilation, fixation and blink rate factor into communication. An example would be the word, "Yes". It can mean completely different things (even in the exact same sentence), depending on HOW it is said. This includes paralanguage, also known as paralinguistics. Paralanguage includes sounds that sometimes do not have a written form (e.g., *uh-huh* means *Yes* or *I'm listening to you*). Let us begin our exploration.

When my daughter Seresa was a baby I listened to her babble one day. She was saying "no," over and over each time with different intonation, (variations of pitch) voice and rate of speed. It was interesting to hear her experimenting with language. Paralanguage is often the most important message in what is being said.

Try this sentence out putting the accent (stress) on a different word each time and notice how the paralanguage changes the message completely.

<u>Did</u> Seresa give Todd a kiss?
Did **<u>Seresa</u>** give Todd a kiss?
Did Seresa **<u>give</u>** Todd a kiss?
Did Seresa give **<u>Todd</u>** a kiss?
Did Seresa give Todd **<u>a</u>** kiss?
Did Seresa give Todd a **<u>kiss</u>**?
Did Seresa give Todd a kiss**<u>!</u>**
Did Seresa give Todd a kiss**<u>.</u>**

Really makes a difference in English, doesn't it!

The "how" something is said is referred to as paralanguage. It includes word emphasis as above with the sentence about the kiss. It also includes intonation, word and syllable stress, and even the body language that goes with it. It is the Nonverbal elements of communication. Paralanguage modifies the meaning and conveys emotion.

Lesson 2: Parts of Paralanguage

Specifically, paralanguage can be broken down as follows in this chapter. One part of paralanguage is voice qualifiers. Voice Qualifiers include these:

Tone of voice	Loudness or softness
Raised or lowered pitch	Convey things like fear, anxiety or tenseness, or designate a question. In tonal languages this is different.
Rasp, or openness	Caused by muscular tension or relaxation of the larynx very raspy may be a choked sound
Tempo fast or slow	Speaking quickly tends to communicate urgency or a high emotional state. Speaking slow tempos may give the impression of uncertainty
Drawling or clipping	Associated somewhat with accent, and whether the speaker is drawing out individual syllables or clipping them. This is most noticeable if you compare a native English speaker to someone who has learned French, or German first.
Gasp	Quick, sharp and sudden inhalation of air through the mouth. A gasp may indicate difficulty breathing, and a panicked effort to draw air into the lungs. Gasps also indicate the emotion of surprise, shock or disgust.
Sigh	A deep and very audible, single exhalation (letting air out) of air out of the mouth or nose that humans use to communicate emotion. May indicate a negative emotion, such as dismay, dissatisfaction, boredom, or futility. A sigh can also arise from positive emotions such as relief. It could also be an indication of lovelorn (unrequited love, forsaken by one's lover)
Moan	A vocal sigh, usually showing suffering or grief

Another part of paralanguage is vocal differentiators. These include crying, laughing and speaking and a halting (hesitant or wavering) manner. The third element is vocal identifiers. These are small sounds that are not necessarily words but are very important in communication and include such sounds as ah-hah, un-huh, and huh-uh.

All of these non-verbal (but tied to the voice) characteristics strongly affect how something is understood and interpreted by the other person, and how we interpret the words. They provide additional layers of depth and meaning to what is said. The key here is that we need to understand that how we say things can be more important than what we say, especially as we learn another language. When looking to diagnose conflict, always consider paralanguage and how it affects the meaning of the words and the conflict involved.

How can this affect you? Chinese is a tonal language. English is not so tonal. People often told me before I came to China that the people in China were always angry at each other. You could tell by their voices. Fortunately for me I figured it out. I used NLP and watched the body language. It was not angry body language. The Chinese language is based on four tones. Some of these tones are the tones the western world uses to show anger in their voices. Westerners hear the tones and think the Chinese people are all angry, all the time. Many of you will go visit the world. Be aware of the paralanguage. Remember that words are only about 8% of the linguistic that are used to communicate.

Lesson 3: Non Verbal Paralanguage

As I (Debrah Roundy) speak (ASL) American Sign Language, much of the sign language is not the words but the paralanguage that goes with the words. As you first look at a signer you may think "It's all Greek to me," but quickly you will note that the paralanguage gives the movements meaning and you may understand most of what is being said. I have spoken to several deaf people both in Japan and China and I can understand more of what they say than I can of Mandarin or Japanese. Signers are very accomplished at paralanguage as they communicate more through its use.

The biggest use of paralanguage as a non-verbal element of communication arose from comic books and is used in modern communication with texting, instant messaging, WeChat and e-mail. Nonverbal and paralinguistic elements can be displayed by emoticons, font and color choices, capitalization and the use of non-alphabetic or abstract characters. An example is a sigh and is usually represented with the word itself, 'sigh', possibly within asterisks, *sigh*. Nonetheless, paralanguage in written communication is limited in comparison with face-to-face conversation, sometimes leading to misunderstandings. It is important to learn to use emoticons wisely in your communication in the office and workplace as it can make or break you in the work environment. Good use of emoticons proves that a picture is worth a thousand words.

Signing a song in ASL with some students for a program in our town square in Rupert, Idaho, USA. Can you tell which picture shows the words, "The bombs bursting in air!"

Perspective: An English professor wrote the words, "A woman without her man is nothing" on the blackboard and directed the students to punctuate it correctly.

The men wrote: "A woman without her man, is nothing."
The women wrote: "A woman, without her man in nothing."

Chapter 4: Language of Love

When we talk of paralanguage it is a good place to mention the languages of Love. Love is such a big topic yet it is often treated as something everyone knows a lot about. Scientists have discovered that there are five different languages for love. We all think we express love the same way, then are often disappointed when someone we love and think loves us, does not seem to communicate that love. When the love is there, often the lovers are communicating in two very different languages.

Five different languages have been identified by social scientists. These are words, touch, giving gifts, service and time. Here is a chart to help you decipher the languages of love.

111

Where do you fit in? Ask yourself how do you like people to show they like you? How do you show others you like them?

Language	Actions	Communications	Avoid
words	Spoken words Written words letters	Encouraging Complimenting affirming	Harsh words criticism
Time	Running errands Sitting at home talking Going for a walk together	Quiet places No interruptions One on one conversations	Too much time in groups Being away from each other for extended time Being alone
Receiving gifts	Giving gifts Remembering special occasions with a gift Small tokens of love	Private giving of gifts Pleasant facial expressions	Forgetting special events
Physical touch	Hugs pats sitting together close touch	Non-verbal Pleasant facial expression	Physical abuse Corporal punishment Lack of touch.

I had a student come up to me and ask about a relationship. He and his girlfriend seemed to be made for each other and their relationship had been burning brightly yet recently it seemed to be flickering a bit. He kept telling her how much he loved her but she never told him she loved him back. Still she would always drop what she was doing to run an errand and even would go to the store and buy him something to eat if he was working late, but she never said, "I love you." I knew the problem immediately. Do you?

I told him about the languages of love and told him that for her running an errand or bringing him a special thing to eat was saying, "I love you," in her love language. If he wanted to really thrill her, do something for her such as planning an evening with just the two of them alone and give her the gift of time. That would communicate to her most effectively in her language.

Think about your parents. Do they tend to show love to you in the same way or are they different? How about to each other? Even at work as you learn to show appreciation to your co-workers though the language they understand best you will find yourself more effective. Some will appreciate a pat on the back while others would prefer to hear the words, "Well done!" and so on.

Learning the languages of love and appreciation can make you more effective in your family, your love life and even in your business career. Enjoy exploring the language of love!

Lesson4: Emoticons

Writing things lacks something that communication face to face has, paralanguage. The written word often is misinterpreted because the paralanguage is left out. Emoticons were developed to give written words more of the emotions and help the message get across as it was intended. What is hard to say in words is often obvious with an emoticon with its tongue stuck out, or a red face, or rolling eyes. We might say that these emoticons speak louder than words. Indeed a picture is worth a thousand words as it gets the subtle message across that words alone cannot convey.

Likely you already use emoticons. If you do not take some time to learn how to use them. There are plenty of tutorials on the internet that will help you. Add emoticons to your informal texts, tweets, emails and posts. Emoticons are not appropriate for formal writing and formal emails, they are for casual posts. A student set me this to tell me how she felt about speaking. Although she wrote no words, I got the message clearly! Do you sometimes feel like this also? 🥺 😳

Lesson 5: Tools to Serve You

Whether you are a businessman or a research scientist you will need to communicate in speech and writing. You have now learned three useful tools. These can serve you for the rest of your life.

- ➢ TOTE - Use to make speeches and essays on how to get a goal. Make the outcome in all three modalities to reach everyone in the audience.
- ➢ LLA – Use the logical level alignment to align a group to a single purpose.
- ➢ Modalities – Use the modalities in any descriptive essay or speech. When you use all three or even all five modalities you are likely to connect with all of the audience. It will not matter whether the person's primary system is visual, kinesthetic or auditory if you include all three.

NLP Model	Description	Applications
TOTE Model	Organizing to get something accomplished	Organize a team, a research project, a family vacation, a research paper
LLA Model	Unite for a common cause	Unite a family, team, research unit or organization to move towards a common goal
Modalities Model	Describe something to an audience	Describe something completely enough to reach all people understand no matter their representation system.

These three NLP models can help you for the rest of your life to quickly organize you self for the goal you need to reach. You can use them for yourself and you can use them with a group. They can be used to put together speeches, essays and thesis. In a large document you can use more than one, for instance you can describe the purpose of an organization in all three modalities. I trust these will help you be more successful.

Enjoy a life time of exploration! Learning to use paralanguage effectively will make a more effective communicator both in oral speech and the new world of modern communication via written language.

Unit 14: Perceptual Positions

Lesson 1: The Blind Men and the Elephant?

There is a famous poem my John Godfry Saxe called "the Blind Men of Indostan." It tells of six blind men who are taken to experience an elephant. Each one encounters a different part of the elephant. One thinks it is like a wall because he flet the body and it is big and broad, another like a fan because it felt the ears. The man with the tail thought an elephant was like a rope and they all disagreed vociferously. Each one was right and all were wrong because an elephant was so much more that what they felt. It is the sum of it's parts.

One's subjective (existing in the mind, persons feelings, beliefs, perspective, or desires) experience may be true, yet it may not be the totality of truth. If the sighted man was deaf, he would not hear the elephant bellow. Denying something you cannot perceive (understand through the use of your senses) ends up becoming an argument for your limitations.

The opposite of subjective is objective. Whereas subjective exists in the mind and can be influenced by emotions and prejudices, objective is having actual reality. Below is an example about an apple.

objective	The apple is red, almost round and has a stem.	
subjective	The apple tastes good and is yummy	

Lesson 2: Perceptual Positions

Just as the blind men from Indostan in the poem only got a portion of the objective (having actual existence uninfluenced by personal prejudices) experience, so we often get only a portion of the experiences we have in life.

In NLP we learn that the person who has the most flexibility (versatility) is the one who will be the most successful in a relationship or partnership. By using the perceptual position exercise you as an explorer can gain greater flexibility. You can then use this flexibility as you talk with others or as you debate a topic. If you can see it from more sides you have a better perspective of the issue.

It is likely that as you looked at the topic of discussion, "how much influence should parents have on their children's career choices?" in class, you gained much greater clarity (ability to understand things clearly) as you saw it from four positions. It may not change how you feel about the topic, but it will help you relate to others and discuss the topic with better understanding.

Lesson 3: The Perceptual Positions

The word perceptual means an awareness through the senses. It comes from the root word perceive which means to understand through the senses. Here is an example in a sentence: He gathered perceptual information about the city, the smells, taste, flow of people and the sounds, before he wrote his tourist's guide.

In 2013 I gave my students this same lesson but I did not explain it well enough. They sent me e-mails asking for more explanation. I got the perception that they did not perceive the meaning of perceptual positions so after class I rewrote the lesson material to make it clearer. I wrote back, "I perceive you are frustrated because you have not got the answers yet so you e-mailed me and now I can understand your frustration for I can feel it in your words. (Sense I am using is the sense of feeling).

We use 4 perceptual positions in the NLP Perceptual Positions Exploration. They are:

1st position.
- You, yourself
- How do you experience the world?
- How do you perceive the issue being discussed?

2nd Position
- Looking at the situation from "another person's shoes."
- A person who is close to you and to the issue. Taking the other's position instead of your own

3rd Position
- Looking at the situation from an "other" or detached point of view.
- Step into the shoes of another person and experience how that person perceives the issue.
- Someone who has a perception of 1st and 2nd people both and the issue
- Teacher, administrator, grandparent, village elder, government official, American or ???

4th position
- Looking from completely outside the situation.
- A world view
- God's eye view
- A universe view
- The Big Picture
- An angel view
- An astronaut's view
- Step out of the world a bit and look at the problem from a global perspective.

When we can take an issue and look at it from many different perspectives we gain flexibility. When one is in a debate it helps to look at an issue from different positions. This will give you greater flexibility and help you score points.

It will help you in life also. As an example, let us say you want to leave a day early from school to go visit your parents. You look at it from your perspective. You long to visit your mother and have some of her delicious dumplings. She makes the best ones in all of China! Then you look at it from your mother's view. You perceive that she would love you to come home but also wants you to do well in school and will worry if you miss a class. So you step into your teacher's position. You note that she feels sad that her class must be the very last one before the holiday and so she works extra hard to make it an interesting lesson. Then you look at it from a big picture. You see that if you are doing well it will not make a difference if you are there or not, but if your score in the class is not good, it will lower your score, you will not have the information you need for the final exam and it could affect your future career.

Now you have a lot more information and you can make a more informed decision. Using perceptual positions can make a huge difference in your understanding of human relations.

It can make you much more effective in the work world as you begin to see the perspective of each person involved in a decision. Enjoy perceiving the world in a whole new way.

 I well remember a great teacher who explained perceptual positions to me. I was sitting in a room full of people. He held up a finger and a piece of paper. He then covered his finger with the paper so we could not see it. He instructed us to raise our hand when we saw this finger again. Slowly he moved the paper and as he did people from one side of the room to the other begin to raise their hand, like a wave at an American ball game. He then explained that he was standing in the fourth position. He could see his finger and all of us. His perception was much larger, broader than ours. When you take a fourth position that is what you are doing. You are seeing every aspect of the situation or the problem.

You have already learned to use perceptual positions to broaden your view of an issue. There are other techniques that will help you in your quest to see the world more fully and expanded. Here is a story of someone who exemplified (showed well) the meaning of empathy. He is a friend of mine and we are developers of two NLP programs, The Harmony Strategy© and Xavier's Strategy for Organizing©. He just happens to be a Chinese-American, too.

"At Whole Foods Market today, I saw a little boy with his dad in the cafe section. His dad was helping the boy with his homework while both were eating pizza. After finishing his drink, the boy diligently got up and put his drink bottle in the recycle bin. His dad was watching, and I could tell the boy wanted to please him by showing him how responsible he was. The boy walked back proudly, but his dad noticing that the boy had put his bottle in the wrong recycling bin ('compostable' instead of 'bottles and cans'), frowned and said, "Can't you do anything right?"I could see how the words affected him. His shoulders drooped and he looked confused and frightened. My heart broke at that moment for the boy. His dad was a good man. I could tell by how he was helping his son with his homework. He had just been careless with his words, and didn't see how much his words cut and will echo forward for his son...I smiled at both of them and said, "Those recycling bins sure are confusing! You know... I just did the same thing myself. But, I think you must be a great dad to teach your son to clean up after himself so promptly."They looked at me with surprise. Then they smiled."

Xavier Lee

Unit 15: Psychogeography

Lesson 1: What is Psychogeography?

Psychogeography refers to where the people in a relationship are in the geography of the situation. This can have both physical and symbolic importance. For instance, a king or an important person will often sit on a raised throne to show his importance.

An idiom of speech is that someone is on their "high horse." The king had to have a higher horse so he would be seen and so people would know he was the important one in the battle or the parade. An example of this idiom, "My friend Cliff was on his high horse when he got an "A" on the biology test." This means he was feeling important.

Lesson2: Personal Space

People have an imaginary space bubble around them that belongs to them. If others enter that space they feel invaded. This bubble varies from person to person as individuals and from person to person in a psycho-geographical relationship. It will also vary by culture. Some cultures tend to stand close while others like their distance.

Lovers will stand close to each other showing by the psychogeography that they are very literally close in many ways. They are comfortable in allowing each other within their personal bubble or space.

Two boys angry and ready to fight who stand that close will soon be in fisticuffs. (A fight)

As a teacher and a counselor I learned to work with troubled youth. There were times when I had to get in their personal space but I did not want to be confrontational. (Meeting face to face, feeling an eagerness to fight) We learned to come up to the youth but stand slightly to the side and look the same way that youth was looking. It's called the non-confrontational position. It is especially useful in building rapport, and in conflict intervention and resolution as well.

Wu Bangguo (L), chairman of the Standing Committee of China's National People's Congress (NPC), meets with Caretaker Dutch Prime Minister Mark Rutte in the Hague, the Netherlands, May 15, 2012. (Xinhua/Liu Jiansheng)
(news.xinhuanet.com)

Note they are in each other's personal space but in a non-confrontational position. They are looking out in the same direction.

Close friends Or confrontational	acquaintances	Non-confrontational position	Looking together, united	Mentor or teacher
Within each other's personal space	Respecting the personal space of each other	Within each other's personal space but no eye contact, looking the same way	looking the same way, united	Mentor or teacher is behind to support, to catch if you fall or fail

Lesson 3: Spatial Sorting

As you did the exercise in perceptual positions you changed the place you stood as you explored each position. This is called spatial sorting. You sort the parts out to explore them.

John Grinder and Judith DeLozier discovered that when people change their psychogeography by changing where they are standing or sitting, they can dissociate or separate themselves from the context of the issue explored. In other words, when you were exploring the issue of homework you started out associated into yourself and exploring how you felt about it as you discussed it with your classmates. You then did the Perceptual Positions Exercise and dissociated from yourself and associated or joined into the position of your parent and others. In NLP work we often associate into an experience to gather more information. If you did this well, your view of the issue expanded and you had more flexibility as you discussed the issue the second time. We find that by getting up and moving around, by changing the psychogeography of the relationship we can keep the parts separated better and get a better exploration. When you are an explorer in NLP programs it is often good to stand up and move around in your explorations as you use psychogeography to cleanly sort each place whether it is you and another person or you and yourself in a different place or time.

You can use perceptual positions and psychogeography in many ways. As you do perceptual positions you become more empathetic. An empathetic person is sensitive to others and recognizes their feelings. An empathetic person is understanding and cares about others. An empathetic person will walk in the shoes of another and experience life from their view point. This will help you not only in speech but in every aspect of your life.

Lesson 4: Six Things That Drive Hiring Managers Crazy

Let us now look at interviews, job interviews being common, let's consider them first. The simplest mistakes can quickly blow your chances for a job because they drive hiring managers crazy. Learn about these all-to-common errors newbies in job hunting make.

-You don't listen.
During an interview you may want to give them as much information as you can about yourself, but the manager may look at you as a "Chatty Cathy" and back off, worried that your constant need to talk will keep others from working.

-You bring a support team.
 Bringing your mother, best friend or spouse tells the manager you are not yet grown up enough to handle a job. Show instead your independence and arrive alone.

-You nag.
After your interview leave the manager alone. E-mails are far too easy to send. Meanwhile s/he is trying to wade through numerous notes and your email is one more on his plate that he did not want. Yes, a follow-up email is good about a week later thanking the manager for the interview. Keep it short and to the point.

-You are overzealous in your applications.
Do not apply for every job in the company. Look carefully at the skills they are requiring and the ones you have and apply specific to what matches you with them.

-You're not fully or properly dressed.
Come to an interview dressed for success. Look at what others in that position wear and dress similarly. If you are doing a video or SKYPE interview consider it as if you were actually there and dress as you would if you were actually there.

-You lack basic interview skills.
When you are interviewing give the manager your complete attention. If you cannot live without looking at your smart phone then ditch it before you walk in so there is no temptation. Brush up your skills by practicing with a friend common questions you may be asked. Learn to answer them quickly and fully with only the information needed.

Lesson 5: More on Interviews

Of course you know you need interview skills to get most jobs but where else can you use the skills? Here are some ideas:

- School interview
- With a new co-worker
- When you are the boss
- Meeting a friend you have not seen for a long time
- Talking with others at a bus stop or on the metro

An important way to prepare for an interview is to practice with another. As you go over common questions it helps to prepare your mind. After you have been asked something have you looked back to the past and said, "I wish I'd said that," as you thought of what you could have said. Practicing helps you avoid that regret. After you have practiced your mind has some time to let things sit on the back burner. This means to put the thoughts aside in the back of your mind for a while and come back to it later while it simmers or come up with ideas.

Lesson 6: Dress for Success

Another good tip for interviews is to dress for success. Remember the lesson on rapport. One way to gain rapport is matching and dress is one thing we can match easily. Find out what kind of clothes most people at the job you are looking at wear and then try to dress one step up from that, just a tiny bit better. If you are applying for a job as a waitress at McDonald's dress a bit better than what you see the people there wear. If you are applying for a managerial position wear what a manager would wear dressed extra nice for work. Here are some common ideas:

Dress conservatively with dresses about knee length. Shirts and blouses should be long sleeved except on the hottest summer days. Girls choose a low heeled shoe. In the USA we suggest a 2" heel. A little heel makes a gal's legs look nice yet she can still walk a comfortable and graceful walk, not the stilted walk of a girl in heels. A suit in navy blue, black or grey are the best choices. Limit jewelry. No dangly earring or necklaces, however a small piece of jewelry that enhances the outfit is a good choice. Do not wear perfume or an aftershave with a strong smell. You do not know if people are allergic to the scents you may choose. However do take time to wear deodorant because you do not want the most powerful memory of you to be bad body odor. A portfolio or a brief case always gives you a professional air.

Do not have/bring

- Gum
- Cell phone
- Coffee or soda
- If you have lots of piercings, leave some of your rings at home (earrings only, is a good rule)
- Cover tattoos

On your letter requesting an interview, resume and/or curriculum vitae remember that the person may see hundreds of these. Most are never read beyond the first page. Make the first page count. Keep your letter and resume each one page long or less. Make it powerful and unique.

In some western countries such as the USA interviewers must follow certain laws to prevent discrimination. Do not put your age, race, color, religion, political party, and do not put a picture on it. If you do, the interviewer may not be allowed to hire you because s/he could be charged with discrimination.

These little tricks may be just what you need to beat the competition when the time comes. Best of luck job hunting. So where does psychogeography fit in to this discussion on interviews. Use what you have learned to place yourself. Remember to shake hands and then shift to a non-confrontational position. When invited to sit, turn your chair ever so slightly so that you are looking out together rather than directly facing each other. Notice how you feel about the other person and gently shift positions if you detect a need and see if it makes a difference. Your interviewer is in control but there are small things you can do to make that person feel greater rapport with you.

Unit 16: Contrastive Analysis

Lesson 1: What is Contrastive Analysis?

Contrastive analysis is the act or process of comparing and contrasting different states, performances or representations looking for the "difference that makes the difference" (the important thing that causes the change to occur).

An example of this is Mary. Mary is one "sweet chick" (nice girl that guys like). She is one creative bright light (outstanding) at work and dreams up the most wonderful ideas but when she is with her boyfriend after work and he asks her to dream up something fun to do for the evening she has no ideas. One day Mary does a contrastive analysis of the two states. She notes that when she is at work she is sitting back at her desk relaxed and with her head tipped up and she sees pictures. She hears a voice in her head say, "that's a great idea."

When she is with her boyfriend she is on the bus. It is the end of the day and she is wiped out (tired). She is looking down at her iPhone and the voice she hears inside is saying, "I'm hungry, let's just grab fast food."

She decides to try a change. She can change the physiology of the situation by leaning back on the bus against her boyfriend and looking up. She can ask her internal voice what would be fun.

Mary tries it the next day. She gets on the bus with her boyfriend and leans back against him with her head tipped up. She waits for a picture to happen just as it does at work. She sees a good restaurant near their homes. The voice says, "I'm hungry." She thinks, we can order ahead. She asks her boyfriend to call. She continues to lean back (on his shoulder) and she sees herself and her boyfriend relaxing at a nice meal. "Why this is just my cup of tea," she thought. (something you enjoy doing and that is easy for you) I knew how to do it, I just needed to change my physiology.

Lesson 2: Why do a contrastive analysis?

As an experiment a basketball team was divided into two groups. One group practiced to learn a new skill. The other group was instructed in the skill and then asked to imagine or dream about themselves doing the skill, but without any practice.

Then both groups played a game. The ones who had done the mental practice actually did better than the ones who had physically practiced. The researchers concluded that their success came from never missing a basket with their imaginary ball. You see when they imagined it, they never missed. Each opportunity was a perfect play.

When you have not done something before, it is strange to you. It does not feel comfortable. When you have experienced it, it feels familiar and "like home." The experience can be in your imagination!

When I had not been to Shanghai before, it felt strange and unfamiliar. Then after being here for four months I went to Japan and Macau to visit friends. As I was in Macau I said to myself, "I want to go home." The home that I was wanting to go to was Shanghai and it had begun to feel like home.

In Contrastive Analysis we take a new desired state and dream about it so it becomes a new home, a new familiar territory.

Lesson 3: Review of the BAGEL

Last term you learned about the NLP BAGEL. We used it when we were learning about gaining rapport. If you can match basic behavior cues with the person you are chatting with you can gain rapport faster. Here we will use the BAGEL in a new way. We will use it to compare and contrast different states of being. Here is the BAGEL.

B	body posture	The way a person stands or sits. Look for little things like is one shoulder up or one foot forward. Watch for how the posture affects the breathing.
A	accessing cues	What modality is being used? Watch for gestures that show such as a movement near the ears can mean they are hearing or one to the heart may show they are feeling.

G	gestures	What are the hands doing, where are they gesturing, are the gestures balanced or asymmetrical? Are they smooth or jerky?
E	eye movements	Watch the movements to help a person by asking questions based on the part of their brain that they are accessing.
L	language patterns	What words does a person use repeatedly that show his or her thinking. I <u>can't</u> do it. I am <u>stuck.</u> I <u>need</u> help. It <u>hurts</u> to think about it. We will learn more about this when we study the Meta Model.

The eyes tell us what part of the brain is being used. As people do things their eyes tend to do the same patterns. For instance when I lose something I tend to look to the right to see if I can picture where I left it, then I look down to the left ask myself where I might have left it.

That pattern works for me and it is what I do without thinking about it. I would never know the pattern if I had not done a contrastive analysis to find out how I found things I had lost.

Lesson 4: Do It!

Now it is your time to try it. Think of a time when you did your homework really well. You just got in and "went with the flow." (Came smoothly and was easy to do) Actually associate or put yourself into the time and be there.

Now think about the BAGEL and notice the little things. Next think of the time when doing your homework left you "down in the dumps." (Discouraged). Do the BAGEL and notice the little things.
Last compare and contrast. What are the little things that made the difference? What could you change to help you "get off to a flying start" (easy to start with everything going well) and "hang in there" (keep working to the end) until your homework is done. Maybe you can even "hit the hay" (go to bed) early.

Now you know how to do a contrastive analysis. You can do it anytime you want to compare two states. You can help your friends when they are stuck. In the contrastive analysis you have done something called mapping across states. You have taken a feeling or behavior from the present state and mapped it across to a future state. People who are successful often use mapping across to prepare for a future event. When they do this it makes the future event seem more familiar and comfortable. This helps them be successful.

An Example

Example of my Contrastive Analysis Exploration

Creating this lesson well:

B	body posture	Sit straight, sometimes lean back to look at the computer and reflect. Breathing is high in my chest and free feeling. Feet tend to be together and crossed at the ankles.
A	accessing cues	Put my hands together near my face (steeple my hands)
G	gestures	Hands work together
E	eye movements	Look up to the right then down at the computer
L	language patterns	I love it when the lessons just roll out!

Stuck in a lesson stagnation rut:

B	body posture	Lean to the right, arm on the desk, head down. Breathing is deep, low and slow. Weight is more on one side with one leg front and the other back.
A	accessing cues	Eyes down to the left right arm by ear (yes, there is internal dialogue)
G	gestures	Toe taps, fingers drum
E	eye movements	Eyes down to the left, tend to stay there
L	language patterns	Sigh This is sooooo boring!

What is the difference that makes the difference?

I actually did this as I was preparing the lesson. When I was doing the homework well state I was sitting up and really enjoying it. At first I had a hard time getting into the "stuck" state. Then when I did get in it I noted that I could hardly even type. I just wanted to sit and do nothing. But I had to finish so I went back to the do the work well state and immediately the words started to come to me and this is what I typed.

Good, generative state

Eyes up, head tipped How can I best meet the student's needs?	Steeple hands symmetrical Let's see what is next	Hands together, relaxed I love it when the lessons just roll out!

Stuck State

Posture is to the right, hands are asymmetrical head to left	Right hand gestures by ear Lots of negative internal dialogue Even my mouth is asymmetrical

Have fun doing the contrastive analysis. Don't get… wiped out (too tired, exhausted)

Get wiped out (too tired, exhausted)

Unit 17: NLP Presuppositions

Lesson 1: Presuppositions

A presupposition is something that we presuppose is true. It may not be true in every case but we accept it as true in order to use it in developing an issue. For instance we supposed there were other planets in other solar systems and scientists began to look for them. They found them and now it is no longer a presupposition, it is true. Interesting to me, as I write in 2015, scientists are again speculating that there are one or two more planets or planetoids even beyond Pluto. They must presuppose that there are in order to research. Maybe you reading this book will find out. I am so curious to know. There are 10-13 presuppositions used in NLP programs depending on the person or organization that is teaching. This unit we will only explore a couple (2 or 3).

Lesson 2: Positive Intention

The first presupposition we will look at is this, Every action has a positive intention. What this means is that whatever a person does, there is a good reason for it even if it does not appear to be in any way a good thing. Every action has a purpose or reason. It is either for pleasure or to avoid pain.

Here is an example, three people are eating watermelon. Are they feeling the same? Maybe not. One is eating for the pleasure of eating, another is eating to avoid being hungry later on. The third may be eating because he is very hungry and wants to stop the hunger pains. All are enjoying the food but for completely different reasons. All three reasons have a positive intention, to avoid hunger, to stop hunger or for the pleasure of eating.

Lesson 3: Maps

The map is not the territory. Every person has his or her own map of the world and no map is the same. Just think of a map. Every person will think of a map differently. No one map is more true than another map, all are valid in some context. The best maps are the ones that have the widest amount of variety and choice imbedded in them.

People build their map of the world from the sensory input given them. Remember the blind men who "saw" the elephant. Each had a map of the world that included an elephant and each map was different. Each map was accurate, but no map was complete.

These are all maps of my home in Idaho. Each is good for some uses. None is good for every use.

Each person creates a map of the world as they live. It is made up of the experiences they have had. One year we had a foster child in our home. He was from an indigenous (native to and originating in a particular region) American Indian tribe, the Sioux.

He had periods of his life where he had not had enough food to eat. His map of the world said that the world may not have enough food and he had better watch out or he would be hungry. One day I went into his room to clean and the closet did not smell pleasant, I opened the closet door up to clean and it had rotted food in it. I first I felt angry, "Why would he stuff his closet with food." Then I asked his counselor and she explained that his map of the world said that sometimes there might not be food to eat so he had better put some away "just in case". When I understood that his map was different from mine. I could help him by giving him some food that would not go bad so he could feel safe.

Lesson 4: Flexibility

The person with the most flexibility wins. In any problem there are always choices. Often we can only see one choice, but there are two obvious ones and one is doing nothing at all. That is a choice.

An example of this would be doing your homework. Let us say you have a lot of homework during Qing Ming festival. When you first look at it you think you only have two choices, doing it or not doing it.

Then you think flexibility. Let's see. I could do it all before I leave school. I could come back a day early and get it done. I could set aside an hour a day to do it. I could reward myself when it is done with a lunch out with my mother. Wow that is 5 choices. They will all get the job done. Now the prospect of getting homework done does not look so daunting.

Some day you may have a child. I hope you do, for children are the hope of the future. You can say to your child, "You must go to bed now." The child has no choices. But give your child choices and you will win. For instance, "You can go to bed now or you can go to bed in 5 minutes. Which one do you choose?" Of course they chose 5 minutes, but instead of going to bed unhappy now the child is happy because he or she made the choice to go to bed. Try it!

People are always happier if they have choices and if they make their own choice. This can be important in a business setting. If you can give your co-workers choices they will be happier in their work situation. It will help them feel like they have control. You want "buy in" (agreement) from others. Then your team works more smoothly and efficiently. It will make you a better boss someday, maybe even a better CEO, the Chief Executive Officer, the highest you can go on the corporate ladder!

Lesson 5: The Presuppositions

Different NLP organizations put out different lists of presuppositions. Some group several presuppositions together as one and have a smaller list. Others may have a few more that they find useful. Below is a list of the common ones used. Remember they may not be true in every situation, they are only a useful tool to base learning and exploration on.

NLP is still a fairly new study, only forty years old in 2015, and it is a flexible exploration and study that learns from others as it is based on modeling. Because of this flexibility NLP varies a bit from trainer to trainer. My major teachers came from NLPU. Be flexible when you discuss with others who have studied from other organizations.

IMPORTANT PRESUPPOSITIONS OF NLP

The map is not the territory

All behavior has some "positive" intention

People work perfectly

Everyone has all the internal resources they really need

The mind and body are connected

The meaning of any communication is the response it gets or elicits

You cannot not communicate

People make the best choice they can in any situation

There is no failure – only feedback

All the information you need can be obtained through clear and open sensory channels

The one (whether it be a person, an organization or a business) with the greatest flexibility will have the most influence / will win

If it's possible in the world, it's possible for anyone

We create our own realities

Unit 18: NLP Anchoring

"It might be a part of a grand event or a very simple moment, perhaps a brief interaction with another person. The grand or the simple, it doesn't matter. Just the remembering will lift your spirits, and warm feelings will fill your soul." ---Marjorie P. Hinckley

Lesson 1: What is an anchor?

You have likely heard of an anchor for a ship. I worked at SJTU and would occasionally visit the museum. On display on the Xuhui campus in front of the SJTU C. Y. Tung Maritime Museum was a very large ship anchor. An anchor is something that holds something else in place. The anchor of a boat holds the boat in place so it does not drift away from where the captain wants it to be. The anchor is dropped out of the boat or ship to the ocean floor where it catches the sea bed and holds the ship tight. A ship may be anchored for the night, of during a storm, or when it is being unloaded.

There is another use for the word anchor. It can be used as something that holds us to a feeling or a thought. Think of your grandmother. As soon as you think of her, what do you feel? Each person will feel something different but likely you will feel a sense of love. You may also feel her warm arms around you or her soft touch. These are all kinesthetic anchors holding you to your grandmother.

Are there other anchors? I like olfactory anchors. When I smell floor wax it brings me back to the memory of my grandmother who always likes shiny floors and would keep her floors waxed. Does your grandmother or grandfather, or your parents make a special kind of food? When you smell it does it immediately remind you of them? Then it is an olfactory anchor for you.

As I travel through Shanghai, I see many ads for Pizza Hut. The ads are very carefully developed to create in you anchors. When you think Pizza Hut what do you imagine? Family, friends, good times. Those are anchors Pizza Hut worked hard to develop.

Sounds can also be anchors. If you hear a fire cracker go off, what does it anchor you to? I imagine a lot of you will say Chinese New Year, or good luck. Not me. Once a fire cracker went off in my hand. When I hear a fire cracker I still remember the pain and how scared I was. I wonder how many of you are anchored to ice cream. What do you think of when you think of ice cream? It is likely something good.

When I was 12 years old, my school had an ice cream bar machine. I really liked Fudgecicles, a chocolate ice cream treat. Each week I would get an allowance of 10 cents. That was a lot of money then. An ice cream bar cost 5 cents. If I was careful with my money, I would have enough left on Friday to buy an ice cream bar. Those bars became for me an anchor in the feeling of being mature enough to manage my money wisely. One night in Shanghai I went to an expat store. They had FUDGECICLES! They were very expensive but I bought them anyway because they were such a delightful memory and anchor to me.

When a boy promises to marry a girl he often gives her a ring. The girl will love to look at and play with it because it is an anchor to her boyfriend and to his love for her. There is a picture of my rings given to me by my husband 40 years ago. They are pretty worn now. The engagement ring was a rose with a diamond in the middle and the band was two leaves. He wanted to buy me a much more expensive ring, but I choose this one because there was no other one like it.I also did not want to start a marriage with a debt. So that was my gift back to him, a simple and unique ring that was well within his budget. It is a wonderful anchor!

Lesson 2: How Anchoring was first discovered

Ivan Pavlov was a Russian physiologist who lived from 1849-1936. He is most famous for his experiment with dogs. We call it Pavlov's Dogs. The Pavlov's Dogs illustration helps us to understand why we respond sometimes irrationally to certain situations. It is all in creating anchors.

The initial Pavlov's Dogs experiment was simply to place a dog in a sound-proof, smell-proof cubicle, with no outside view - a controlled environment in other words. Each time a bell was rung when food was given to the dog. Then the amount of salivation the dog produced was measured. After repeating this several times, the sound was made but no food was given. The dog still salivated. The sound had become an anchor for food.

 Pavlov's Dogs provides a wonderful and true example for anyone seeking to explain or understand how our past experiences can prompt certain behaviors in the future. This can even include fears like the fear of speaking in public, taking a test, spiders, or of flying. The first time we do something new we may be a bit frightened and if nothing relieves this fright it becomes anchored with the thing. My daughter Alyssa, one night, stepped barefoot into the bathroom. A big, fuzzy spider was there and she stepped on it. Oh, my goodness. Now some may say she has an irrational fear of spiders but certainly that fear was tightly anchored that night.

Anchoring is, then, the process of connecting or associating an internal response to a trigger in the environment or in the brain. We call this a stimulus-response. Given a stimulus a response happens on the behavior level. It is reflexive. You do not think about it, it happens. It is outside of your cognition.

NLP takes this a step farther. We learn to consciously use anchoring so that it can become self-empowering tool that we can purposely access when we need or want it. We can use it to re-access times when we were particularly effective at creativity, learning, peace, and other valuable resources so that as we return to that state we can again be at our best. NLP anchoring creates a psychological anchor that helps us to stabilize in internal state we wish to use similar to how an anchor stabilizes a ship at sea at a place we want it to be.

Lesson 3: Using anchors

People can create self-anchors. When you are particularly deep into something you can quickly create an anchor. You just touch a part of you where you would like the anchor stored in your muscle memory such as a finger or your ear. Then each time you touch there it will bring back the memory. You may ask, how long will the anchor last? Some fade quickly, but if they are used often or made under powerful circumstances like a fuzzy spider in the middle of the night, they will last a life time and you can add more things to it to make it stronger, too. (No, please not fuzzy spiders)

I used anchoring for myself. I normally do not touch the top of my little finger so I chose to touch there when I was in a very quiet and peaceful state. Now when I need it I simply touch that finger the same way and it is easy to access a peaceful state again. I also anchored the students in my classroom. When they were being particularly good I would rest my hand on their right shoulder and whisper, "Good job." The touch and the voice became a double anchor. I would do it any time they were being good so it would be a strong anchor. Then when a child was having difficulty I would come quietly to him or her and rest my hand on their shoulder. They would immediately settle down and then I would add, "Good job."

Was it powerful? It was so powerful that once a child was having a seizure. No one thought you could change that. I quietly walked up to him and touched his right shoulder. Immediately the seizure stopped. I was amazed and everyone else asked, "What did you do. It was magic." No it was not magic; it was the power of a good anchor.

You can also use an anchor is speech class. I you are in one of my classes you might note that I use geographic anchors a lot. I do not always stand in front of the podium but when I am giving a serious lecture I will be there. When I want you to relax and listen to a story I will move away and maybe even down to the desks. That is because I want to anchor you as students. When I am lecturing I want you to pay attention and if you are not I will wait often for you to so I can keep that anchor for you. It will help you in your learning.

I would like you to relax a bit as I tell a story. It is a break state that gives your brain a rest. A break state is when think of something else and leave the thing you are discussing on the back burner for a while.

My lectures are crafted (created carefully, not just made) to maximize your learning potential. Surprise!

Anchors can help you in giving speeches. Your speech may have a special point you want to anchor, a nugget of information that is most important. Just as Pavlov's dogs had to be hungry for the stimulus to anchor with the response, you need to create a hunger in your listener. It is important to create in your audience a state of readiness. There is a feeling of openness and connection that tells you the group is ready. Often a story, a joke related to the material or a metaphor engages the audience, then when the engagement is full, the nugget is delivered. The audience may have an "Ah-ha" moment. The speaker is not just delivering information but providing a stimulus that gets connected to the reference response of the learner. Good teachers do this often creating link to learning in their students.

Chapter 4: Pentagon of Excellence

We will use an exercise similar to the Circle of Excellence to create for you an anchor of your own. It is called the Pentagon of Excellence (©Debrah Roundy 2008) and uses an imaginary pentagon, a five sided polygon. My class and my athletic teams all used the same anchor. It is the OK (okay, acceptable) sign in the English world. Do know that in Brazil it is not ok to use this sign, it is a dirty (filthy, derogatory sexual) sign. If you are in Brazil chose another anchor.

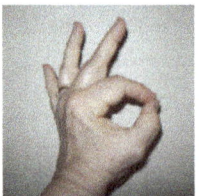

Pentagon of Excellence Strategy   ©Debrah Roundy 2008

1. Create an imaginary pentagon in your head
   Give it color or colors that mean excellence to you
   Shiny, swirly or sparkly
   smooth, rough, or bumpy

2. Step in your pentagon and think of a time you did your best. What did you do? Where were you? What did you hear, see and feel. Remember it all and enjoy.
   Step out and shake it off (break state)
   Test it by stepping in again. (This is using psycho –geography to create a state)

3. Step in your pentagon and think of another time you did your best. Remember it all and enjoy.
   Step out and shake it off
   Test it by stepping in again

4. Step in your pentagon and think of a third time you did your best. Remember it all and enjoy it, too.
   Step out and shake it off
   Test it by stepping in again

5. Step in your pentagon and hear someone say "Good Job" to you, or cheer you on.
   Really hear it in your imagination
   Enjoy what you hear

6. Now put all of them together and then make your anchor (ok sign or any other you choose) while you are feeling really excellent. Try to anchor at the point that the feeling is the strongest.

7. Future pace
   Think of a time in the future when you will want to be excellent
   Imagine yourself getting ready for the event
   Just before the event stars, fire your anchor
   Feel yourself feeling excellent
   Go and do your best

When you shake it off, it means you are "breaking state." It means that you were in one state (a state of being, the quality of having existence) and now you are shaking that state off so you can go into the next part of the exercise clean of that state. You are educating your body to remember quickly what excellence feels like to you. Then when you need to feel excellent, maybe for a speech contest, a dance production, a sports contest or a job interview, you can pull up quickly the feeling of excellence and use it.

Have fun. Can you create and anchor a state of excitement, good test taking, or of inner peace? Tai Chi practitioners anchor an inner peace in their stance as they commence Tai Chi. It is a great example of an anchor.

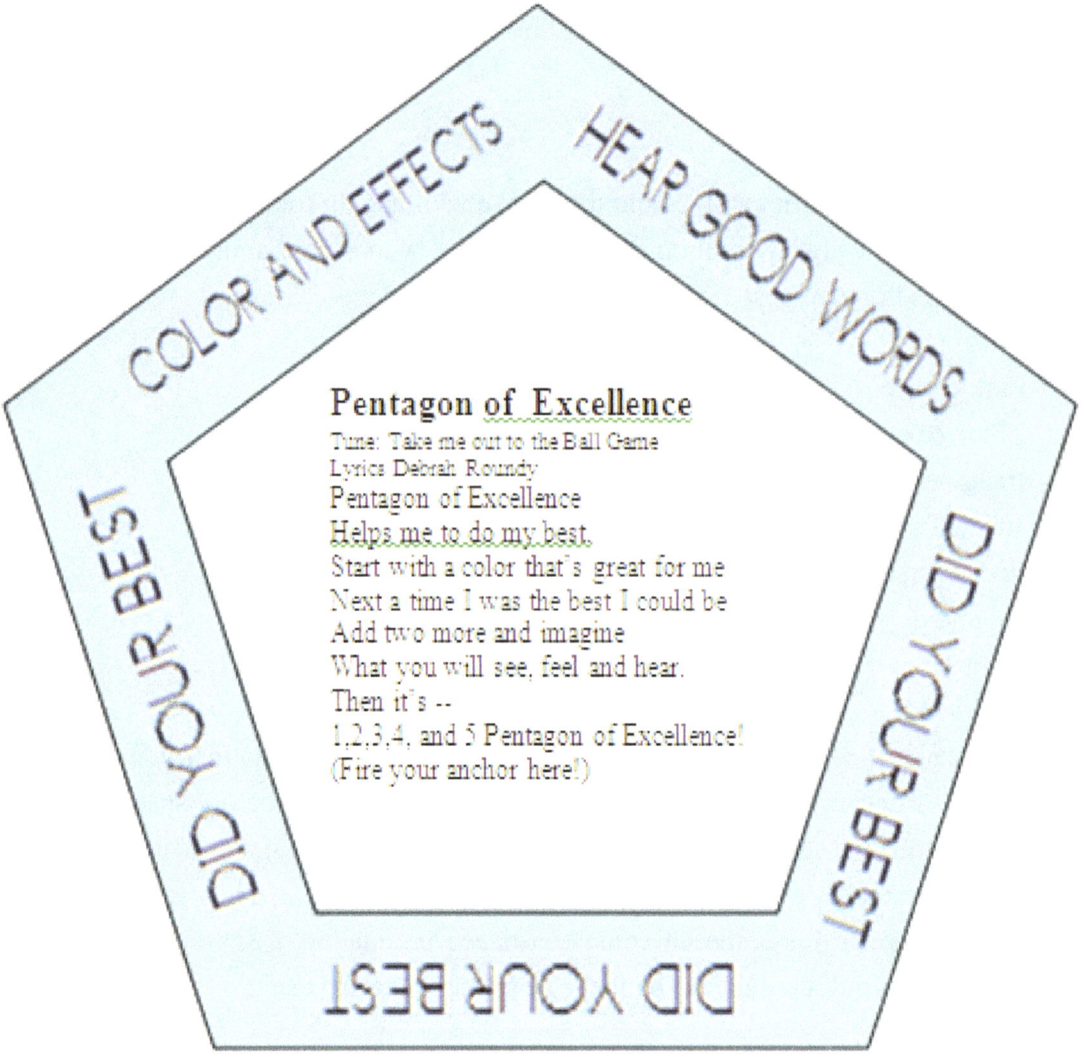

Pentagon of Excellence

Tune: Take me out to the Ball Game
Lyrics Debrah Roundy

Pentagon of Excellence
Helps me to do my best.
Start with a color that's great for me
Next a time I was the best I could be
Add two more and imagine
What you will see, feel and hear.
Then it's --
1,2,3,4, and 5 Pentagon of Excellence!
(Fire your anchor here!)

Sides of pentagon: COLOR AND EFFECTS, HEAR GOOD WORDS, DID YOUR BEST, DID YOUR BEST, DID YOUR BEST

Lesson 4: Stacking Anchors

Now that you know what an anchor is personally you can learn about stacking anchors. When you have a good anchor that you would like to keep you can continue to add to it, or stack more onto it. Each time an occurrence happens similar to the anchor you touch again the original anchor and make it stronger. Michael Colgrass, a very innovative composer and writer as well as an NLP trainer, has an anchor he created many years ago. He adds to it each day when he sees something beautiful. It is a simple one where he just holds a finger and his thumb together and squeezes for a brief second. Over the years this anchor has strengthened and become an important tool for him. Each time he begins a performance he fires (accesses his anchor by doing it) his anchor and recesses those beautiful feelings he has built up over his life time.

You may wonder how long an anchor will last. Anchors can be connected with impacting events and although they happened once the anchor, good or uncomfortable, may last a lifetime. Other anchors last only a few hours or days before drifting away. If you continue to pursue NLP studies you can learn how to use anchors to re-access states and how to decrease the strength of an anchor that is less than resourceful in your life. You may find that anchoring is a rich exploration to explore in life.

Chaining Anchors

Unit 19: NLP Meta Model Language Patterns

"If what is said is not what is meant, good vanishes and society comes undone." -- Confucius

Lesson 1: What is the Meta Model?

Have you ever said something to someone and then realized that what you said and what they understood were two completely different things. You just didn't understand it and you are confused and bewildered.

Words are a model, or a symbol of your experience. They are only a drop in the bucket. They can never fully describe what you mean. In NLP we may say that this small drop is the surface structure of language.  Surrounding this small drop is the rest of the drops in the bucket. The bucket is the whole experience. We call this the deep structure. The deep structure is the way your represent the world internally in your body and mind. It is the tail wagging the dog. This idiom means you only see the tail of the dog wagging frantically but what drives the wagging is the dog. (a small part is controlling the whole of something)

We will study the NLP Meta Model to make understanding of our speaking and writing move to a higher level as we clarify the words we speak and write so that they are no longer clear as mud but instead are as clear as day. We will go from the surface structure into the deeper structure so that we can be specific in what we mean. We will also learn how to use vague words as tools to reach a larger audience in our speaking and writing. Using the Meta Model can go both ways, towards greater clarification and towards ambiguity.

Lesson 2: History of the Meta Model

You learned a bit about Richard Bandler and John Grinder earlier in the book. They were the co-creators of the study of NLP. They watched two different and expert therapists (Virginia Satir and Fritz Pearls) talking with their clients. They melded it with their work in Transformational Grammar which seeks to explain the relationship between the surface structure of words and the deep structure of the entire experience. Through this they developed the Meta Model explaining how people link language and experience. They discovered that when people speak they tend to do three key things naturally. The delete, generalize and distort. This helps us explain our experiences in words without going into long-winded and detailed explanations that would cause the listener to die of boredom. The results of their work were published in 1975 in the book, *The Structure of Magic*.

These are normal processes we do all the time. For instance you may say, "They are going to go sit on a chair." You leave out a lot of details. Why are they sitting on a chair? What kind of a chair is it? Who are they? Much of this comes through in speaking through paralanguage. You gesture to the people, you gesture to the chair. You wipe your brow and the listener knows they are tired and will take a rest and so on. If you went into all the detail that was needed you would work the thing to death adding too much detail and everyone would be bored listening to you.

In our speaking and writing, therefore, we tend to delete information, not giving the whole picture. We also make generalizations by extrapolating from on experience to another. Lastly we also tend to distort things letting our imaginations run wild.

This is how it works: we take in information by our senses. We then run it through the filters of our life deleting things we do not think are important, generalizing things from previous knowledge and fleshing out (adding to as a sculpture adds clay to give a bust skin and life) the information with distortion. We then take this information and meld it into our own view or map of the world. We will study more about maps of the world later this term.

For further explanation, think of a car wreck. The police come to take a deposition or testimony from those who saw the wreck. Each person will give a different story. Yet it is the same wreck. Why?

Experiencing the World Around You

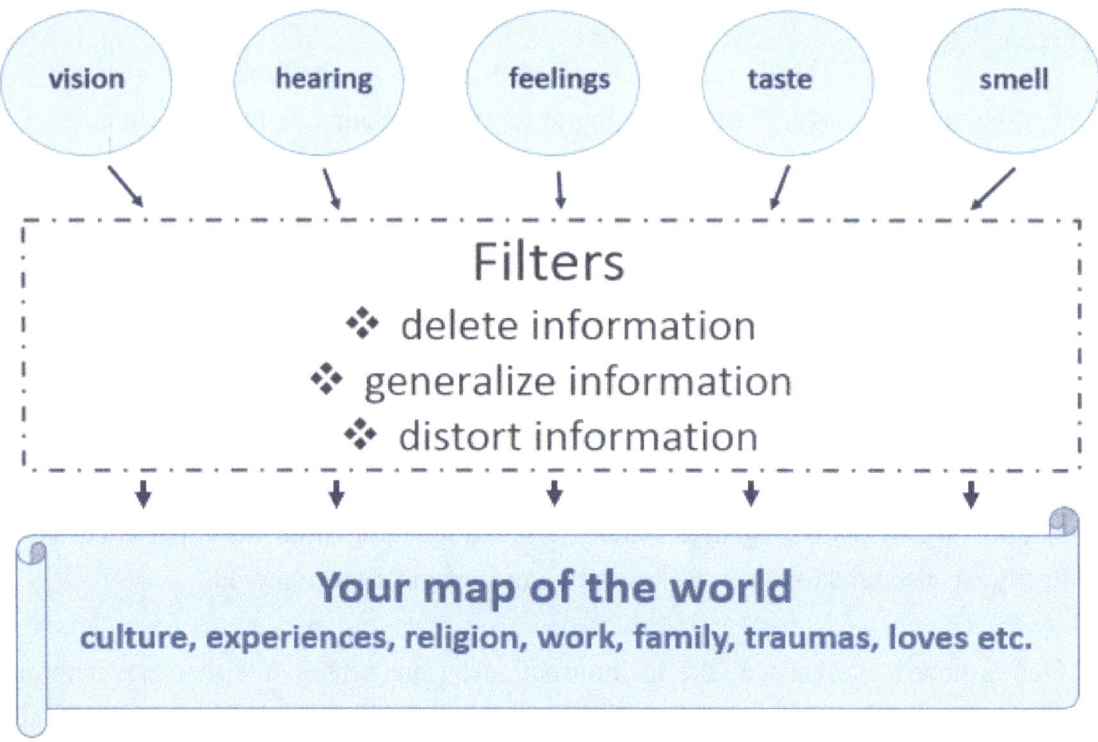

Each person takes what they imputed from their five senses, then generalize, deleted and distorted according to their experiences and lastly they put it into their own map of the world that was formed by their own experiences. One person may have seen a car wreck where everyone came out ok and another was in a car wreck where a loved one dies. Their personal maps of car wrecks would be completely different and would put a different spin on what they saw happen. (They would interpret the car wreck in a favorable manner to their map of the world)

Our study will look at the Meta Model patterns one by one as we learn a series of questions that will assist us in clarifying the deletions, distortions and generalizations we use to make our English writing and speech more clear and understandable so it will no longer be clear as mud. You will often recognize these questions because they are ones you normally ask when you need clarification. The difference you will find is that you will be more aware of the deletions, generalizations and distortions in your writing and speaking. It will help you in conversations, too as you learn to gently ask the questions to clarify what the person is saying so that you have better rapport with him or her as you fully understand what they really meant. By questioning you will find a clearer picture of the real experience and have tools to find it. You will find that your essays will be clearer and more concise as you become aware of the Meta Model in all you communicate.

This is going to be a useful study and you are going to appreciate even more the skills you have learned and are yet to learn using NLP to acquire greater English skills. Glad you have jumped on the bandwagon.

The Meta Model was developed by Richard Bandler and John Grinder in 1975 as a way to identify problems people had in the words they used in a therapeutic environment. They identified and categorized the Meta Model patterns then created questions to use to help people make the patterns become stepping stones instead of traps. Word Traps is taken from NLP Meta Models and Violations. My source for these lessons was my training at NLPU 2007 with Michael Colgrass a Pulitzer Prize winner. I sometimes call these word traps or violations. Those familiar with NLP will recognize this as the Meta Model of Language Patterns.

The basic principle behind the Meta Model is the presupposition that *the map is not the territory*. In other words each person looks at the world through their own map based on their experiences, current needs, joys and problems and the people they interact with both currently and in the past. Our mental and verbal maps have three basic areas that both help us and cause us problems. They can be a help because we can generalize things and not have to relearn at each step of our lives, and help us in further growth. But they can also cause us problems because we can be stuck or trapped by the same processes that assist us. These processes are generalizations, deletions and distortions.

Generalizations occur when we put a lot of information together mentally. For instance, a generalization would be the word cat. If I said "cat" to you, you might generalize a soft bodied animal with four legs and a tail. If you work in a zoo your mental picture of a cat might be much more vicious, the feel coarse-haired and muscled, and the sound you hear in your mind might be louder and deeper than my picture of a little fuzzy house cat with a tiny meow. Still the generalization of cat would lead us both to some of the same information. The trap would be that we would each have a mental map of a cat completely different from the other person and yet we might very well mistakenly think we are both thinking of the same animal.

The second basic trap is deletion. We tend to lump things together and delete unnecessary details that otherwise may occupy and clutter our minds. Deletion helps us reduce the world down to a size we can handle. It is proven we can handle about two to seven bits of information at one time. Because of this we must delete a lot of information or we would be on constant sensory overload. An easy example of deletion is being in a crowded room with a lot of people conversing, yet you only pay attention to your conversation, deleting the others from your conscious mind.

Distortion is the third Meta Model process in common use. We daily distort information that comes in to us. We might have a meeting with the boss and imagine what will happen going through several scenarios in our head before we choose the best one. It is this wonderful ability to distort or fantasize information that has given our world beautiful art work, lovely musical compositions and exciting novels.

Bandler and Grinder identified twelve categories of Meta Model processes that may cause linguistic problems in our communication. In the class I took with Pulitzer Prize and Emmy Award winner Michael Colgrass, he added a thirteenth in his workshop on The Language Maze. These include simple and comparative deletions, unspecified referential index, unspecified verbs, nominalizations, universal qualifiers, modal operators, complex equivalence, presuppositions, cause and effect, mind reading, and lost performatives.

In this lesson not all traps are addressed. We will look at some generalizations that can trap us, holding us from doing what needs to be done. Learning to escape word traps is an important life skill for you, the student. I have been amazed at how becoming aware of the meta model has made such an incredible difference in my student's writing.

Lesson 3: The Can't/Must Trap

As you do your homework, maybe you hear yourself saying, "I can't do this." "I must do that." Maybe you said, "It cannot be done, it is **impossible**." Children in the USA often say a little poem when other children saw unkind or mean words to them.

> Sticks and stones can break my bones,
> But words will never hurt me.

Do you think this poem is true or do you think words can hurt you?

Words can hurt you. You can even hurt yourself by using words wrong. In NLP we say using words wrong is a **trap,** something that stops you. One trap is called The **Can't/Must** trap.

I can't do English.
I must do English.
It is impossible to do English.

Do you ever hear these at school? Do you ever say them? You are probably thinking, "Yes, I hear them all the time. Sometimes I even say them." You need an escape for yourself or your friend who is stuck in the trap. The escape is simple. Ask, "What stops you?" or "What would happen?" Here are some examples:

| A. | I couldn't go on stage and do the show in English. |
| B. | What keeps you from it? |

| A. | I can't make much money. |
| B. | What would happen if you did? |

| A. | It is impossible to get rid of a headache. |
| B. | What makes it impossible? |

The purpose of the escape is to reframe the problem, to look at it in a new away. Remember the presupposition, the person with the most flexibility wins? Well when you look at the problem in a new frame you gain flexibility and often can create a win. We call this reframing.

A.	I must go to the dentist.
B.	What would happen if you didn't?
A.	I would get cavities. I might get an infection from the cavity and possibly lose my teeth. It is better to go to the doctor than to lose a tooth. Yes, I <u>get</u> to go to the dentist and prevent dental disease. Now the trip to the dentist looks worthwhile, I <u>get</u> to go.

So, what is going on in the brain to make this a trap? When you say you can't do something your right brain really believes you can't. Sometimes it is true that you can't do something. Your mom may say that you can't go to the store. If you go anyway you will be in big trouble because you did not do what your mother told you to do. That is not a trap.

The **Can't/Must** Trap is when you say you can't do something but you really could. You might say, "I can't do math." But could you if someone helped you out? Could you if you had a pencil? Could you if you had enough time? The question to ask yourself is, "What is stopping me?" Then decide whether it is good or bad. You make the choice. Don't let the **Can't/Must** Trap trap you into a choice.

The other word in this trap is must. **I must** tells your brain you are being forced into something. Are you being forced, or are you being trapped by your words? Words can help us or trap us. Choose your words.

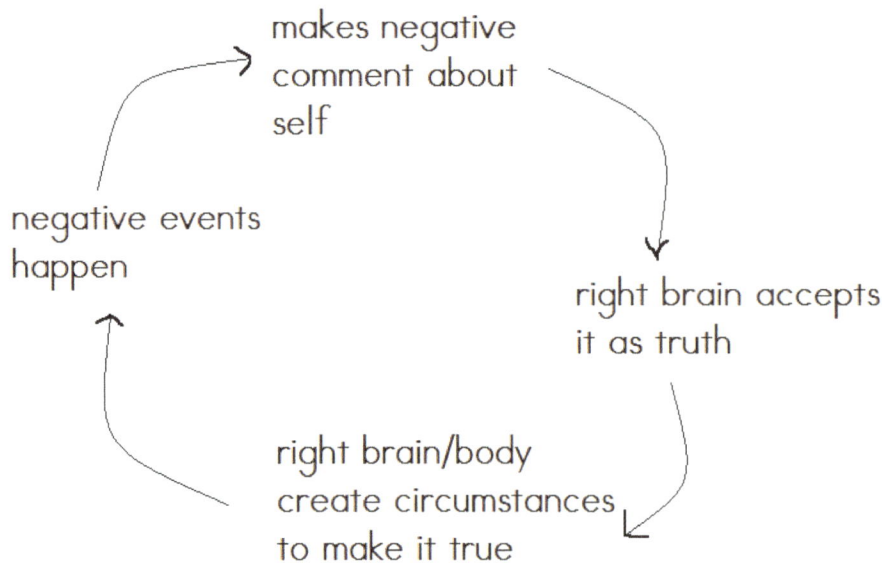

Lesson 4: I Don't Know Trap

Another **trap** that stops us is the "**I Don't Know**" Trap. Have you ever said it? When we use this trap our brain does not know what to do. It is trapped. Our brain often has the answer; it just does not know how to get the answer. Many times the brain is saying "I don't know what to do, the chunk or amount of work is too big." It might even be saying, "I give up."

When we hear the **I Don't Know Trap** it tells us the person needs help reframing the problem. If you say it to yourself in self-talk (internal dialogue) you now know your brain does not know what to do, the chunk is too big. You can learn the escapes to ask yourself to chunk (gather all the bits together into one amount) it down and take care of, or solve the problem.

The **I Don't Know Trap** includes others ways or forms of saying, "I don't know." They include:

> I am not sure (or I'm unsure)
> I am not clear (or I'm unclear)
> I haven't the faintest idea

There are 5 escapes you can use to help you get out of the **I Don't Know Trap**. The escapes will help your brain think up new ideas and ways when you use them. It is the way to help a friend, too. Here are the escapes:

> What would you say if you did know?
> Guess
> Make it up
> Imagine you do know
> Who would know? What would that person say to you?

To hear how this works read the example below.

Student:	I don't know how to do this English translation.
Teacher:	Imagine you do know.
Student:	Oh, I see. I would do it like the one on the board that we did.
Teacher:	Good job! You came up with the answer yourself.

Each time we get in a word trap we can use an escape to help us reframe our problem and see it in a new way.

One last bit of advice. It is not always a good idea to use an escape. Sometimes the person we are talking to really just wants someone to talk to, a sounding board to hear the problem out loud. Maybe a friend needs to vent, to talk about a problem and get it off her chest, to let go of stress. That is a time to listen, not to use an escape. It is a time to be a friend. The more you practice the better you will get and the better you get, the more successful you will be.

Lesson 5: You make Me!

Another word trap we want to escape is the **You Make Me Trap**. You remember that your right brain believes everything. If you say, "You make me." It believes you are being made or forced to do something. No one can really make anyone do anything. But you can be forced into doing things. Forcing does not feel good inside. Forcing feels like you are not in control of yourself, and you are not. The <u>**You Make Me**</u> Trap tells your right brain you are a victim. It tells you that you are being forced and that you are helpless to change. It says that you are not in control of yourself.

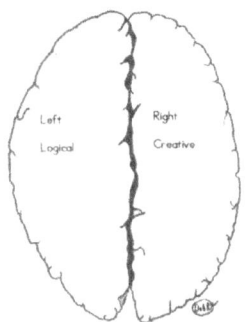

Sometimes people use the **You Make Me** Trap to keep from doing things. A little child may say, "Soup makes me sick." The soup doesn't make him sick, he just doesn't want to eat it. Still after saying that he has a problem. His right brain heard what he said and thinks soup should make him sick. Next thing he knows, soup really does make the child sick and he doesn't even know why, but you do.

Every trap has a way out of it, or an escape. Sometimes the best escape for the **You Make Me** Trap is to ask "How?" or "Always?" These will help you rethink the words you say and say them in a better way.

Know that sometimes the **You Make Me** Trap is real or seems real. For instance if someone is brandishing a knife at you, it really does make you feel scared. If it is true then you can explain the reason why.

This lesson covers just a few of the common Meta Model patterns. It is good to take a break and then come back to them later so that is what we will do. Watch for more in a future lesson.

Language Trap	Brief Description
Deletions	
Deletions	Omits which, how, when
Unspecified Verbs	Vague, generalizing verbs (exercise? Jog or swim)
Unspecified referential Index	Fuzzy noun or object. It, they, this, people, him
Nominalizations	Verbs frozen into nouns (can you put it in a wheelbarrow?) We are fighting for truth. You can't put truth in a wheel barrow We are fighting for money. You can put money in a wheel barrow.
Generalizations (setting limits)	
Model Operators necessity	must, should, need, have to, necessary, could
M O of possibility	Can't, impossible, won't, couldn't,
Universal Qualifiers	Always, never, all, every, no one, everyone
Distortions (sematic ill-formedness)	
Presuppositions	X is assumed true so Y is also true
Mind Reading	Crystal ball (I know you aren't happy)
cause/effect	X makes me Y When X then Y happens
I don't know	I don't know
Complex Equivalent	2 different things are stated to be the same They both are exchange students so they had got good grades.
Lost Performative	Lost who? Says who? According to whom?

Unit 20: NLP SCORE

*"The world we have created is a product of our thinking.
It cannot be changed without changing our thinking"* -- Albert Einstein

Lesson 1: Roles in NLP Exploration

We have done a lot of NLP explorations by now but we have not yet looked carefully at the role of each person in the exploration. As we get into more interesting work it is time to look at each role individually.

EXPLORER – The explorer is the person who is exploring the program. He is in charge of where it is going.
- Goes into new territory
- Is curious to find out
- Leads the exploration
- Relies on the guide to guide the exploration

Guide – This is the person who quides the explorer. Like a person who is going to climb Mount Everest, he has been there before and knows the territory.
- Guides the explorer
- Follows the explorer's lead
- Asks open-ended questions to enrich the exploration.
- Holds the place for the explorer

Observer – this person takes on a third or even fourth position and is not directly involved.
- Watches to learn
- Keeps the time
- Protects the space
- Answers questions if asked
- Asks for help if needed

Your Team
- Make sure each member of a team gets to do all three positions.
- There is learning in each position.
- Sometimes we use only two people, the explorer and the guide.

You may have noticed the guide uses open-ended questions but do not know what these are. An open-ended question is a question that cannot be answered with a simple answer such as yes or no. It takes more. Here are examples of open and closed ended questions.

closed   Do you want a bagel? (yes or no)
open   What kind of bread would you like to eat?

closed   Do you like this class?
open   What is the most interesting program you have learned about in this class and why?

closed   Do you have a problem?
open   What problem that you have would you like to explore today and why?

Often students want to rush through an exploration with the idea that the team that gets done first is the winner. This is different. The team that explores deepest is the winner in this exploration. It is not the team to get to the top of the mountain first that is the winner, but the team that sees the most fabulous views and finds the most wonderful treasures. As you explore be among the teams that get it all, the fun, the views and the treasures!

Lesson 2: What is the SCORE?

NLP practitioners work with a lot of problems. Some practitioners work with people who have problems such as in counseling or life coaching. Others work with businesses helping them find solutions (answers) to their problems. Everyone has problems and every business has problems to solve. A problem is the difference from where you are to where you want to be. If you are happy where you are, then you do not have a problem. The SCORE model is a good way to solve a problem.

Early innovators Robert Dilts and Todd Epstein often found that the simple method of the TOTE model was not always adequate (enough). A new program was developed with more steps to find solutions. It was called the SCORE.

Each letter of the SCORE stands for a word. These are

S	symptom	What causes the problem, things that stop you from getting your goal
C	cause	Where you are when you want to be somewhere else
O	outcome	Where you want to be, your goal
R	resources	What you need to solve the problem, your operators
E	Exit or effect	Where will you be when the problem is solved, what happens after you get your goal.

The SCORE helps a person or a group move from a problem to a solution, the desired state, what does the person or team want to have happen. It is more intense that the TOTE model because it will look for a cause of the problem. It will also extend beyond the solution to what will happen next, what will be the result of the solution. Note that the SCORE is not done in order, but all the letters are there and this helps to keep things organized.

The word score has many meanings and several are pertinent to the SCORE model. It can mean to keep track of things such as scoring papers. The model helps people keep track of the steps and resources. Also score can mean to get a point in a ball game, it is an outcome just as the SCORE model leads to an outcome.

Lesson 3: How to set up the SCORE?

The SCORE model uses psychogeography. We start by creating a space on the floor where we are working. It can be a very small area or a large area. I had one person once who had wanted many resources and she liked to move. We made her SCORE very large, half a gym size. The person who is the explorer, the person who is doing it, gets to decide on the size. The explorer sets down the papers if you use them to set the space.

Once the area is set up the guide, the person who guides the explorer, protects the area. Help others step around it and keep it clear until the explorer is done exploring. Part of the quide's job is to protect the explorer and to protect the space. Always leave a nice big space for resources. You will also choose a place off the time line where you can see the entire time line from second position, outside of it. This is refered to by NLP practitioners as Meta Space. A space outside of the working area.

Lesson 4: Doing the SCORE

After the explorer sets up the space for the exploration, the guide asks the explorer to step into the symptom or problem and tell a little about it. That is a good time to practice BAGEL skills for the guide and the observer.

Next the explorer steps back a step into the symptom place and explores why the problem is there.

After this the explorer walks around the resource space. Do not walk through it yet. The explorer steps into the outcome space and explores what the outcome will be. Again use that BAGEL. For the fourth step, step into the Effect. What will the effect of the outcome be? Explore that.

The guide may begin to notice differences that are often opposites. The explorer may do one thing in the symptom place and something just the opposite in the outcome place. It can be as illuminating to be the guide if you have watched the BAGEL well.

Now the fun begins. The explorer starts at the cause and moves to the symptom then takes a step into the resources. This is where the right brain gets to do its work. Ideas will come to tell the person how to get the outcome. When an idea or two – or even many ideas come, the explorer then steps into the outcome and last of all the effect.

Next both go to Meta Space. What is that? Well anywhere that is off your SCORE area and where you can see the entire program. The root of the word meta is Greek and means over, between or above. Meta space is taken from this Greek meaning as you are standing between the spaces looking over them. You can talk about it and decided whether to walk the SCORE again. The explorer then goes back to the beginning and walks the SCORE again. This time see if more ideas come. Often they will. I have the explorer walk their own SCORE at least eight times. That gives the right brain lots of time to dream up ideas. It is interesting to note that when it is done, the SCORE feels complete.

When the explorer is done then both the explorer and the guide may talk about the ideas. The guide may have written the ideas down and will give them to the explorer. The guide really helps the explorer solve the problem. When it is done, pick up any papers or rocks or things you have used to make the spaces. If your partner did a nice job, give them a fish (Positive Affirmation).

Lesson 5: Real Life SCORE

I would like to give you an example of a SCORE I have done. Here is a SCORE worksheet so you can see an example. I did this one as a demonstration model at NLPU in 2011. My guide was Robert Dilts, the man who developed the program. It was a humbling privelege to get to do it with him as a guide.

program	My words and thoughts	What is going on
Cause	I have done three weddings and I know they take a lot of work.	I remember my other children's wedding. They were a lot of work.
Symptom	I am worried. I want my daughter's wedding to be beautiful.	I feel overwhelmed. There is so much to do. My eyes are down. My body is droopy. I want to do the wedding myself as a gift to my daughter
Resources	Find a picture back drop Get lots of bread Get friends to make soup Buy a cake Get a new dress Get a place to have the wedding	

| Outcome | Everyone is standing in line at the wedding and happy. | I can picture the wedding and lots of people there. |
| Effect | Daughter is happily married and I am not too tired. | I can see myself relaxed and happy the next day. |

It worked. Every time I started to get overwhelmed, I would think of my SCORE and the next step to take and the entire wedding fell into place beautifully. Your SCORE will also.

Lesson 6: Dancing SCORE

> When asked what one of her dances meant Martha Graham said.
> "If I could tell you it I wouldn't have to dance it."

In 1993 Judith Delozier, a Neurolinguist and a dancer, developed from the SCORE a somatic version called the Dancing SCORE. Those who are kinesthetic will especially love this one. This version takes no words but uses instead the wisdom and knowledge of the body, the somatic mind. The components include spacial sorting physical movement, intuition and the energy of the explorer. (spacial- of or pertaining to space. Example: driving a car one has to have spacial awareness of where other cars and pedestrians are to be a safe driver)

Some of you are already thinking I can't dance. I have two left feet (clumsy) and cannot do this. Ah, but you are Neurolinguists now and you know that the greatest flexibility will win for you. I have seen Dancing SCORES with only small movements and I have seen one that took up an entire gym. I saw a wonderful one once moved by a martial arts practitioner that was crazy-wild. A friend who was a singer found that a song emerged (come to the surface) at each space. Some SCORES are long and complicate and others are simple. You go with the flow. (do what comes naturally.)

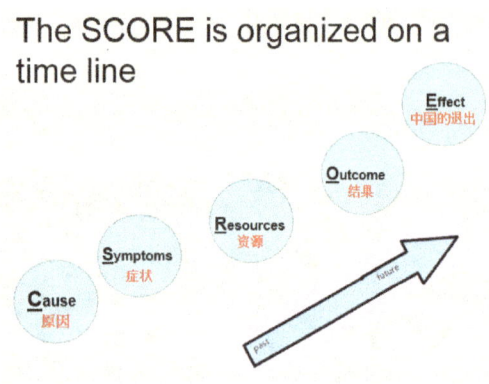

Just as with the SCORE you have already learned, you lay out your space with five areas: cause, symptoms, resources, outcome and effects.

Next step into the Problem Space and just experience it as a movement. The guide helps you by noticing the BAGEL of the movement and helping you do it again until you have the components of the movement.

Next you step back on the time line to the cause and allow the cause of the problem to emerge as a movement again. No words are needed, just let the movement tell the story. Go back and forth between the two spaces until the movements flow or even make a bit of a dance.

Now you step out into your Meta Space away from your SCORE. With your guide, explore what you have done and where you want to be, then step into the Outcome space and allow a movement of where you want to be emerge from deep within you – then step forward into the exit and feel it emerge as yet another movement. Again your guide is remembering your movements for you and helping you.

Back into your Meta Space away from your SCORE. Shake it off and with your guide, explore what you have done. You may want to go back and try it several times before you are ready to step into the resource step. You are the driver and you decide when you feel you have the spaces ready.

Now the fun begins. Step into the Resource Space and very slowly move through it. Allow the movements to emerge. You will find that your body will be drawn to the Outcome space. The movements will become resources to get you there. Some people know what the resources are that match the movements and may want their guide to write them down. Most people just move through the space feeling the dance emerge. You may move through your Resource Space several times and new movements may emerge. That is quite alright. Keep going over until it feels complete.

Back to Meta Space to talk with your guide. Do you need more? Then go back and move it (dance it if it is a dance) again. Does it feel complete? Then go back and move it again several times. I encourage my clients to do it at least 8 times. This is called the installation of a strategy. Each time you practice it the strategy will become stronger and move deeper into your neurology. It will become a driver to get you to the Outcome you have chosen.

Finally you go back to Meta Space one last time and discuss it with your guide. If it feels complete you are done, or are you? Some problems are solved with one time through the Dancing SCORE, others take repetition. When I worked on removing liver disease from my body in 2007 I did the Dancing SCORE over and over, at first every night, then every week. I still do it and add to it years later. I have even had it posted on You-Tube and danced it at a Woman's Day Program in Shanghai in 2014 to inspire other people to overcome problems in their lives. It has evolved over time as I have added more resources to it. For me the Dancing SCORE was a powerful tool for healing. It will be interesting to find out how some of my students use the Dancing SCORE in their future.

Unit 21: NLP Meta Model Language Patterns 2

Lesson 1: What is the Meta Model?

Once upon a time there were two sweet little girls named Posy and Neg. Both girls loved to dance and were beautiful dancers. They were asked to do a very special part on their community program. They were to get up in front of all of the people in their community and do a dance together for the Independence Day celebration in their city theater.

Posy and Neg were very excited. They ran home after school to tell their mothers. Their mothers were proud of them for being chosen for such a special part. Posy's momma said to Posy, "I am so proud of you. You have a lot of talent. Get up and do your best for your community. "

Neg's mother said almost the same thing. She said, "I am so very proud of you. You have such a lot of talent. Don't be scared to get up in front of your community."

The girls practiced every day. Finally the day arrived and they got up to dance. As Posy started to dance she could hear her mother's voice in her imagination saying, "Do your best for your community." She smiled at Neg and squeezed Neg's hand. She would do her best, just as her mother had told her. She started to dance and her smooth steps and quick smile filled the hall with beauty.

Neg stood beside Posy. She started to dance and she heard her mother's voice, "Don't be scared." "Oh, no!" thought Neg "Scared, I am not supposed to be scared, I am scared. All of my community, old people and young people are here and I am scared."

Neg's legs started to shake. She felt like wobbly pudding inside. She was glad Posy had

squeezed her hand. She didn't know if she could make it through without that had squeeze of reassurance.

When it was over all of their community friends came to tell the girls what a great job they had done. Posy thanked everyone and some of her friends asked her if she had been scared. She told them she wanted to do her best for her friends and that is what she did.

Neg's friends told her they were proud of her. She told them it had been very scary and she didn't know if she would ever do that again.

What made the difference?

Lesson 2: What made the difference?

Words are very powerful. They shape our world. Both girls have the same ability to dance, but the words made all of the difference. I learned this over and over as a teacher watching parents build their child's reality.

So what happens? The left brain is very logical. It hears the words said and questions them. Are they true? Are they in the correct order? How do they relate to other things I have learned in the past? How can I use them?

Not so the right brain. It is very believing. It hears words and accepts them as true then moves to make them a reality. Let's do an experiment. Think of anything **BUT** a pink rabbit.

What did you do? Well of course first you had to think of a pink rabbit and then you had to search in your mind for things that were not pink rabbits. That is the way our brains work. Neg was told not to be scared so first she had to think of being scared and then switch it with not being scared, but it was toooooo late. She had already matched scared with dancing in her brain and now it was becoming true. Worse yet, each time she thought of dancing she was going through the "don't be scared" scenario again.

Something else is at work here. Your mind cannot think in negatives. It only thinks in one direction. First it has to form an image of the positive, then it comes up with the opposite. The same thing happens if someone says to you, "Don't think about your problem." You start thinking about the problem right away. If someone says, "Don't worry." What do you think the first thing you do is? Worry!

NLP has learned why this is true. Our brains do not know how to put things into negative words. In order to know what not to think about, our brains first have to think about it. We can change our **thoughts**, the things that form in our minds, from what they are to what we want them to be by using positive words. This changes your brain. It helps your brain help you get what you want instead of what you don't want.

This brings up a word trap **don't/won't** we have studied. Instead of using don't or won't, use what you do want to happen. Use positive statements. Find out what a difference it will make. Knowing that your mind must reverse negatives, how can this be used? Tell people what you want, not what you do not want. When I was 36 I thought to myself, I have always wanted to be a life guard, was I too old? I went to the pool and asked. No, not at all. They needed life guards of all ages so I decided to take the classes. After I completed my training I guarded. I watched the other guards when children ran near the pool, blow their whistle and call out, "Don't run." Inevitably the child kept running for a bit. I started calling out "Walk, please." Almost instantaneously the child would slow down and begin to walk. How many ways could you put application to this?

Unless you become a Neurolinguist you do not need to memorize them. What is important is that you recognize the Meta Models and know how to escape them. It will make your presentations and writing clearer and that is the purpose of studying the Meta Model.

Lesson 3: More Meta Model

Here is the list of Meta Model patterns and the common words you see associated with each one. We have already explored the first five. Learning to recognize and question these will help make your speak and write more clearly.

Language Trap	Abr.	Brief Description
Model operators of necessity	MO	must, should, need, have to, necessary, could
Modal operators of possibility	MO	Can't, impossible, won't, couldn't,
Universal Qualifiers	UQ	Always, never, all, every, no one, everyone
You make me	MM	You make me… It makes me… It causes me to…
I don't Know	DK	beats me, no idea, don't get it, don't understand, baffled
Deletions	D	Omits which, how, when
Unspecified referential Index	URI	Fuzzy noun or object. It, they, this, people, him
Lost Performative	LP	Lost who? Says who? According to whom?
Unspecified Verbs	UV	Vague, generalizing verbs (exercise? Jog or swim)
Nominalizations	N	Verbs frozen into nouns (can you put it in a wheelbarrow?)
Presuppositions	P	X is assumed true so Y is also true
Mind Reading	MR	Crystal ball (I know you aren't happy)
Cause/effect	C/E	X makes me Y When X then Y happens
Complex Equivalent	CE	2 different things are stated to be the same

Now that you have a good background knowledge of the Meta Model and why it is important to us, let's look at these one at a time.

Unspecified referential Index (URI) are often pronouns and do not specify who or what is meant. A referential index is a person, place or thing to which the statement refers. Using URI's is one of the most common errors I find in grading student work. To challenge this linguistic pattern ask for clarification. Example is below:

> The students do not study.
> Which students do not study?
> The four students in the fourth period class who sit on the back row each week and play with their cell phones are all getting bad grades and do not study.

Lost Performatives are patterns of linguistics where who is left out. Lost who? Says who? According to whom? To challenge it you ask for clarification of who made the value judgment and how it was made. Here is an example for you:

You should eat at McDonald's as the food is so good.
Who said the food was good?
It sure wasn't the American Medical Association, they think McDonald's is contributing to an assortment of diseases, it is my little eight year old cousin and he likes to go out to eat there but my mom will not take him because she agrees with the AMA.

Unspecified Verbs are linguistic patterns characterized by too little information about the verb. The verb is vague, and generalized. To meet this you just ask for clarification, for further information. Here is an example:

The girls danced.
What kind of dancing did they do?
Oh, they are the greatest jazz dancers, you should see their smooth moves.

Nominalizations are patterns of linguistics where unspecified verbs are converted into nouns. Judith Delozier taught us that nominalizations are nouns you cannot put into a wheelbarrow. What she meant was that you cannot see, feel or touch them. They are not persons, places or things but are ideas. Here is an example:

We are fighting for truth. (one cannot put truth in a wheel barrow)
Challenge: Who is truthful to whom and in what way? What is truth in this situation?
We know that much of our food is GMO, and are fighting to have it put on the labels so we can make our own choice as to whether to eat it or not.

These are the pieces of information that make your essay or speech strong as you then explain what the nominalization means to you.

Nominalizations can be an important tool for you. Politicians use them all of the time. Each person has a different map of what truth, justice, power, love and so on are. When a politician says, "We are fighting for truth." Each listener has their own map of what is truth and feels that the speaker is communicating with him or her about something they feel strongly about not realizing that everyone in the audience is making a completely different picture in their mind of truth depending on the map they are living. In this way a politician can reach a large audience and get buy-in for the cause they are fighting for.

Presuppositions are linguistic patterns where "X" is assumed or presupposed to be true so "Y" is also true. I got caught in this Meta Model violation when I was in college. I had a girlfriend when I was a little girl who was Japanese. She was really cute and my best friend. Unfortunately my family moved and I did not see her for ten years. She was in my college class and she was still just as cute and petite as she was when we were young girls. I said to someone, "Vickie is cute, she must have a lot of boyfriends." Unfortunately I was wrong. Vicky was shy and had never had a boyfriend. I felt badly for presupposing something that I did not know. The Meta Model challenge is to challenge the thing that is being presupposed.

Mind Reading patterns occur when someone indicates they know what you or others are thinking. Michael Colgrass calls it the Crystal Ball. It is as if you are a fortune teller and can see inside another person's head. Marintha is walking down the street with her handsome boyfriend, Steve. A beautiful girl with long black hair walks by and Steven turns. Marintha jealously says to him, "I know you are thinking how beautiful she is." The Meta Model response to this is to question it. "That is interesting that you would think that way because I was actually thinking I know her, she is in my physics class and so I turned to smile."

Cause and effect patterns occur "when X makes me Y" or "When X exists then Y happens." When it rains I always get a chill. This example is best challenged with a counter example or an example of the opposite. "Was there a time when you did not get a chill when it rained?"

It is interesting that some allergies are built this way using cause and effect without knowing the power of the linguistics on the neurology. Suzi Smith has a CD out with the allergy process. It has helped many people. If you have an allergy you would like to live without, give it a try. Find out how very well it works for you. With severe and with life threatening allergies you must work with an experienced life coach. Consult your medical professional and a professional NLP coach before doing medically related NLP work. There is not an organization that licenses NLP Coaches. Some people put up a shingle (idiom for open a business) with as little as a week end of training. Your author, Debrah, has had over 1000 hours of training and coaching experience and countless hours of teaching. Choose wisely. Because it is an unregulated profession anyone can be a coach.

Complex Equivalent are linguistic patterns where two different and unrelated things or ideas are stated to be the same or equal to each other. For instance, the feeling "A" s equal to the feeling of "B." An example of this would be, He forgot my birthday therefore he does not love me. The meta model response to this is to offer a counter example. Let's break this one down.

> He was late for our appointment. He has no respect for my time.
> Have there been times when you have been late for an appointment because of traffic? Does that mean you did not respect the person?
> or
> What does being late have to do with respect?

Lesson 4: Still More Meta Model Information

The meta model patterns can be organized into three general categories. Sometimes words can fit into more than one category depending on how it is used in the sentence. If this is of interest to you there is a whole area of study that could engage you for the rest of your life.

deletions	Generalizations	Distortions
Information gathering Recovering missing links and details.	Setting and Identifying Limits Words that put limits or boundaries to a person's model of the world.	Sematic Ill-formedness Processes people use to judge and give meaning to behaviors and events.
Deletions Comparative deletions URI Unspecified Verbs Nominalizations	Universal Qualifiers Modal Operators Presuppositions You make Me (Colgrass) I don't know (Colgrass)	Complex equivalents Cause and effect Mind Reading Lost Perforatives

When we work with a problem such as when we are going to give a speech or write a paper it is good to write down the topic sentence and analyze it with the meta model patterns to find where you need to expand and clarify your words. Using the information from the analysis can help the writer or speaker clarify for the audience. Here is an example:

| UQ | URI | CD | UV | URI | URI | UV | URI | URI |

All of the scientists get too busy in their explorations and lose sight of their final goal.

All five of the scientists in Lab 4 get absorbed in their explorations of the molecular structure of the genetic material they are analyzing and lose sight of their final goal not to analyze but to find the gene that causes the deformity in the rats.

This sentence clarifies what the audience needs to fully understand the sentence presented.

Former students of mine how repeatedly told me that becoming aware of and using the Meta Model, even on a superficial level, has made great improvement in both writing and speech. As I have taught it I find that mine, also, has improved significantly. You will find that it also helps you.

Unit 22: NLP Disney Strategy

Do what you do so well that they will want to see it again and bring their friends.
---Walt Disney

Lesson 1: What is the Disney Strategy?

It is likely that most of the world knows who Walt Disney is. Shanghainese certainly do as they wait and anticipate the opening of Shanghai Disney Land. Walter Elias Disney is a legend in his time (someone who is famous while yet alive), His simple, yet appealing animated characters make him popular with all age groups. People thought his dreams were flights of fancy (Not practical for real life), but he took those dreams and made them a reality.

NLP modelers used Disney to model for his creative genius. What was the difference that made the difference? He was able to look at things from different perceptual positions. The comment was once made that-

"There were three different Walts; the dreamer, the realist and the spoiler.
You never knew which one was coming into your meeting. " (1)

It was this ability that made him a creative genius, and as we know, NLP'ers wrote down his strategy so others could increase their creativity also. Modelers followed him around for several days writing down every movement, word and gesture until the program he used was fully recorded and understood.

Walt's' creativity included a process called story boarding. It is used by animators of every cartoon. He learned how to make a big picture then chunk it down into smaller bits until the smallest bit; an individual movie frame began its creation. He would first dream a big dream and draw a few pictures to represent it. Next he would take these big chunks and break them into smaller parts by adding what comes next. Finally he would break that into even smaller parts adding what came in between the larger pieces. Disney would literally chunk his dream down into pieces, and it worked.

Disney once said, "The story-man must see clearly in his own mind how every piece of business in a story will be put. He should feel every expression, every reaction. He should get far enough away from his story to take a second look at it…to see whether there is any dead phase…to see whether the personalities are going to be interesting and appealing to the audience. He should also try to see that the things that his characters are doing are of an interesting nature."

Robert Dilts describes his version of the "Disney Strategies" (there are actually more than one) in his books "Tools for Dreamers," "Skills for the Future," "Strategies of Genius Vol. I" and "Visionary Leadership Skills." There is also a summary in the Encyclopedia of Systemic NLP and NLP New Coding by Robert Dilts and Judith Delozier. It can be found under "Disney" at http://nlpuniversitypress.com/. NLP Modelers such as Dilts created a program that people could follow to be more creative. It works for both individuals and teams. It is useful in many venues including school, work and the arts. Anywhere one needs to enhance creativity, one can use the Disney Program for Creativity.

Lesson 2: Dreamer

The first step to creativity is the dream. When Disney went into the dream state one of his workers said of him, *"When Walt was deep in thought he would lower one brow, squint his eyes, let his jaw drop, and stare fixedly at some point in space, often holding the attitude for several moments ... No words could break the spell ..."*

The secret of Disney's success as a dreamer, and your success too, was to go into a trance of dreaming. He would look up in space and see a picture there. He was looking at a dream in the future and he was very much into himself. In fact he was so into himself that if others talked to him he might not even hear them.

We can do the same thing to dream our dreams. Look off into space, into the future and notice your dreams emerge. Be relaxed as you stand symmetrically (balanced). Enjoy the creative process. It is your right brain at work doing what it does best, Imagineering! If you are doing it by yourself, you might want to write down the ideas, or draw them as Disney did. If you have a guide, the guide might want to record them for you.

This can be done with a large group. The ideas can be written on a chalk board or a white board, put on big pieces of paper and hung around a room and so on. We often talk about how it is good when the creative juices are flowing. When the creative juices are flowing, write down every idea, even if the ideas are silly, or ridiculous or out of this world (better than the best, extraordinary). Often those ideas become a spring board (start) to the best work.

For coaching, good questions to ask are what, why, where, when, how and who questions. Let me share with you the first time I did the Disney Strategy. I was studying in California on the University of California Santa Cruz campus at an NLPU workshop. The teacher, Judith Delozier, needed an explorer and I volunteered. It was amazing. As she guided me through the dreamer I saw a book emerge  before my mind's eye. It was a teacher's manual of NLP programs for young teens like I taught. One year later I had produced this dream. It is called NLP for Me, by Debrah Roundy, of course.

Lesson 3: Critic

Now that you have a dream may may say, "but it is out of this world. I cannot really do that." It is time for a critic, you. The critic has an important task of looking for the problems.

When you are a critic you need to step completely away from the dreamer. Not too far, but far enough to see the dreams. Your eyes and head are down, your head is tilted and your body is angular. Often you put most of your weight on one side of your body. That is the physiology of the critic. Whether you are working aone, with a guide or in a group, the idea is to pick apart the dreams and decode what is needed to make them a reality. The critic physiology really helps.

Are you coaching an explorer? Why, who , when, what and how questions are good. Who would question your dream? Why would they? What is wrong? When would this dream not work?

I challenged my students to create a dream in 2008. Their dream was to go to the 2010 World Special Olympics Games. There is a picture of us in 2009 at the invitational. We failed to make the cut for the games. But we held fast to our dream and in 2010 we made it, we got our dream. We got to go to the games greet the performers with a song in ASL and watch them. It was out of this world!

Warning. Occassionally someone will want to criticize the dreamer and tell the dreamer that s/he is a lemon, no good at all. That is not the purpose of the critic. The dream belongs to the dreamer and the dreamer should feel free to explore all options, to freely fly as high as a kite (dream big). The critic is not against the dreamer for you see, a house divided against itself cannot stand. (a group that is not united will fall apart and not achieve the goal)

Lesson 4: Realist

Now let's move, literally, move to another place a bit farther away. The realist feels the dream, the longing and the hope. The realist looks squarely at the problems the critic has found. Here the realist can see clearly both the dream and the problems that the critic has found. The realist has the job of making the dream become a reality.

The realist gives the dream a framework using what has been learned from the critic. S/he acts as if the dream were achievable and gets down the brass tacks to make it happen. (becomes serious about it).

The realist answers the questions that a good coach might ask:

- How will the dream happen?
- Who will be over each part of the implementation of the dream?
- When will it happen? (and when will each step happen)
- Where will it happen?
- Why is each step necessary?

Lesson 5: Meta Place

As a person works through the three areas, sometimes the explorer needs to see the big picture, so see everything as if from 3rd or 4th perceptual position. The place for this is called meta space. It needs to be off from the rest so that all three places can be seen clearly. The explorer and the quide can go there, look at the entire creative process and decided where the explorer needs to go back or revisit. This strategy does not have a certain form to go through, the explorer can go back and forth between the three positions as needed. For instance, if the explorer is in the critic state and finds he needs more ideas, it is ok to go back to the dreamer place and dream up more dreams. Nice! That is icing on the cake, you already have it good and now you are getting even more. It is excessively much, It's over the top! So the entire program is laid out something like this:

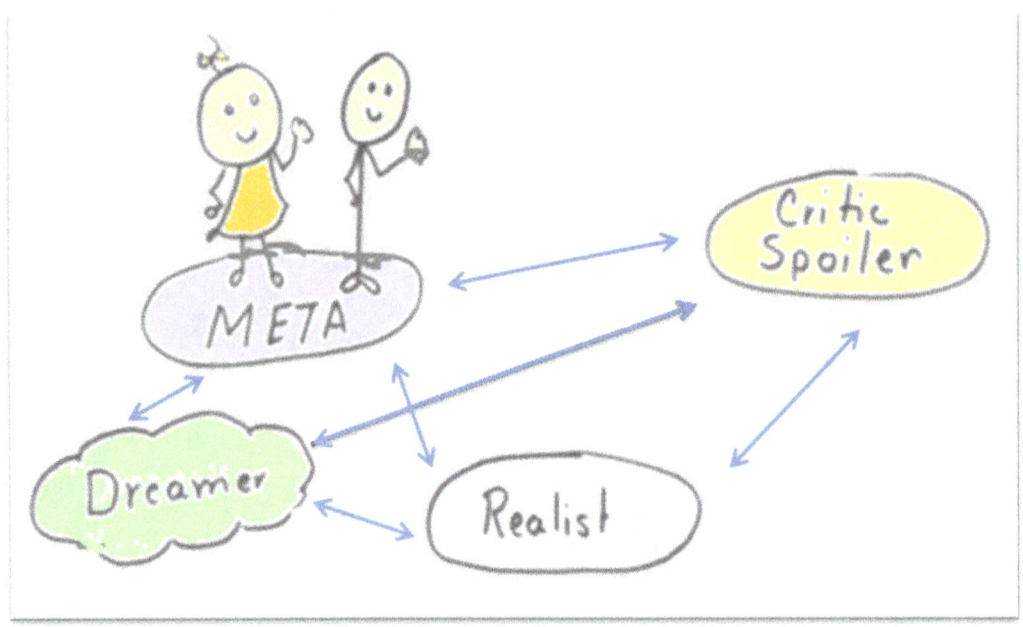

And here are ways you can move through it. Of course you always start by creating the dream. You will know when you are done when you stand in Meta Space and notice that it looks complete, it feels complete and you know it is done. Then the real work begins as you make your dream come true. Happy dreaming!

Debrah and Judith Delozier at a presentation with me showing my
NLP for Me book for young children and children with special needs.

My students complete a Disney Dream to create a play they did for the school. Here are some pictures.

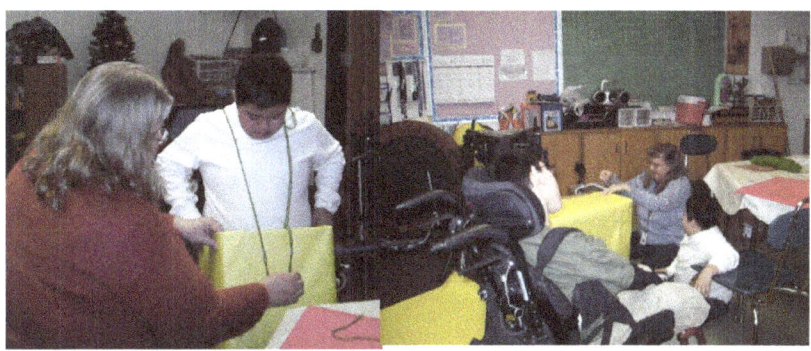

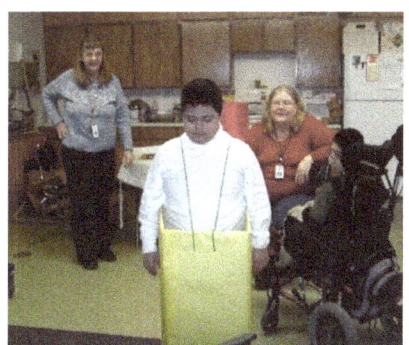

Unit 23: Metaphors

Failure is the condiment that gives success its flavor."
— Truman Capote

Lesson 1: What is a Metaphor?

One bright spring morning my little granddaughter, Chloe brought in a leaf to show grandma and attached was a cocoon. We put it in a jar in hopes that it would hatch. Several days passed and a small opening appeared. Chloe sat entranced. Nothing seemed to happen for a while and she would run off, then return, but still no progress seemed to be made. It seemed the creature inside was stuck.

Chloe decided to help the butterfly so she ran to my sewing room and grabbed a small pair of scissors and carefully enlarged the hole. Quickly the butterfly emerged, but it had a swollen, funny-looking body and small shriveled wings, not the majestic wings of a butterfly.

Chloe did not know what a newly emerged butterfly was supposed to look like so she continued to watch excitedly and called me to join her, Grandma, come quick. The butterfly is out and it sure looks funny!" Any minute we thought the wings would expand, but nothing happened. Finally I looked at the cocoon and saw the scissors sitting there and a straight cut made where the hole had begun. I knew what had happened. The poor butterfly would never fly, crippled by kindness and haste, for it is the constriction of the cocoon that forces the fluid from the body of the butterfly into its winds so it is ready to fly once it has overcome the struggle of the fight for freedom from the restrictive cocoon.

Sometimes struggles are exactly what we need in our lives. If we were allowed to go through our lives without any obstacles, it would cripple us. We would not be as strong as what we could have been. We could never fly!

Metaphors are powerful learning tools. A metaphor is simply a figure of speech that compares two unlike things. Samples of metaphors include similes, stories, parables, personification, hyperbole, fables, songs and analogies. The story is an example of a metaphor. How does it apply to you as a student?

Lesson 2: Why Metaphors?

*[But] we accept irony through a device called metaphor.
And through that we grow and become deeper human-beings."*
— *Haruki Murakami, Kafka on the Shore*

Metaphors are very useful tools in speech. They will lead a person to learn something without directly teaching them. They work on the subconcious level. Metaphors are right brain. The left brain is literal and hears the story as it is. The magic happens with the right brain. It hears the story and starts making connections. In those connections learning happens, behaviors may change, and new understanding emerges. Metaphors are very powerful tools for learning and change.

There are two types of metaphors, shallow and deep.

Shallow Metaphor
Shallow, Simple metaphor – comparison, simile.
A shallow metaphor makes simple comparisons and creates a better understanding

Deep metaphor
A story with different levels of meaning. A deep metaphor has stories with many different levels of meaning. It connects with the unconscious mind and is used to gain understanding at the unconscious level. Each person understands the metaphor based on his own life experiences. Each person gets an individual meaning to the metaphor. The famous Jewish teacher, Jesus, was especially skilled in the use of metaphors called parables.

Lesson 3: Uses of Metaphors?

"Know a man by his metaphors."
— *John Connolly, The Wolf in Winter*

Here are some uses of metaphors.

- Can help clients to better understand something about the object or idea to which the metaphor is applied.

- In therapy.
- Helps you create rapport with a person
- Helps you create rapport with an audience or a team of co-workers.
- Makes speaking, and writing more lively and interesting.
- Can communicate a great deal of meaning with just a word or phrase.
- Can create a mind shift particularly when someone or a group of people are in a stuck state, a state where they cannot seem to move forward.
- Since they imply rather than directly state relationships, people think about what they are hearing and take on new learnings and ideas.
- They can be used to change the direction of a person or a company.
- Metaphors reach each listener at her/his own level.

Think about the story of the butterfly. It never said anything about people and yet when you read it you likely saw yourself as a butterfly. You may have thought of your struggle in school and how the struggle helps you to fly in your future.

What if your mother heard the story. She likely would picture in her mind an entirely different outcome and your grandmother, yet something different for she has lived even more life. A very well written metaphor such as a parable, will speak to people on many different levels. It will take a person from where he or she is at to a new level of thinking.

Lesson 4: More About Metaphors

"Metaphors are dangerous, Metaphors are not to be trifled with.
A single metaphor can give birth to love."
― *Milan Kundera*

One important thing about metaphors is that they are interesting. Your left brain enjoys the story. Your right brain is making connections. Your brain likes the challenge in seeing things in more than one light (more than one way).

Another important thing about metaphors is that they grab people's attention. It is good to start a talk with a metaphor because people are likely to listen. You get their attention and then you make your point (the message you want to give), After you make your point, you tie it back (bring the thought back) into the metaphor. That stregthens your point in the mind of the listener. A good debator will also use the power of a metaphor. Instead of just reciting endless facts, the debator will tie it into a story. You will often hear someone say, "This reminds me of...." then they will proceed with a short sentence or story illustrating the point they are debating. It may be very short yet extremely effective.

Here is an example. A business team is meeting to generate more ideas for the next year's marketing. They are doing well and the boss wants them to come up with even more ideas in the future, He says, "This reminds me of a hot air balloon, as the ideas start to pour in from all of my colleages the balloon rises higher. We are rising higher with our ideas, let's generate a few more so we can have a successful year." If he is really clever he may only need to say, "Today was like a hot air balloon. We have really risen. Thanks for working with me." He would need to say nothing more. Everyone would feel validated for the work that day.

This reminds me of my friend Suzi Smith. Suzi is a master of metaphor. Notice her picture from her website. Do you see metaphors of what she does in the pictures? She guides them like a compass to soar to new learnings like a bird and to provide light to lives as a fire. She has a collection of metaphors that she always has ready. She is a presenter and sometimes she will have just a few minutes to fill before the presentation should be over. People have paid money to hear her and do not want her to finish early or they will feel they have not got their money's worth (the value of the money they paid). She can quickly pull out a story that will take the right amount of time to fill the space and people love to hear her stories because they always learn more than what they expected, and each person learns something different. Now that is a good story. For a real treat go to: http://suzismith.net/?cat=4 where she has posted some of her best metaphors. It will be a feast.

Unit 24: Conflict Integration

*"We don't get harmony when everybody sings the same note.
Only notes that are different can harmonize. The same is true with people."*
— *Steve Goodier*

Lesson 1: The Process

In life we all face conflicts at one time or another and of one sort or another. A conflict is a mental struggle that occurs when people have different maps of an issue. When we are frustrated and cannot find a solution we feel we are caught between a rock and a hard spot where there is no desirable solution to the conflict. Conflict can occur within us or it can occur between people. Individuals are multi-leveled as you learned by doing the Neurological Level Alignment. An example of this on a behavior level would be a person who says, "On the one hand I would like to play this video game tonight, but on the other hand I know if I do I will not get my work ready for tomorrow and will regret it. On a belief level it might be, "I believe playing video games will strengthen my eye-hand coordination yet I believe I get too engaged once I start playing and have a hard time stopping." Moving higher up the continuum a person may have two conflicting identities. "I am a person who always prepares the day before for my next day, and I am a person who takes time to relax and balance my energies."

Conflict can even occur subconsciously within the body. Take this example, "I like to be thin and svelte yet extra weigh gives me power when I have conflicts at work." Or "I really do not need to wear glasses but I like all of the extra attention I am getting as I get glasses." There are two commonly used idioms for this conflict within, to be "of two minds" or to be "at odds" with oneself.

Conflict also occurs between people and groups as you will know. We all have different maps of the world and when our map intrudes on the map of another conflict will occur and we will be "at odds with each other."A popular English idiom is "it takes two to tango." The Tango is a partner dance that takes two dancers to move together, but often in opposition to each other. The idiom means you have to have two people with different ideas in opposition to have a conflict. NLP provides many tools. Using tools such as Meta Model, calibration, and non-verbal linguistics such a paralanguage can also help.

Lesson 2: The Procedure

The NLP procedure for Conflict Integration takes two contradictory or incompatible parts, sorts them and resolves them. It is a core program to resolve many personal, physical, and interpersonal problems as well as in negotiation by looking fully at both sides and attending to their concerns, then working out the problem, often with compromise and new solutions that present themselves as the program is worked through.

This program was developed by Bandler and Grinder and first presented in their book *The Structure of Magic Volume II (1976 page 45)*. These are the steps to the program looking for the positive intention is a piece of the program that was added later.

- Start with a conflict, there are two sides to a problem
- Put your hands out and put the two sides of the conflict, one on each hand. You will find that your hands will know which one gets each side.
- Start with one side and do the LLA, then do the other side. You are looking for the positive intention of each side.
- Create an unbiased meta position where the two sides can be heard distinctly from an unbiased position.
- Allow the parts to discuss freely as needed giving each a turn and making sure both are heard. Sometimes one side wants to talk and interrupts the other. If you make this a game, sit on that hand to quiet it. If you are working with two people remind the talkative one that both sides get an equal time to explain their view.
- Make sure each side of the conflict recognizes the positive intention of the other side. They do not have to agree, only to be recognized.
- A conflict cannot be solved on the same level as it is created. When the parts of the conflict are laid out clearly look for a similarity and work with it. It will be on a higher level.
- Explore alternatives to solve the problem. At least three choices can usually be generated. Let each part offer choices, then the other part tell what is and is not acceptable and offer another choice. Remember the NLP saying, "If you have only one choice there is no choice. Having two choices is a dilemma. There is magic in having three choices. " Continue to adjust the solutions until one solution is agreed upon. Often it is completely different from what either one had come up with.

Find a conflict to explore. If you want to study with someone else the two of you can come up with something to work though together. Make a worksheet like this but you will likely take a whole piece of paper, as you find out all of the small pieces of the conflict.

	Problem on left hand	Problem on right hand
Environment		
Behavior		
Capabilities		
Beliefs and Values		
Identity		
Purpose or positive intention		

Now that you have done both sides let your hands talk out the problem. As they talk it out see, how they can agree and how they can compromise. I sometimes put puppets on the hands of my clients and let the puppets talk it out. The idea is to take the conflict outside of you so you can see it more clearly. It is important to let both sides talk it out until they are both satisfied that their needs and desires are addressed and will be met and the positive intention is served for each side.

When they have talked it out and come up with the compromises they will agree on, then let your hands come together and be friends. It is important to let them come together on their own. Do not force it. Then bring your hands in to your body and let yourself take back or integrate the conflict. Then ask your subconscious mind to work on it and leave it alone. It is always interesting to see what happens.

Lesson 3: Stories

This can be very powerful. I used it when I made the choice to live or die after I had been diagnosed with liver disease. You can see that I chose to live. The program can also be done for fun little things. My friend Suzi used it for chocolate donuts.

Here is her story. In college NLP trainer Suzi Smith heard chocolate donuts called her name each morning at breakfast. Now she would let her healthy part look at the part that wants chocolate donuts and eventually he found the positive intention of both parts.

	Problem on left hand	**Problem on right hand**
Environment	college	college
Behavior	I do not want to eat chocolate donuts	Eat a chocolate donut every day for breakfast
Capabilities	Choosing to make good food choices	Choosing a donut that I really like
Beliefs and Values	I believe chocolate donuts are not a healthy choice for my breakfast	I am in college now and I am free to choose to eat what I want to and I like chocolate donuts
Identity	I am a person who makes good food choices	I am a person who is grown up and can choose what I like
Greater purpose/positive intention	My good health will help me complete my school and get a good job so I can support myself without the help of my family	I can feel happy about my choices and so I will work hard at school so I can get a good job so I can support myself without the help of my family

As her hands talked it out, her right hand really longed for a donut and her left hand recognized this and asked for a compromise, she would have a chocolate donut once a week to satisfy her love for the donuts and she would make healthy choices the other days to satisfy her desire to be healthy. They both agreed and the hands came together. Both sides could now feel that their positive intention had been met. She brought them in to her happy tummy which knew it would still get chocolate donuts even if it was not every day.

Lesson 4: Sandra

Several weeks after school began the first year I taught school in China, one of my favorite students (all of my students are my favorite students you know) lingered after class. Sandra, not her real name, was going to leave SJTU. She looked down because she really did not want to leave. Her breathing was slow, her shoulders were slumped and her voice was soft and inconsistent. She was a good student and I questioned why. Sandra was in a quandary and uncertain of what to do. Her parents wanted her to be an English teacher and she had made it to SJTU successfully, yet her grades were falling because the conflict was so severe. You see, she did not want to be a teacher even though she liked teaching and children, she longed to be a writer. She loved the area of China where she lived and wanted to write the stories of her countryside and was passionate about it. She was so passionate that she was threatening to drop out of SJTU to pursue her goal. The conflict was obvious and easy to see.

We had barely started school and she had little experience with NLP yet her passion made me want to help her immediately for leaving was a serious threat. It is hard to get into SJTU and I worried that she would regret her decision in the near future as a degree from SJTU would give her a big boost in the job market. We let the two sides of the conflict emerge, to follow her heart and be an author or to do her family duty and be a teacher. We went up the neurological levels and found that at the level of purpose she wanted to be successful in supporting herself and helping support a future family. She then brought her hands into her heart and we decided to shelf it or set it aside and see what would come up.

A few weeks later the conflict was solved. She knew what she would do. She would finish her education at SJTU and do her best. She would get a job as a teacher for beginning writers usually do not make much money. Most writers are not like J. K. Rowling, the lady who wrote the Harry Potters series. Most make little money from their books. She would write in her spare hours. Then when she became successful she would stop teaching and devote her time to writing. I could tell from her physiology that she as congruent with the solution. She stood straight and talked. Her face was light and her breathing has high in her chest. There was excitement and strength in her voice.

Luckily I taught there a second year and had her in my class. I asked her about the conflict. "Oh," she brushed it off, "everything will turn out fine. I realize now that getting a diploma at SJTU will help not only a teaching career, but also a writing career. I have made the best choice." I knew she really believed it.

You remember the presupposition **People make the best choice they can in any situation?** By using conflict resolution, Sandra was able to add greater flexibility to her choices and arrive at a choice that had never occurred to her before and one that would satisfy the needs of both sides of the conflict. She has found that the presupposition, "The person with the most flexibility wins." was true. She was the winner! You can be the winner too.

What is the conflict!

Unit 25: Swish Pattern

Lesson 1: History

The Swish pattern is a powerful and useful NLP process developed by John Grinder in 1985. Typically it is used to help people who have a specific image that is creating trouble for them. Examples include cigarettes and sweets which tend to be compulsive and obsessive. Things we desire and crave and often things we are addicted to. The Swish Pattern is based on behavior psychology and in self-organization theory these images are held in our mind by some kind of an attractor. The image itself can also be an attractor. We have within us learned pathways that our body knows well leading to attractors both wanted and undesired. The idea is to use the pathway for an undesired behavior to create a new and desired behavior pattern. If your unwanted behavior is eating chocolate which you would "die for" yet seems to make you break out in zits (pimples) and your wanted behavior is passing on the chocolate with clear skin, you have your pictures and you are ready to go.

The above paragraph mentions self-organization theory. You may not be familiar with it. This branch of study arose from the study of chaos. When enough complexly interacting elements were brought together instead of creating further chaos, they tended to spontaneously organize. An example is this. When I was growing up I had a girlfriend named Kathy. Her parents collected clocks from all over the world. Many of the clocks had pendulums. Surprising to us all, all of the clocks pendulums tended to swing together. When a new clock was purchased, after a while, it ordered itself with the rest of the pendulums in the house. Self-organization theorists speculate that self-organization processes also occur in our nervous systems. These are a result of associative connections between our nerve cells. These are thought to follow the Hebb rule. Hebb was a neurologist who was awarded the Nobel Prize. He discovered that if two interconnecting neurons in a similar state responded at the same time their connection was strengthened as if a kind of rapport was created. Indeed the Hebb rule may be the basic strategy for establishing rapport as taught by NLP and involves the mirroring of another person's behaviors and cognitive patterns being used.

This is where the idea of attractor basins used in NLP emerged and was strengthen. You will see it used in the Swish pattern below, but first take a look at this diagram.

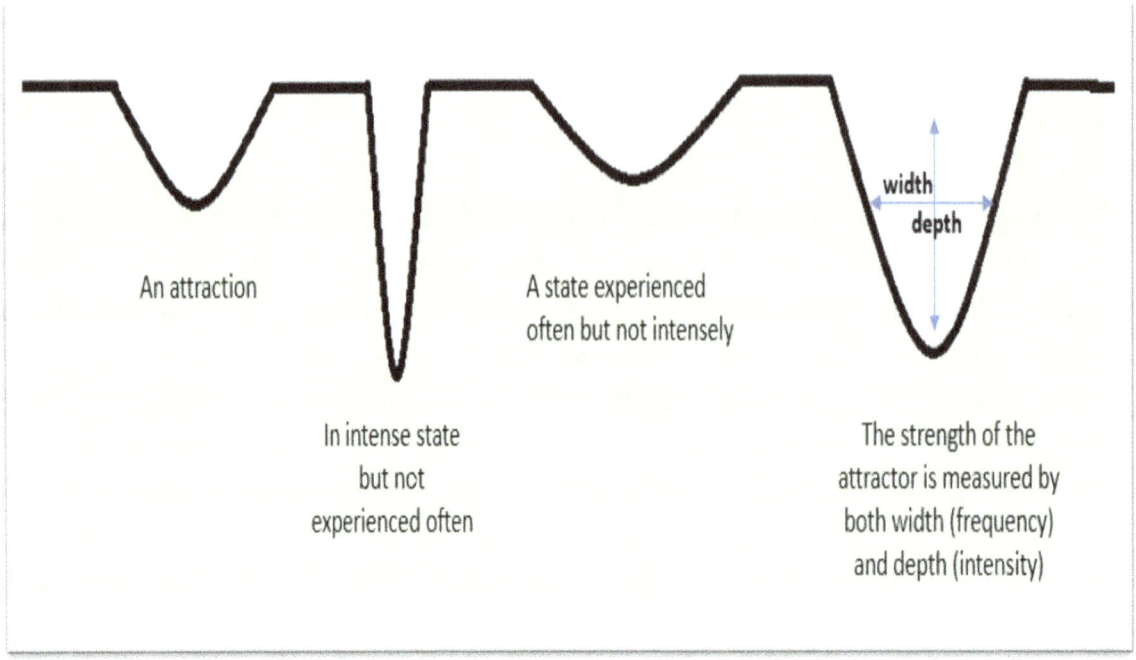

You will remember from a previous lesson that there was a ball. The ball will roll into a state and it is stuck there. If it is a good state that is ok, but if it is a bad state, you are stuck in a bad state, not so desirable. The idea is to make the desired state basin both bigger and deeper by increasing both frequency and intensity. This can be done with practice and using programs such as the Circle of Excellence which provides both frequency and practice making the attractor basin larger so the ball falls in.

Lesson 2: The Swish

The first step in the Swish Pattern is to have a problem and typically this is a problem with something the person keeps coming back to. It may be a habit, an addiction or a compulsion. When the person sees the object he or she associates right into the picture. For girls, chocolate is a common compulsion and when you think about chocolate you associate right into your favorite kind of chocolate and you crave it. This does not do much for your wise food choices.

Your next step is to check ecology. Is it ecologically ok with you and with what is going on in your life right now. It is important to make sure change is positive to all parts of your life. Just as an aside note to the ladies, the Swish is reversible if you find you really do want access to chocolate in your life again.

1. Now create your cue picture. Picture the trigger of the undesired behavior and associate into it. If you are doing the chocolate you might picture your favorite kind of chocolate in all its luscious richness.
2. Play around with the image to find the critical sub-modalities. For me it is the luster and lusciousness of the chocolate, the smooth and robust mouth feel as it melts, the sweetness, and the creaminess. I like the weight of chocolate in my hand, it is just right. Use a sub-modalities work sheet until you are familiar with the process.

3. Now break state. You might remember that this means to change your state or frame of mind. Talk about something else, walk around a bit or even do a wiggle dance to change your state. This allows you to break from the pictures and emotions of the state you have created.
4. Now a second image is to be identified or formed. This is an image that will take the place of the one you are well associated into. You may remember the term "Nature abhors a vacuum." You are going to remove the compulsive image and this will leave an empty place or vacuum. You will want to have something ready to fill that space created in your mind. This will be something you are attracted to but the image is not yet as strong as the one you have a compulsion for. You will be dissociated from the image at this time. You will learn some tricks to change that. For me it is a time I went to a wedding banquet and was presented with an amazing feast yet felt very balanced and in control. I had just a little bite of everything and finished the entire banquet nicely satisfied but not stuffed.

5. Now enrich your picture of your desired state by using sub-modalities again. Concentrate especially on the sub-modalities that were strongest in your cue picture. For me the chocolate looked luscious and lustrous so I want to enhance what I see in this new picture making it look even more luscious and lustrous. I like the mouth feel of the chocolate so I need to enhance the feelings of the food in my image. I notice how I savor each small bite of food and enjoy the different textures of each one. I note that I felt very in control of myself and I add that to my full picture. I enhance the sub-modalities.

6. Break State again.
7. Recall your cue picture and put a frame around it. Make sure it is in the same place as you created it before. This is important. Then recall the desired state image in its fully enhanced state. Squash it down into a small, dark dot in the bottom left corner of the framed cue picture.
8. Now, with a swishhhhh sound, enlarge or even explode the picture until it completely covers the cue picture.

9.

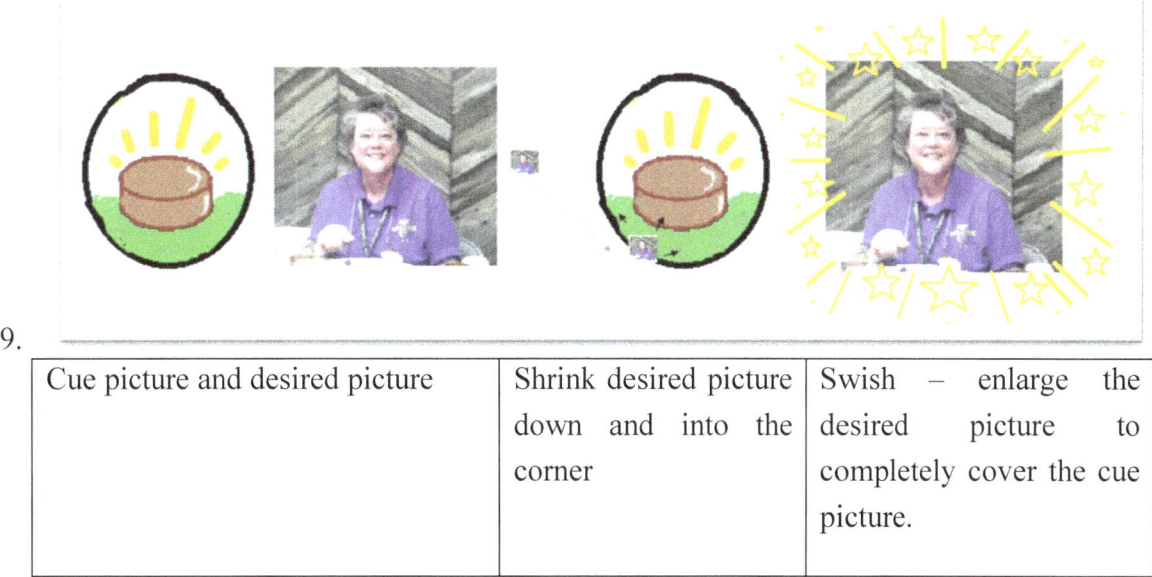

| Cue picture and desired picture | Shrink desired picture down and into the corner | Swish – enlarge the desired picture to completely cover the cue picture. |

10. Break State
11. Repeat the Swish several times to install the strategy firmly in your neurology.

Some people, particularly people whose primary representation system is kinesthetic, find the Swish will be more effective if they use their hands bringing them together quickly as they squash the undesired picture as they allow the desired picture to expand. For me personally I felt the sound was distracting and prefer to do it without sound. Feel free to explore what works best for you. For the person with the most flexibility wins. Ladies, with chocolate you may have to do it again on occasion. Chocolate is a girl's best friend so enjoy those Valentine Chocolates for a day then SWISH them away.

There are other ways of doing the Swish. My, Debrah's, first experience with the Swish was with diabetes. The next chapter will be a shortened version of the experience. You can read the entire story in my book, *Journey Through Liver Disease*.

Lesson 3: My Journey through Diabetes

It was my first session with an NLP Coach. My coach had experienced Multiple Sclerosis in the past but now was symptom free. I had liver disease and my Medical Doctor had told me that I would eventually die from it. I had turned to Traditional Chinese Medicine and although I was not completely cured, I was almost there. But something stopped me. Sharalee, my coach, invited me to choose what I would like to work on. I started thinking. I couldn't think of liver disease, I knew at that time that it would eventually take me home, (I would die) but I had diabetes and the process of dying of liver disease would be much nicer if I didn't have diabetes. I knew the symptoms of diabetes were impacting my life and compounding the problems I had with liver disease. I was doing much better with the Chinese Tradition Medicine treatments and I thought, "what if? I had nothing to lose." I asked, "Did you ever work with someone who had diabetes?"

"Yes, I have." She replied. "Does it feel like you are, (pardon my French,) damned?" (Going to hell)

"It sure does but spelled different, dammed." I wrote in my journal, "Exactly! Something is stopping me, damming me, as it were, from utilizing insulin. I detect it in the core of me. So I am ready to begin my journey."

Again from my journal, "I do not know what to expect, but I see clearly on Sharalee's countenance that she is excited to take the journey and has no fears. So the road ahead, though it has many twists and turns, must lead to an exciting vista. Her look reminds me of my children when they beat me to a mountain top. 'Come on, mom. You won't believe this.' I was never disappointed.

The first session we did the SWISH Program. It was the weirdest thing I had ever done. She had me imagine that diabetes being drawn out of me and taking an imaginary form. Much to my surprise, it did. It was a swirling ball similar to Japanese lanterns and the swirling was like the artist drawings of the outer planets. Then a gold band emerged gently yet very securely wrapping it. As I gazed, suddenly the blue and swirling ribbons of color part for just a second and I noticed the interior was a glowing, fiery, burning red. It scared me. I had never had anything like this happen to me before. She asked if I wanted to explore it. "No, it might hurt." I wanted it to go away. I was frightened. Even as I wrote the words in my journal I could feel the fear.

Sharalee then helped me construct a second me, in the space in front of me. The me we created was healthy. We explored what she looked like, how she saw the world, what she heard, and what she felt. What she smelled was added and I knew the smell I loved, lilacs. How about a taste that was her, mandarin oranges. She was dressed in a pastel peach dress and.....she danced! Sharalee then taught me the Swish. I learned to put the new me in the exact place of the swirling ball.

Looking back I think I must have been the weirdest client she ever had. I had a question for everything. What is it? Who is this me? And most important, "Well, where does the ball go when I SWISH it." I have since done the program with others and they just SWISH it away, but not me. Then I think that is the way I have always been. I want to know how and why things work. It was that questing for knowledge that lead to me wants to know more and eventually lead me to studying NLP at NLPU with Michael Dilts, Judith DeLozier and Susi Smith. It was that questing spirit of me that lead me to wanting to create NLP curriculum for my students and share with them some of the empowerment, the magic of NLP.

She sighed. No one asked such questions. She must have thought, where can it go as she paused then said, "Put it in your past."
"Where is my past?"
"Don't you know where your past is? Where do you think it is?"
I was stumped. I had no idea. Past was past and now was now. I knew where my future was, though. It was in front of me. I had that much solved. Oh, so my past must be behind me then. I gestured behind me. She agreed and disagreed. Yes, it was behind me but not on my right side, but my left. Now after years of NLP I understand that some gesture I made or bit of body language gave her a clue to where I put my past but I had never been aware of it before.

I constructed the diabetes ball that had appeared very near to me in my present time space. (Now I know) Then I looked into the future and constructed the Well-formed Me. I was healthy, I was not young, but just me, an appropriate me for my age. I could smell lilacs. I could see me dressed in a beautiful peach color. I could taste the freshness of oranges. I could hear that I was healthy. I was calm and assured.

I then moved the Well-formed Me from my future to the present knocking the diabetes out of the present and into the past. As did it I felt a small quirky feeling and I think I even made a bit of movement. Something happened. I knew it. I could feel a difference inside of me. We practiced it several times to make sure I knew how to do it on my own. It was strange. I had never done anything like that before.

 I went home. I felt good. My blood sugar levels went down, but more important, I felt good. That night I woke up. A great ball of energy shot through my back. What was it? I had never felt anything like that before. Sharalee had told me that something might happen but she did not know what. She had told me it would be ok and to just relax and enjoy the experience. That must be what she meant. It did not hurt. I was ok. I glanced at the clock. It said 3 a.m. I learned later that this is a time when the liver and organs associated with the liver in Chinese Tradition Medicine process and work. Before morning the energy had awakened me several more time. Now I knew something was happening that was not threatening and I relaxed and found it interesting.

The very next day I noted that my blood sugar was down, and I felt so good inside. It was a wonderful, freeing, intensely happy feeling and I liked it.

Lesson 4: Wrap Up

Often in NLP work there is a single powerful attractor that is not wanted. This often happens to a person when they are under six years old but can happen any time in life. It can be a car wreck, a bad reaction to a food or smell, or any other impacting event. After one of these impacting events the event seems to lurk in the back of our minds almost like a virus on a computer. Using principles learned in Self-organization theory those attractors can be mellowed out much as a virus cleaner removes the virus from our computer. The ball of our state falls into the bigger and better attractor basin making life easier to live.

A similar program has been developed for many allergies. Often an allergy is formed in a single learning. This happened to me. I had a bad head cold when I was a teenager that occurred just as the beautiful lilacs came into bloom. They were my favorite flowers and as I buried my head into their sweet fragrant blossoms a sneeze! Quickly my body linked lilacs with sneezing and being stuffed up in my nose. From then on lilacs became the enemy running a virus in the back of my mind. The lilac virus soon recruited friends and over the years more and more flowers and scents became "the enemy' an allergy.

Using an NLP process called the Allergy Process I was able to unlearn the program my body had developed and in 1 hour was able to enjoy all of the scents that make life so wonderfully fragrant. This program can be learned from Suzi Smith, an NLP professional, or can be found on an Mp3 at http://suzismith.net/. It is not a part of the Practitioner

Certification. Some experts say that approximately 85% of all allergies are created by the single learning process and can be destabilized and unlearned in a very wonderfully short time.

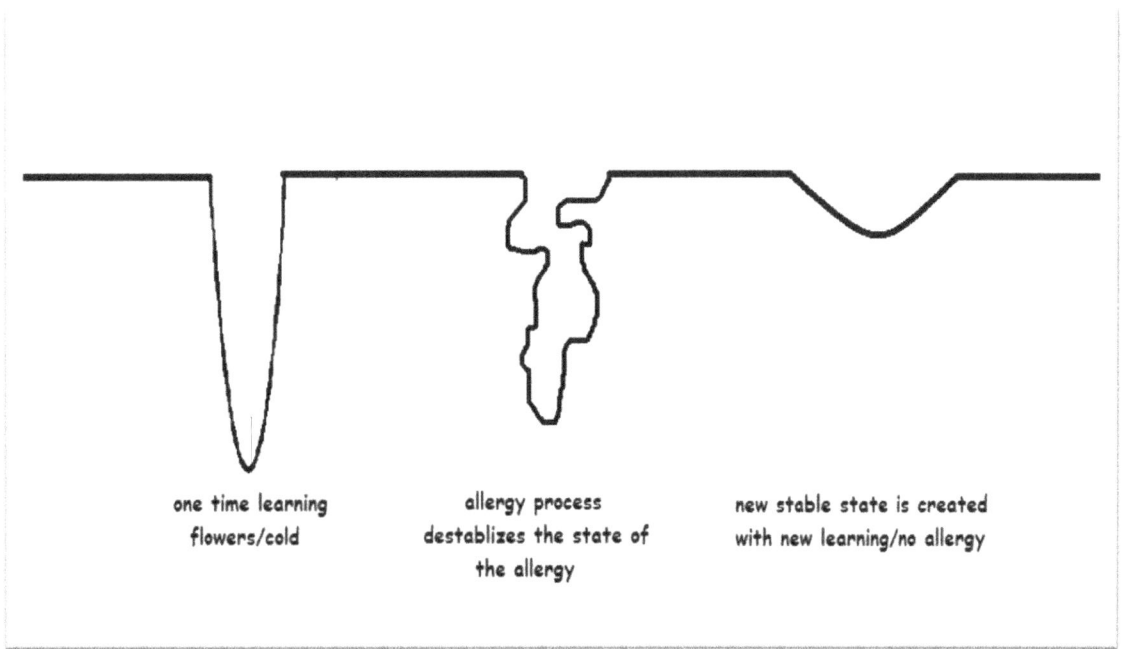

Our brains are very powerful. If and when we can harness the power of the brain almost anything is possible. I do hope you are ready for an exploration of a lifetime as you learn to use your brain in new and more effective ways to achieve what you want in life.

Unit 26: V-K Dissociation

Lesson 1: History

The V-K Dissociation Process was developed in 1976 by co-founders Bandler and Grinder. It was only a year after NLP first began and is one of the earliest therapeutic techniques to be developed. It was a synthesis of techniques used by Milton H. Erikson, M.D., and processes used by Fritz Perls. This very effective NLP program has been used effectively for many years and its effectiveness is well proven.

Lesson 2: About the V-K Dissociation Process

V-K Dissociation is a powerful NLP process used for painful, stressful and traumatic experiences. In this process the person will dissociate or separate into parts or units the emotional response from the visual stimuli of the experience. The person is then able to replay the experience over again without the emotional response that was previously attached to it. This helps a person distance themselves from the event and become better able to assess it and cope with it. The goal is to separate oneself from one's feelings by moving the entire visual picture of the event outside of one's body through the use of the imagination. Sub-modalities are important in this process to help create a dissociated state. By manipulating sub-modalities the event is made less impactful. Likewise the use of accessing cues is important to put oneself in the observer perspective dissociated from the event. Linguistics is also used to help facilitate the dissociation with words such as "he, " "she," "the younger me," etc. V-K Dissociation can be done on a two or a three place dissociation depending on the impact of the event being worked with. All of these common NLP tools help to make the dissociation easy and ease the trauma of the event.

As the process progresses a type of Change Personal History is used to recode perceptions of the event by anchoring new resources into the memories adding knowledge and resources that were not present at the time of the event. This is done with anchoring. A form of reframing is also used to explore choices to satisfy the positive intention of the negative feelings associated with the event.

Finally the new choices if the resources and responses are future paced into possible future events that could occur so the explorer will have more resources when a presenting event or a similar one surfaces in the future. As you can now see, V-K Dissociation uses many NLP techniques.

Lesson 3: The V-K Dissociation Process

Before you start the process establish your set. You are going to be in a movie theater. I like to have my explorer sit in front of a blank computer or TV or a big screen depending on what is available. Next find a place in the audience. Set a chair there and make sure the screen is just right for watching the movie of an event in your life. You want to be sitting so your head and eyes are looking upward just as they would in a movie theater.

Now imagine yourself leaving your body on that chair and then go sit in the projection booth. You might remember that projection booths are above the audience slightly so the projector can project the movie down to the screen. You are going up there so you can watch yourself sitting in the movie theater watching the movie of an event in your life. Again your eyes should be looking upward at about a 20 degree angle. Your breathing will be shallow and in the chest. Shoulders are relaxed and back and there is little or no tension in your facial muscles. Anchor this state.

Now you in the projection booth are going to create the movie that is going to show to you in the chair in the audience. On the movie screen project the movie or snapshots of the event starting at just before it happened. Watch yourself in the audience and if the movie is too impacting play with sub-modalities by moving it farther away, making the movie black and white, making the picture smaller or very bright or very faded. Adjust until it is just right. It helps if you imagine you have a computer that you can manipulate to change it, sort of like a paint program on a computer that you manipulate by pressing the mouse. Occasionally an event is so impactful it is a good idea to suggest to the explorer that safety glass could enclose the projection booth so the explorer feels safer.

As the explorer manipulates the movie the guide asks questions such as, "What was happening there to the younger you?" and "What is she doing?" "What does she need that she did not have?" Now run the movie again adding the things that were needed. Check to make sure everything that is needed is there.

Now go into the audience. This is a time when you really need to do this and use separate chairs. So move up into the chair and play it again. Check to see if it is enough. If you need more go back to the projection booth and add what is needed. Check it out again. When it is complete return to your audience seat and run it again. Do this as often as is necessary to get the resources you need.

Next you may want to put yourself (associate) back into the event and notice how bringing in the new resources and changes make a difference.

Finally future pace the changes by imagining a future which could trigger the anxiety state and call on your new resources to check it out. When I, Debrah, have used this process I have added more steps. Before we finish we run the whole movie in reverse first slowly and then quicker and quicker each time until it is down to a couple of seconds just as you would do with a DVD in your computer. Finally we burn it to a USB drive in our imagination and decide where to store that USB so it as away from us and yet available if it is ever needed.

Lesson 4: Real Life Example

How about a real life example. I was taking a class one time with a lady, RoAnn, (not her real name) who was having difficulty with a real event. We were sitting around the campfire bowl as she told me about it. She had been working at a cook in the camp kitchen just a few years before. While she was working with a crew of other ladies, suddenly a crazy man jumped in through the window and grabbed a knife. He stabbed one of the ladies in the kitchen. She ran and escaped. I could see from her strong physical body response that it would be something good to work on right now.

We set up our space with a screen in front of us in the campfire bowl where the skits were held and RoAnn sat on a seat. The story was pretty interesting and it was after a training session and so others requested to stay so we had a good audience. We made sure everything was set just right and then RoAnn and I moved to the back of the bowl to set up the projector.

Now she started to play the show. She flashed the pictures on the screen. Working in the kitchen. Intruder entering through the window. The knife! Blood squirting and splashing all over. Everyone running. The man is apprehended. Safe at last.

What did she need?

Of course this was unexpected and an occurrence not likely to happen to anyone, but it had happened to her. She had needed someone to yell, Lock the window!" She had needed someone to grab the knife and move it out of his reach. She had needed to grab her friends' hands and run, especially the friend who was stabbed. We added these and tried the movie again. It helped. She was ready.

RoAnn went back to her seat in the audience and as it played again she told them what was happening and what she had needed. Her friends talked about it. I think most important they reached out and touched her gently letting her know they were there for her. Then we all agreed it was time to run it backwards. Back it went. Remember the destabilizing of the basin we did in the last lesson. This is the same, we are destabilizing the event. At first it was slow to make sure everything was there. Then she pressed the back button on her imaginary computer and went right back to the beginning of the scene. Chi-click, it was done. She tried it a few more times to the encouragement and cheers of her friends. Then I presented her with an imaginary USB drive and she accepted it. Where would she put it? In her back pocket. She safely tucked it in knowing it was there if she needed.

Lastly we talked about how she could use that knowledge in the future realizing that it was not likely she would ever need it. She commented that being a bit calmer would help so we added it in. Then we all got up to leave and as we did I noted she was calm, no longer agitated and walked with a sure gait, Mission Accomplished.

Lesson 5: Flexibility

It would be nice if no one in the world ever needed this powerful program but it seems almost everyone has something powerfully and impacting occur in their life. Life is real, we live it warts and all. One girl who needed it was blind. We did a sound booth instead of a projection booth. Enjoy your exploration of this powerful process as you allow something from the past leave its learning and resources with you while removing the impact of the event.

Unit 27: Xavier's Strategy for Organization

First comes thought; then organization of that thought, into ideas and plans; then transformation of those plans into reality. The beginning, as you will observe, is in your imagination. -Napoleon Hill

Lesson 1: History

In 2009 I (Debrah) took a workshop at NLPU in beautiful Santa Cruz, California. I was excited about the possibilities of new learnings. One thing scared me, however. That was modeling a strategy. Could I do it? I did not think so. I felt scared and timid, especially when I thought of Robert and the wonderful strategies he has developed. Thinking, too, of Judy who has developed my favorite strategy, The Dancing SCORE. I so admire Grinder and Bandler, and their incredible work. Even the thought, I found it the scariest thing about NLPU trainers. I felt petrified.

Then the day came and we just transitioned into it so easily it wasn't quite so scary. Still I was apprehensive. Fortunately I worked with Xavier and he was such an easy person to work with. He also confessed to feeling a bit tentative at the challenge and we decided to support each other and work together. His strategy that I modeled was clear and obviously good. Here is his story as I recall it.

Xavier Lee worked for a bus company that organized and drove groups of people to see sights around the south western United States. Often the groups were exchange students or similar foreign groups. One day as he was sitting at work he got a phone call from a panicked driver. The bus had broken down in Death Valley. Death Valley is aptly named because so many people die there of the heat and it was the middle of summer where temperatures often are over 100°F (38°C) Death Valley is the lowest place in North America as well as the hottest with a record high temperature of 134° (56.7°C). This was truly a recipe for disaster if a remedy could not be found quickly.

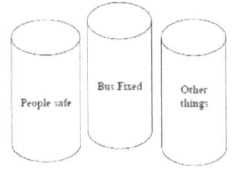
His strategy was one to organize information quickly, sort of a triage, in his head. Xavier told me how as the bus driver gave him information he would quickly put each important piece of information into an imaginary silo organizing the information as it was given and creating

silos as needed. He then leaned back a bit to see clearly all of the silos and manipulated the silos by importance until everything was done.

Some of the information he needed was how much water was available, where was the nearest repair shop, was there shade and how he could keep the people in the shade as the bus was quickly heating up like an oven. After the information was loaded into the silos and the silos were triaged by importance, he leaned forward again and in his imagination pulled the "Safety" silo forward. He made decisions and called the bus driver telling him to get the people out of the bus and into the shade of the bus. He instructed people to be careful with water and to share. He advised them to wear adequate clothing so they would not sunburn and asked if those with sun screen would share it around. He then put down the phone and pulled out the next silo. The bus had to be fixed fast. He called the repair station that was nearest but they could not come quickly enough, it was just a small shop in the desert. He knew speed of the essence. He made a few more calls and found a company that could dispatch a repair truck immediately. It would cost more but time was of the essence. He made the arrangements needed and sent it off.

He leaned back in his chair again and looked at the big picture. It was time to go back to the bus and put the people at ease. He leaned forward again and picked the phone up to call the driver to see how everyone was doing and tell them that a repair truck had been dispatched for them and would arrive in two hours.

Again he leaned back to look at the big picture. The crucial things that meant life and death had been done. Now it was time to look at other issues. He continued on with his day getting the insurance forms needed, calls made and so on. A disaster of epic proportions was averted. The day, though traumatic, went well and soon the people were rescued and again on their way to the Grand Canyon.

Having learned to model I watched Xavier's every move. Where were his eyes, his head and his body. How was his breathing, his posture, his speech? Then I had a magnificent thought. As he went thought his story many times for me so I could take notes, he first told of the bus driver calling him and getting the news, Xavier had a look on his face I had seen many times before. It was the same look my precious students would get when they had their schedule rearranged such as at the beginning of a term. It was the exact same. As I modeled I began to feel that this strategy was better than just a thing that works for Xavier. I thought, "I think it will work for my special needs students." This was beyond my wildest dreams. If often took two weeks for them to settle into a new schedule and the panic look would come up often. I could tell when I modeled the strategy by trying it on myself that it was good and easy to chunk down. It would be easy to teach and easy to model. There would be a bonus from this project, I would use it in my classroom.

In August, just a few weeks later, it was time and I taught it to my students. I told them they got to be the first kids in the whole world to learn this strategy and it made them feel special. The aides in my class were there and listening in, of course. They were immediately applying it and instead of just presenting a strategy, we were doing it as a class. It was incredible. Best of all, the adults in my room were taken with it even more that the students and immediately using it. I mean it was immediate. They could see it would work and put it into play then and there. We were actually doing it as we went and making changes. It worked so well it became automatic. The next day I sent this note to Xavier.

> Today was when I saw it really work. Those kids are using their silos and some are already using their imaginations to create the silos. I was not telling them to use the silos, they were turning to them on their own because they knew it worked.
>
> Xavier, your little strategy is a miracle for these special needs students. They have just taken it and flown. It has given them a way to organize that they can understand. When I saw them pull out the silo for the class they were in and check it-WOW! This has been one incredible experiment.
>
> Yesterday was a difficult day as we transitioned to new classes and I had two of my 12 students "blow." (have a behavior that is not acceptable, a temper tantrum) Still it was working. Only two blew. The rest were doing ok and some seemed to be almost clinging to the strategy for support and congruence. I think the thing that blew one was that we ended up with a lunch schedule we were not planning on, and so the one blew at the end of lunch. I think the other one kind of got sucked in as he was right there when the other child totally blew up. It disturbed him and made him feel anxious.
>
> This has been so much fun!

When I chunked the program down, we used real little paper silos that the children could write on. We taped them together to make a full day with a silo for each class. They could each make their own silos and put down what they felt was important on them. As I went to other classes to see how my students were doing I noted that they brought their little silos with them. As the class ended they would look at the silos to see where to go next and what they needed. I do not know why this worked better than a piece of paper with the information on it like the mainstream children would use, but it did.

It went beyond this. A few days later a proud student informed me that they had had a time in their family the night before when then needed to organize something and he had taught his whole family Xavier's Strategy. His mother told me that indeed he had and it had worked very well. One thing I wanted my students to do was to generalize their learning across settings. That is often especially challenging to special needs students. It was amazing how these students internalized this strategy into their neurology and it worked so effectively that they quickly generalized it.

Lesson 2: Xavier's Strategy

So let's chunk down the strategy. I taught it with real little silos that we made of paper. Then one of the students realized the silos would fit nicely on their fingers and soon all of them used them this way, but you may just want imaginary ones as Xavier did. I will use pictures. First you need information you need to organize. Some suggestions include your next day schedule, a new project or a series of tasks that must be accomplished.

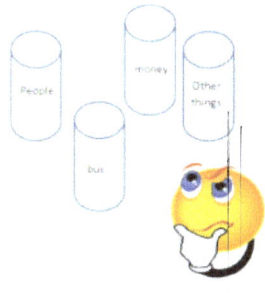
Sit up and look squarely at the problem you have chosen to work with. Your feeling should be alert and engaged. You may find yourself leaning forward a bit and your breathing will likely be high up in your chest. Your feel will be flat on the floor or even tucked a bit behind you. Next chunk the big problem into smaller chunks or pieces. In NLP we call this chunking down. Create in your mind's eye individual cylinders like silos to hold the smallest chunks of information. Label them. Take the small pieces of information and put them into the correct silos so that all is organized.

Now lean back a bit. Relax and look at the big picture. You will find that you will breathe deeper and lower. Your legs will likely reach in front of you and maybe even cross. Your eyes will look up and out farther as you see the big picture. Let the silos organize as you manipulate them into order according to importance or another way as you desire.

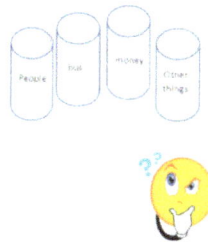

Decide which one is the most important for you to look at first, triage, and bring it forward from the rest. Again the physiology for this is to lean forward, eyes on the silo, feet on the floor or tucked under, breathing goes high and thinking is clear and focused. You will likely find you are sitting very evenly. Look at the problem and analyze it as needed. What needs to be done? What resources do you need? Who do you need to help you? Where and how will it happen? When you are satisfied put it back and go back to the big picture.

Continue with the strategy as needed pulling up a silo of information, finding the solutions and then returning the silo and looking again at the big picture. When the entire piece feels complete look at it as a whole and then work the ideas that have come to you to solve the problem or organize the material needed.

Naturally you do not need to do all of this on paper but can make silos or whatever else works best for you as you know the power of being flexible.

Rupert, Idaho's water silo   Grain silo in the Rupert area

Lesson 3: The Story Continues

Xavier's Strategy for Organization is useful to organize a lot of information quickly. Studies have shown that people can only hold seven plus or minus two things in their head at one time. It does not matter whether you are a cognitively impaired, normal or a genius, all brains are capable of no more than seven $\pm$ two things This is a tool to help chunk up information into groups and chunk down the groups of information in an organized way so that the mind can quickly and efficiently process the information.

The school year went on that year of 2009. We did many NLP strategies including the New Name Strategy before a big meet and greet meeting with Special Olympics and well-formed outcomes for year-long goals. We used NLP programs for our Life skills class where we were to learn the skills we need in life.

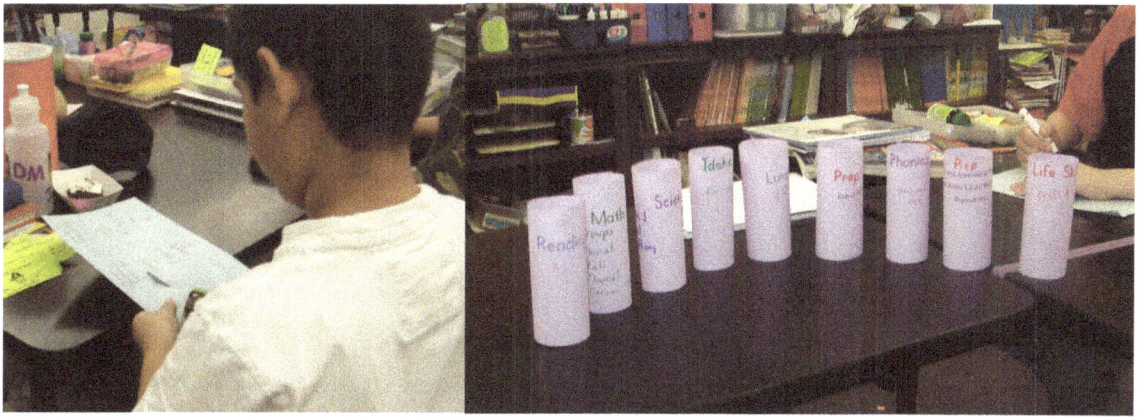

We completed the term and a new term was to start. The students were excited as they knew Xavier's Strategy and we were making our paper silos. Friday night they went home with their silos lined up on their desks ready to go Monday morning. Monday arrived but it was not as planned. The principal came into my room and sadly informed me that a scheduling problem that had arisen and he had worked all week end to rearrange schedules because of it. All of my student schedules had to be changed, every one. In the past this was about the worst thing imaginable. The students do not understand change and to add a change on top of a change was unthinkable, but the unthinkable had happened. It would be hard to keep the chin up.

When the students arrived I explained to them what had happened and asked what could we do? Quickly they got to work without my direction and pulled apart their row of silos then asked us to help them put them in the new order. We gladly did and re-taped them. Then they put them on their fingers as they headed off to class. It was incredible. The magic little silos gave them control, gave them autonomy they needed to be successful.

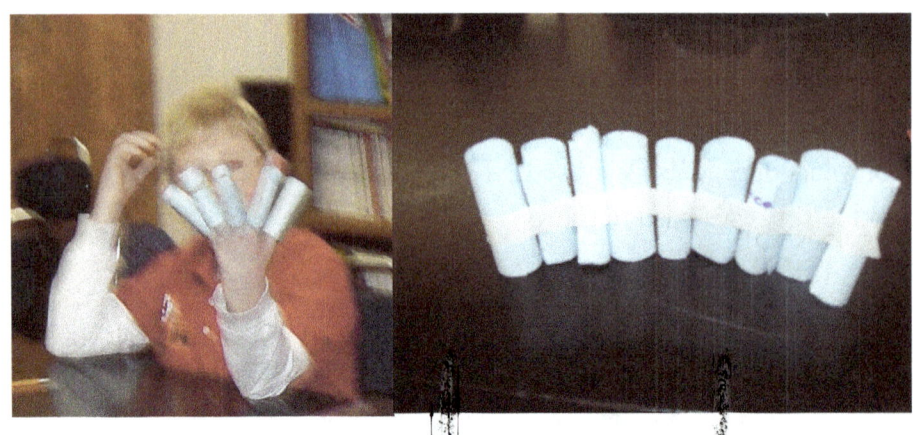

Now maybe I have a little piece of how Robert, Judy, Bandler and Grinder felt when they modeled a strategy, broke it down, then taught it and saw it work. Fun, fun, fun! Invigorating. YES! What I find most interesting is that everyone has within them some of the strategies. The trick with NLP is that you can learn all of the strategies then use the ones that are applicable to you. NLP is wonderful and versatile. For my students, all of my students whether ordinary people, special needs students or the brightest university students in all of China and indeed in the world, it is magic.

Lesson 4: Sample

Problem: Creating a lesson that will teach English acquisition skills to English language learners utilizing the NLP program Xavier's Strategy.

Lesson 1	Lesson 2	Lesson 3
At NLPU	problem	7 ± 2 things
frightened	catagories	chunk up/chunk down
Xavier	small chunks in	back to story
Strategy worked	catagories	worst case scenario
looked like my students	use physiology	students gained
secondary gain	up close/big picture	flexibility
	flexible continue until	autonomy
	complete	control
		It was magic

Unit 28: Reframes

"If a problem can't be solved within the frame it was conceived,
the solution lies in reframing the problem."
— Brian McGreevy

Lesson 1

When I was young we lived in the desert country of Idaho. There was little rain on the desert, but the mountains would catch the rain and fill the bubbly springs which, in turn, would flow into the mighty rivers. We had a garden and in order to make it grow we had to 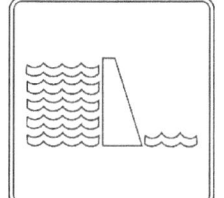 irrigate our garden, bring water in from the river. Idaho has a vast network of canals to take the water where it was needed. Once a week my dad would open our irrigation box and let the water flow onto the thirsty ground. The water would have to be controlled so at the end of each row he would build a small dam of dirt to stop the water. Only by going over the dam could the water continue to flow.

An example of this is one I see and hear almost every day in my classroom. My students will say or write about how hard their work is or how hard they must try. Hard becomes a dam. Hard is a powerful word that means difficult, maybe even almost impossible.
"I have to work so hard," one might say.
I ask, "What would happen if you used diligent instead of hard? Diligently means steady and constant. I have to work diligently, try it."

Another example. My work is hard.
"Try, the work is challenging, instead. Challenges are interesting and lead you forward."

How about have to? If we have to do something there is little choice. Try instead, I get to. "Get to" leaves a choice open. It is something that is interesting and engaging to do. I get to do my homework. Even better add a future. I get to do my homework now so that I can play a computer game before I go to bed. Now the homework becomes an opportunity to do what you want to do. Interesting way to look at it, isn't it? That is a reframe. Looking at something in a new and different way that changes your frame of reference.

Lesson 2: Life Experiences

Working with children we often have the experience of when a very small happening appears to them to totally take over their life. For example, when I was twelve years old my mother enrolled me in ballet lessons. I was on top of the world. I had always wanted to dance and now I had my chance. I was a faithful student, never missing a lesson.

One day my mother dropped me off in front of the studio door and just as she drove off I saw that I had left my dance shoes on the front seat of the car. I was devastated. I sunk into the depths of despair. How could I have done that to myself?

Tears welled up in my eyes. I chased my mother's car, but of course I could not catch it, then stood in the middle of a very busy street unable to move. You are likely laughing by now but to me this was the end of the world in my twelve year old mind.

On older man walked up to me and gently led me out of the road asking what had happened. I told him through sobs that I had left my dance shoes on the front seat of the car and now would not have them for dance lessons.

He now worked to reframe it. "Could I dance without them for one day?" That had never occurred to me. I began to see that the shoes were not the whole world and gradually realized I could find other solutions to the problem. Fortunately for me, however, my mother had heard my call, driven around the block and returned to the drop off spot with the slippers and I danced up a storm again in another dance class.

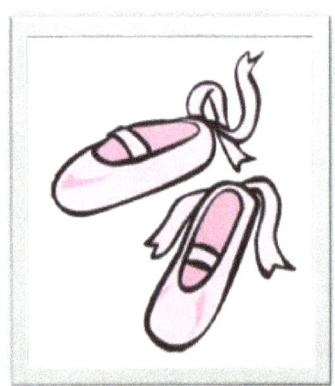

Looking at the pictures above, first notice how the slippers loom large in the eyes of the twelve year old me. The gentle old man framed it as a problem that could be overcome. Notice now how the reframe of the dance shoes as a small part of the tapestry of life makes it much less important. It is actually a very small and insignificant little incident in a very wonderful life. Seeing it again the big picture widens the perspective and makes a difference in how it impacts us, and how we react to it.

My students often look at exams in much the same way. The exams loom large in their minds and take over their thinking. Sometimes they appear so daunting the exams seem to take over their lives. They neglect food and sleep that will help them ace the test. A good friend can reframe it and make the study a bit gentler as their friend realizes it is not the end of the world. This is especially important if the friend did not feel they did well on the exam. Even when the friend rejects the reframe he is still listening and beginning to think in a new way.

Lesson 3: Two types of Reframes

In NLP we look at two types of reframes, context and content. An experience will have a different implication depending on the context in which it occurred. I did not like gym class. If I had instead been dropped off at a gym class and left my shoes it would have been great. I would have had an excuse not to participate in gym class and instead read a book or even help the teacher out by being a water girl. Maybe I would be lucky and she would let me go an empty corner and practice a dance which I would gladly do, even barefoot!

The behavior of leaving the shoes is simply a behavior. It is not good or bad. Leslie Cameron-Bandler (1978, p 131 Contextual Reframing) said that NLP "accepts all behaviors as useful in some context." Reframing the context allows us to view the behavior as merely that, a behavior. We can then shift our attention to the issues related to the larger context, what to do about no shoes.

When I was teaching my students to set well-formed outcomes I had one young man who managed to get in a fight every single day. The other guys knew it and would egg him on. I think they delighted in seeing him get in trouble and it became a joke to them. But he did not like it, he wanted to make a change and he chose that to be the subject of his TOTE. He was going to stay out of trouble for one term. He was committed to his well-formed outcome.

It was successful for many weeks. He learned what caused him problems and how to avoid the problems. Then the fateful day arrived. We went on a field trip and had to ride in the close quarters of a school bus. The guys who were the perpetrators in the past sat near him and the challenge was on. They kept at him until finally he blew and another teacher, not understanding what was happening, wrote him up. He came to me, head down, and crushed. He had failed. It was time for a quick reframe to get him out of his rut.

"Mike," I said, "Look what you have done. You went nine full weeks without getting in trouble Have you ever done that before?" (Mike was not his real name)

He shook his lowered head mournfully no.
"Do you realize that you have gone longer than you ever had before? You may not have won the war, but you have won a lot of battles. Take your detention and pay for the problem and we will make a short TOTE to go that one last week with no trouble."
The reframe was all he needed to pull him out of the rut and get him back on the right path and I am happy to report that he made it.

The other type of reframe is a content reframe. People behave in response to the world as they see it. I have a student in China I will call Chan. (That is not his real name.) He is talking an audio course where the students watch videos and then hold discussions. I have the students do a small quiz every week with a few vocabulary words and a discussion answer on it. Chan did not like this and would hand in his work late and with snide remarks on it concerning having to write in an audio class. It was time for a reframe.

> Oh, Chan, "Have to write" or "Get to show your understanding of the material and pick up personal writing tips from a foreign professor who really cares about you and wants to help you be successful in the world?" I do not have to read each student's work but I do because I think each and every one of you are worth it and will make a difference in the world.

Another example of content reframing you have likely used by now as an NLP explorer. Remember when you learned about representation systems and that people literally see, hear or feel the world in different ways. Maybe now when someone has gone on and on about the boring and tedious facts of his project when it is as if you can see the entire project before your eyes, you understand that he is working in an auditory digital mode and cut him a little slack instead of getting frustrated. Have you done that yet?

Another use of content reframing will be found in the next chapter on the Six Step Reframing Program. There you will learn to find the positive intention of a behavior you are doing that causes you problems, illness, or even pain. You will find the positive intention and then look at possibilities of other behaviors that can satisfy the positive intention but without the problems.

Lesson 4: Health Applications

I often wonder how often our words affect our neurology and, in turn, affect our health. Can our words create illness? Can our words create health? As a student of NLP this will be a constant and new exploration for the rest of your life.

First let's look at a visit to a friend in the hospital. We come in to see your friend and the first thing we likely say is, "How are you?" Unbeknownst to us, (until now) this immediately sends the friend's brain on a search, a search for what is wrong. The brain goes back into the illness and may get stuck creating a new dam to go over. Reframe your question to, "how is the healing going?" Or "tell me what is better today." That sends the person's brain on a search for healing allowing them to flowing over the dam and into a great healing state.

As a teacher in a middle school for several years I often had students with snuffle-y noses. I started paying attention to what was being said to them. "Oh, you are catching a cold." Is what I often heard. We tell the child what do and then soon the child really does catch that cold. A quick reframe was in order. "Got the sniffles? Isn't it wonderful how the nose knows how to clear itself and keep you healthy? Think of all those germs you are going to blow out into that tissue and throw away from you. You don't want those old germs any more" Again with a simple reframe we have told the nose what to do and the child moves towards keeping healthy. In my last five years of teaching special needs the students just did not get sick. They had learned how to direct their minds in a healing direction.

Another example of a medical application is diarrhea. It happens to us all on occasion, more often in China if we have a penchant for street food. I have a friend who is an archeologist in Guatemala. Before I first came to China I asked him for advice. He had spoken at the 2010 World Expo in China. He had also survived the food in Guatemala. As he gave me sage advice I couldn't help but notice that he did not get upset about a bit of diarrhea. "Oh, it just cleans you out and keeps you healthy. Your body knows what to do. Just figure it will take about six weeks for your system to adjust, eat the local yoghurt and you will be just fine." It worked. While others complained of intestinal discomfort my husband and I celebrated that our bodies were cleaning out the germs and adjusting to the local food. It did not bother us. Do know that we did not do unwise things like drink water out of the taps because even the locals do not do that. We just followed their lead and made wise choices. Chinese food is great.

Lesson 5: Increase Your Ability

Now that you know how useful reframing can be, you will want to practice it. Often all it takes is changing a single word that is said from one that has a negative connotation to one that is more positive. You saw that in the first chapter of this unit as I reframed student's words from hard work to challenging as well as others.

Bertrand Russell once said, "I am firm; you are obstinate; he is a pig-headed fool." Using this same idea I could say, your homework is interesting, his is hard and hers is a real killer. The homework has not changed but the person's attitude has.

A favorite reframe of mine comes from my life in the rural area of Idaho. We had in our county a sugar factory. (A county is an area of land where the people share a local government. It could contain a few cities. Idaho has about 44 counties each with a small government for affairs larger that the city but not big enough for the state or nation.). The sugar factory was a large part of the local economy. Farmers grew sugar beets. They hired workers to work the fields. They bought farm equipment from the farm implement dealers, and hired repairmen. Their children attended the local schools and they shopped at the local stores. The sugar factory itself hired a lot of workers and paid them a fair wage. However there was one problem, very honestly, when you go past the sugar factory it smells, and it smells bad. REALLY BAD! After we first moved to Minidoka county, my husband and I would often comment on the horrendous smell until someone reframed it. A friend was going somewhere with us and as we passed took a whiff and sighed, "Smells like money!" I never complained about the smell again. What a reframe.

Play around with reframes and be an asset to your friends as you change their problems into opportunities. Enjoy!

Unit 29: Six Step Reframe

"The moment you change your perception, is the moment you rewrite the chemistry of your body."
---Dr. Bruce Lipton

Lesson 1: About the Six Step Reframe

Bandler and Grinder developed the Six Step reframe as a result of their study of the programs and processes of genius in the work of Virginia Satir and Milton Erikson. They would coach people to negotiate not with other people, but with various parts of themselves. You will remember that most of our neuro system communicates nonverbally and because most of our body cannot communicate in words, another form of communication is established.

When this process was being developed John Grinder and Judith Delozier were working with patients at St. Paul's Hospital in Vancouver in 1976. They were involved in a project where they would teach the psychiatric staff NLP skills in a workshop, then return a few months later for a two-day follow up workshop where they would demonstrate the skills on chronic patients the first day then discuss what had happened the next day.

Both had been traveling in Europe and had returned with Walking Pneumonia. They were very ill with high temperatures and what they really needed was a day in bed, but they were scheduled to teach the workshop. They had been developing the Six-step reframe at this time and made an agreement with their bodies that if the bodies would give them a "top quality performance" day, they would return that night, have a good, stiff drink, then sweat and sleep it off. Several times during the day they would check in with their internal selves and again affirm to do as promised.

At the end of the day they went directly back to the hotel, had their drinks and went straight to bed. They slept fourteen hours. The next day, much better rested, they could not really remember the day before. They arrived at the hospital and checked on the blackboard. There in Grinder's handwriting was the process. Yes, they really had been there and taught it even as they used it.

What had they done? They had communicated with a part of themselves that had a behavior in place meant to protect them physically but keeping them from doing what they had committed to do, teach the psychiatrists at the hospital. They had been able to negotiate and gain the time they needed to teach with the promise to take care later.

This story, told by John Grinder, illustrates well the Six Step reframe. It is more than just communicating with your body or even gaining insight on the positive intention. It is bargaining effectively to find or create other choices to the presenting problem. This is a critical part of the technique.

Lesson 2: My Experience

> Be happy with your body…It's the only one you've got, so you might as well like it
> —Keira Knightley

Talking to my body. I thought this had to be ridiculous, crazy as a loon. Still that first year I tried it. I paired up with a young doctor from Europe, Dr. Dave. It was a good match because we were both pretty skeptical. We got in a relaxed, if very skeptical state and he asked if I had any pains I wanted to work with. I really did not have any big things but I thought my knee had been kind of hurting not bad but I had noticed it. It was more achy than painful but it was the best that I could come up with. The doctor began in his mind to put together a medical strategy of what I would need yet did not share it. That was hard for him but he played the game and we tried the strategy. After all, we had paid well for the course. So we followed the steps and made communication, and it, the achy part, was willing to talk. I do not now remember what internal signal emerged to establish communication, but I do recall that, to my surprise, it did. Not too much later I knew the answer to the pain. I like to sit with one leg tucked under me, a very kinesthetic position. We had a nice set up that year with sofas to sit on and I am short. My feet do not reach the floor so I would tuck my leg under me. That would sit me up straighter and feel comfortable. As we established communication, my knee talked. Yes, it was aching and yes it had a message. The message, we are not twenty-one years old anymore. The body is a bit tighter and the position is too tight for me, loosen up a bit, give me an inch.

Ok, I thought, I will. I literally gave it an inch, not tucking quite so tightly. The ache went away and never, not ever to this day almost ten years later, has it come back.

After we finished the good doctor gave me some wise medical advice of who to see and what could be done, but I never needed it. I learned a lot. I am getting older and I need to honor my body and allow it to gently age into each decade gracefully. Beautiful learning.

I understand that NLP programs are developed by modeling those who do it well. I wondered, who does this crazy thing of talking to themselves, besides me, of course? They must be out of their mind! One day I was chatting with my classroom aides and we got on the subject of NLP and were talking about the various programs, I told them simply about the Six Step Reframe. One of the aides piped up, "Oh, I do that. When my back hurts I just ask it what is wrong and then I listen." I have found my example and it worked well for her.

Lesson 3: How Does It Work?

"Understand that you have the ability to get healthy and stay healthy."
Dr. Christiane Northrup

The intent of the Six-Step reframe is to gain cooperation with the internal body part related to the problem behavior by listening to its positive intention, acknowledging that intention and finding alternatives that will meet the positive intention in a system-friendly manner.

The first step is to identify the part that is causing the problematic behavior and establish communication. We often find that the part that is causing the problem does not have a lot of communication with our normal consciousness. You remember that we have numerous neurological organs within our neurological system. These include our neocortex, cortex, limbic system (the triune brain) the heart brain, the gut brain, plus all the communication systems that are involved including the sympathetic, parasympathetic, autonomic and skeletal nervous system. To add to this, every cell of the body save the red blood cells has a nucleus that has a capacity. Of all of these only one is capable of communicating with speech, the neocortex, our thinking brain.

> ## The Systems of Our Own Neurology
>
> - Triune Brain Neocortex, cortex and limbic system
> - Heart-Brain
> - Skeletal Nervous System (conscious, move muscles)
> - Autonomic nervous system (unconscious)
> - Sympathetic (freeze, fight or flight)
> - Parasympathetic (rest and digest' or 'feed and breed')
> - Enteric (second Brain)

It is usually fairly easy to figure out which part has the problem. It hurts or communicates in some other very similar way. That part is doing its darn level best to shout at you, but it has no words so it shouts with pain or something similar. So now we need to establish a communication system. There are many ways to communicate but often a lift of the finger works well. It simple needs to be subconscious so the cognitive brain isn't in control. We refer to these as ideomotor movements, movements we make that we are not conscious of and do not control. The person may be able to use a muscle twitch or a feeling inside as the means of communication. I know, for some of us this sounds like the person has bats in his belfry, but those who do it all the time know that it works.

With communication established, the positive intention of the problem can be discovered, such as my knee needed less pressure so it ached. Knowing the real problem, alternatives can be created or discovered and the part can bargain or negotiate acceptable alternatives that will ameliorate the problem, for me the amelioration was to let my leg have a little more give room. To find alternatives we need to think in a way different from the way that caused the problem. In my case it was thinking how much I enjoyed having a leg tucked under. I needed to add to that thinking that my body was changing and those changes needed to be allowed and nurtured so that I may age gracefully. Generally the guide in this process needs to do as Dr. David once did for me and let the individual generate their own ideas and choices. We ask the person who is exploring to access his or her creative part, the part of our brain that emerges when the creative juices are flowing.

The person usually wants to come up with at least three alternatives that can be tried that the part with a problem will accept. In severe causes more may be needed. When I have worked with wrist-slashing clients I have them come up with ten or more alternatives that will be acceptable. Then they have a plethora of choices with it is needed. If some or all of the alternatives presented from the creative part are not accepted, then more need to be thought up until acceptable ones are found. Occasionally this will mean finding out if there are other parts involved that have been quiet and need to also have a say. Ask the part with a problem if there are other parts involved and if so, give them a voice through another ideomotor signal.

When three or more alternatives have been found person then needs to check with the individual's cognitive brain to check the ecology of the new choices. Will they conflict with something else? If so allow that part to have a voice with another ideomotor signal and allow the parts to negotiate a workable solution. This reframing cycle is repeated as needed with discovering the positive intention of the second part, finding suitable choices and negotiating an agreement with the two, or even more, parts involved.

When at least one, or hopefully at least three suitable choices have been agreed on, it is important to finish the entire program by thanking all of the parts involved for their work. It may sound a bit weird but the body needs to be honored and thanked. If promises are made such as a stiff drink in John and Judith's story, those promises need to be honored so that body will trust your cognitive mind.

Lesson 4: A Few Details

> "There is more wisdom in your body than in your deepest philosophies."
> Friedrich Nietzche

The Six-Step Reframe is an example of pacing and leading to establish rapport. You as a guide or as an explorer are pacing a body part and then when rapport is established, you are leading it on a voyage of discovery about what will work to solve the problem. We pace by acknowledging that the body part as having a real problem with a positive purpose and addressing it. We also pace by acknowledging that the part cannot communicate with words but that it can be understood. We then lead by assisting the part to find an answer to ameliorate the problem by addressing the positive intention with answers.

Choices are an important concept in this reframing process. Choices are alternatives that are a part of the person's map of the world. We can give them numerous alternatives but alternatives are external to a person and may provide no real choice. Choice involves having the capability and the context to be able to internally select the best options of what is available and have agreement on the conscious level. There is a saying in NLP. I have heard Judith say it often but I do not know who originated it. "One choice is no choice at all. Two choices is a dilemma. It is not until a person has three possibilities that he or she is really able to legitimately choose." Next time life presents you with a pain, try the Six-Step Reframe and experience the wisdom of the body.

"Everything you need to know is within you. Listen. Feel. Trust the body's wisdom."
Dan Millman

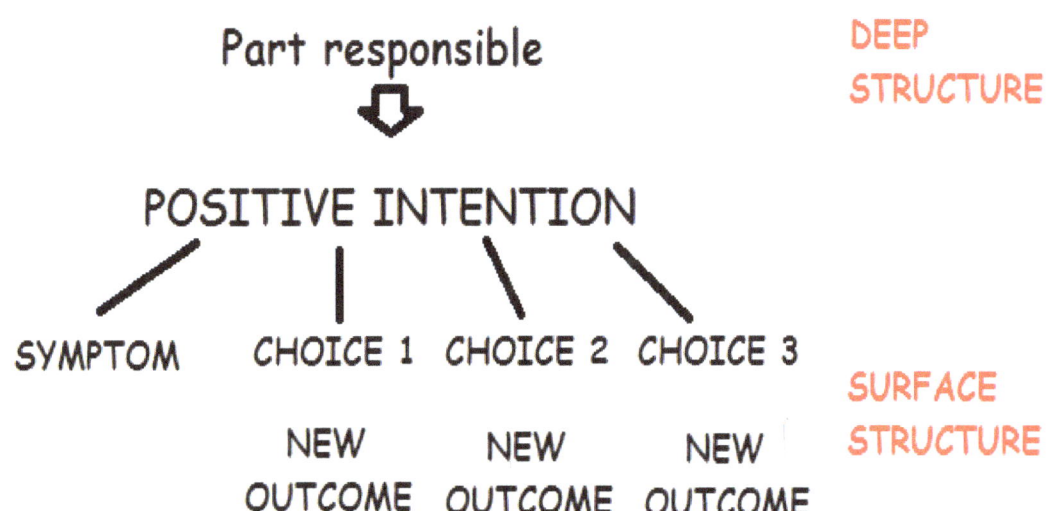

Unit 30: Intervision

"Act as though it were impossible to fail"   --Ralph Waldo Emerson

Lesson 1: What is the Intervision Strategy?

Intervision is a strategy (the science or art of using all the tools available to execute the plan) developed in 1990 by NLP innovators (visionaries, people who are changing the world) for group problem solving. It was developed by a group of leaders. The thought is that the group knows more than the person and no one person has the answer, but the group can synergistically generate more solutions and create an answer.

The opposite of intervision is supervision. In supervision it is assumed that one person has the answers and can supervise or help the others to also get the answers. This method included coaching and teaching. Supervision is often used in discovery teaching, For instance in a chemistry class the teacher may give the students a problem to solve with chemicals. The teachers knows what will happen and can guide the students if they need help.

But not every situation has a distinct, already discovered solution. Not every group has one person that knows all of the answers and can guide the others to the solution. The Intervision program assumes that all of the team is equal, there is no one who has the exclusive anwer that all must arrive at with their guidance. The problem to solve is a stuck state that you or group is stuck in.

The word intervision means mutually visable. In the intervision process no one knows the answer but all can see the problem and contribute to findng the solution. Each person has a different and unique perspective (way of seeing things that is individual and like no one else) and bringing out the perspectives can create novel (new and not like anything formerly used, unique) and unique solutions to problems.

Lesson 2: The Intervision Strategy

Teamwork makes the dreamwork.   --- Bang Gae

This is a strategy to work out a problem in which no one really knows the answer or solution, a quandry or dilemna that is perplexing. It is best to work in a small group of 4-6 people. One person is the explorer and will present the problem. The others are going to help find a solution.

What are some ideas for problems?

Personal: I want some ideas to stop smoking.

Family: We do not spend enough time together

Organization: we need to raise money for our group to go to a conference together

Business: my employees are arriving late to work every day

Neighborhood: the children are staying out too late at night and waking the babies

Here is the process:

1.	Explorer in group explains problem or goal to others in the group. Questions can be asked to clarify the problem but no solutions may be offered or even hinted at.
2.	Each person, including the explorer, individually draws a picture representing his or her own understanding of the problem. It may be a sketch, a metaphor or a symbolic representation. It will be interesting to find out how each person sees the problem a little differently.
3.	In turn, each intervisor (person who is helping advise in this inter-related group) then shares and explains his or her picture. They do not give any advice, just present their picture of the problem. Then ask the explorer a question about the area of potential solution space. The explorer is not to answer the question, but only to acknowledge it. The explorer goes last.

4.	Each group member, including the explorer, who goes last, makes a representation of the solution space he or she thinks would be of the most value to the explorer from his or her point of view. The intervisors may: Make a new map or drawing Add to their previous drawing Add to the explorer's drawing Present a simile, metaphor or analogy
5.	If it is a personal problem. Each person gives the explorer his or her pictures to help him/her get the best solution. If a business group working on a common problem, then all use the pictures to help in coming up with a solution.

The Intervision Strategy is a fun and creative way to look at a problem and to get many capable people to work together to solve it. It uses the idea of synergy, the sum of the whole is greater than the parts. Enjoy the synergy of the Intervision Strategy.

Lesson 3: Sample

In a class I taught all of the students had to take a math s test in a few days and they were all very concerned. They chose to work on it for the intervision exercise.
Below is a sample of one of the papers that was done.

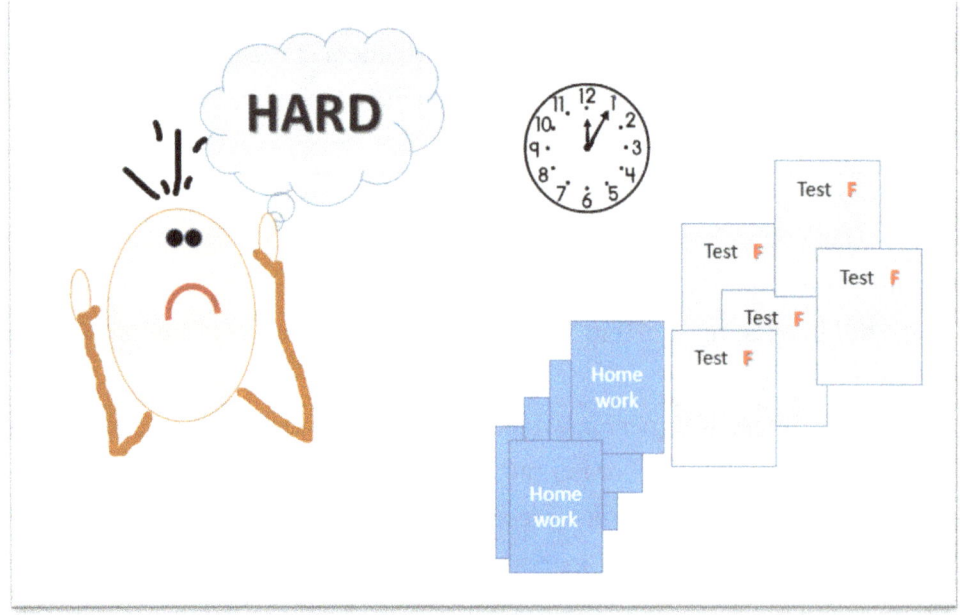

When my children were young we went to a Scout camp. There was an incredible hike. It was 6.5 kilometers and my children were ages 3-13. It looked HARD. We changed the words to diligent, we would hike steady and consistant and be persistent in getting the goal. We made it and so will you by setting aside hard and working diligently, steadily, consitantly and persistently for the goal.

Lesson 4: Conclusion

"The whole is greater than the sum of its parts." — Aristotle

The Intevision program is a creative way to find new answers to a problem and to gain greater flexibilty. The more choices we have the more flexibility we have and we know the one with the most flexibility will have the greatest influence, or as my teachers would say, "The greatest flexibility wins."

I often use Intervision as my speech final as it gives students the opportunity to create their own speech with their own visual aid to assist them in being successful. Maybe you will also get the opportunity to use the Intervision for your final.

As a closing to the entire book I would like to express to you, the learner of NLP that the journey into NLP has been a great gift to me as a teacher. In my special needs class I watched students do things that we were told special needs students could never do. They learned to dream dreams and to make those dreams come true. What greater gift can a teacher give her students than to make dream come true.

Yet there were other gains. I had students whom doctors said were working above what their IQ levels would indicate was possible. I had students who were always sick until they got to my class miss hardly any days in school. I had students who did not want to leave the classroom because they felt safe and accepted. It was a teacher's dream. My own personal NLLA purpose in that role of my life was to maximize student potential and it was so much fun to DO IT.

Now I am a college professor,an honor, not because of my years in education and service to education.Now I watch with awe as my students who are among the most intelligent and well driven in the world take this same material and soar with it. They too are dreaming dreams. Their dreams are appropriate for their abilities. They are getting scholarships, accepting exchanges and internships and seeing potential for the future. With this assignment I took on a new NLLA purpose, to make the world a better place by teaching English skills, often by using NLP as a vehicle. I have been priveleged to enhance the skills of English majors who will interpret for many people, who will translate books and articles, who will travel the world. I have taught scientists who will present the findings of their research through out the world because of their English skills. I have taught ordinary citizens who will have better lives for what they have learned. I have taught older and retired people who will learn the magic that happens when they change for the better and their change filters down through their generations to their children and grandchildren never realizing what a profound influence they could have on the future of the world. Someone once said there is a power in the flutter of a butterfly wing that can be felt around the world. I will be a butterfly and I will teach butterflies to flutter with greater power and stregnth to make the world better in their own individual way. Join me in the flutter of goodness we can be.

Life is like Disney land!
When you come in you pay one price.
When you leave, if you haven't ridden all
The rides, it is your own fault.

Kenneth Dusty Dill

Sources:

Encyclopedia of Systematic Neuro-Linguistic Programming and NLP New Coding by Robert Dilts and Judith Delozier. NLP University Press PO /box 67448, Scott's Valley CA, USA 96067 CR 2000. <http://nlpuniversitypress.com/>

Romilla Ready and Kate Burton. Neuro-linguistic Programming for Dummies. John Wiley and Sons West Sussex, England. CR 2010 Book.

R. Ready and K. Burton. Neuro-Linguistic Programming Workbook for Dummies, R. Ready and K. Burton, John Wiley & Sons LTD, West Sussex, England 2008

Unit 1
Microsoft Clip Art
Chloe Slatter. Personal photo taken by Alyssa Slatter.
 Michael Colgrass.7/15/013. Used with his permission
Circle of Excellence.Created by Debrah Roundy using Microsoft Clip Art.
Minico Spuds. 9/11/11. J.Peg personal Photo

Unit 2
Lecture notes
Microsoft clip art
Photographs belonging to Debrah Roundy
Picture of Michael Colgrass from his Web site.

Unit 3
Photographs belonging to Debrah Roundy
Drawings by Debrah Roundy

Unit 4
Drawings by Debrah Roundy

Unit 5
Photographs belonging to Debrah Roundy
Drawings by Debrah Roundy
Chart by Debrah Roundy

Unit 6

Pictures:

All pictures from Microsoft Clip art except as noted below.

Robert Diltz from www,NLPU.com

Dr. Charles Wilcher http://drwilcher.com/index.html

Chinese Dancers

Unit 7

Wikipedia

Reference: Taken from "A contemporary view of selected subjects from the pages of The New York Times, January 23, 1996. Printed in Themes of the Times: General Psychology, Fall 1996. Distributed Exclusively by Prentice-Hall Publishing Company.

chroniccandida.com

Pears all, Paul, Ph.D. The Heart's Code. Random House, zinc. New York. 1998. book.

Unit 11

Eye and Head Turning Indicates Cerebral Lateralization; Kinsbourne, M., Science, 179, pp. 539_541, 1972.

Eye Movement As An Indicator of Sensory Components in Thought; Buckner, W., Reese, E. and Reese, R., Journal of Counseling Psychology, 1987, Vol. 34, No 3.

Individual Differences in Cognitive Style_Reflective Eye Movements; Galin, D. and Ornstein, R., Neuropsychologia, 12, pp. 376_397, 1974.

Lateral Eye Movement and Cognitive Mode; Kocel, K., et al., Psychon Sci. 27: pp. 223_224, 1972.

Neuro-Linguistic Programming Workbook for Dummies; R. Ready and K. Burton, John Wiley & Sons LTD, West Sussex, England 2008

NLP Vol. I, Dilts, R., et al, Meta Publications, Capitola, CA, 1980.

Roots of NLP, Dilts, R., Meta Publications, Capitola, CA, 1983.

Patterns of the Hypnotic Techniques of Milton H. Erickson, M.D. Vol. II, Grinder, J., DeLozier, J. and Bandler, R., 1977.

The Effect of Eye Placement On Orthographic Memorization; Loiselle, Fran_ois, Ph.D. Thesis, Facult_ des Sciences Sociales, Universit_ de Moncton, New Brunswick, Canada, 1985.

Unit 13

Pictures of Seresa, Fabric market, Minico Spuds signing all by Debrah Roundy. Mistletoe is Microsoft Clip Art.

Unit 14

Apple Microsoft Clip Art

Xavier Lee by Debrah Roundy

Lesson 15

Wu Bangguo (L), chairman of the Standing Committee of China's National People's Congress (NPC), meets with Caretaker Dutch Prime Minister Mark Rutte in the Hague, the Netherlands, May 15, 2012. (Xinhua/Liu Jiansheng) (news.xinhuanet.com)

Boys fighting Microsoft clip Art

Carlos and Debrah in Macau.

Conlan, Catherine.Six Things That Drive Hiring Managers Crazy.Monster Contributing Writer. Monster. 2015. Web February 3, 2015. <http://career-advice.monster.com/job-interview/interview-preparation/things-that-drive-hiring-managers-crazy/article.aspx>

Lesson 16

Pictures on Debrah Roundy taken by Carlos Roundy.

Lesson 17

Picture of people eating from Microsoft clip art

Maps from Google Maps

All photographs taken by Debrah Roundy

Unit 18

SJTU Anchor picture by Debrah Roundy

Picture of OK and my wedding ring set both by Debrah Roundy

Drawing of spider by Debrah Roundy

The Pentagon of Excellence NLP Program was adapted by Debrah Roundy for Idaho Special Olympics Athletes using the NLP Circle of Excellence, a basic NLP program developed by John Grinder and Judith DeLozier

Unit 19

Cartoons of traps by Debrah Roundy

Unit 20

Picture of SCORE by Debrah Roundy

Unit 21

Pictures of Grandchildren at the Rupert Square dancing "Me and My Shadow" by Debrah Roundy. JULY 3, 2010. JPEG.
Pink Rabbit drawing by Debrah Roundy

Unit 22

Pictures
<http://ts1.mm.bing.net/th?id=H.4978284674351846&pid=15.1&w=148&h=110&p=0>
Picture of Walt Disney. Idioms list http://www.buzzle.com/articles/idiom-examples-of-idioms.html
Thomas and Johnson 1983 from NLPU Encyclopedia, NLPU.com. 2000. Web Encyclopedia. 4May 2013. <http://nlpuniversitypress.com/html/D32.html>

Quotes
1. Dilts, Robert. NLPU Encyclopedia, NLPU.com. 2000. Web Encyclopedia. 4May 2013. <http://nlpuniversitypress.com/html/D29.html>

2. Dilts, Robert. NLPU Encyclopedia, NLPU.com. 2000. Web Encyclopedia. 4May 2013. <http://nlpuniversitypress.com/html/D30.html>

3. Dilts, Robert. NLPU Encyclopedia, NLPU.com. 2000. Web Encyclopedia. 4May 2013. <http://nlpuniversitypress.com/html/D32.html>

Further Sources:
Photographs included are of my East Minico Spuds 2007-08 and are used with parental permission.

Unit 23

Pictures

McMillan, Ron. Picture. The way to Change Minds

Further Sources:

Metaphors. Excellence Assured. 2013 Web. 22 May 2013. <http://excellenceassured.com/nlp-training/nlp-resources/metaphors>

My personal notes from NLPU 2012 Course run by Dilts, Judith DeLozier and Suzi Smith

The Encyclopedia Systemic of NLP and NLP New Coding by Robert Dilts and Judith DeLozier. CR 2000 by NLP University Press, Scotts Valley, California 95067. <http://nlpuniversitypress.com/>

Unit 25

Photographs are the property of the author. Drawings and art work were drawn by Debrah Roundy.

Unit 26

Photographs are the property of the author. Drawings and art work were drawn by Debrah Roundy.

This book by my NLP Coach is also a resource.

Corless, Earl and Sharalee S. Clawson. And Then a Miracle Happens. CreateSpace Independent Publishing Platform (October 31, 2014). Book. ISBN-10: 1500838500. ISBN-13: 978-1500838508

Unit 27-30

Photographs are the property of the author. Drawings and art work were drawn by Debrah Roundy.

Study Guide

Unit 1: Introduction and New Name Strategy

Name	
number	

Match the vocabulary to the meaning.

1		Franklin D. Roosevelt	A	more than once or twice
2		automatic	B	happens without you consciously thinking about it
3		exemplars	C	developed with another person two people have equal work in developing something
4		elder	D	A president of the United States, had a great strategy for remembering names
5		core	E	Someone older than you
6		phobias	F	An ideal example worthy to be copied
7		several	G	An irrational and powerful fear
8		co-developed	H	Center or most important part of something
9		NLP	I	lacking a pattern or plan
10		random	J	Neurolinguistic Programs

Quiz:
1. What principle do NLP practitioners work on?
    a. success and failure are not random
    b. culture creates identity
    c. people cannot change

2. Who were the original founders of Neurolinguistic programming?
    a. Richard Bandler and John Grinder
    b. Fritz Perls and Milton Erikson
    c. Robert Dilts and Judith DeLozier

3. What is a part of NLP curriculum?
    a. Mathematical formulas
    b. New age phenomena
    c. Modeling and learning programs for excellence

4. How are new programs brought into being?
    a. Years of scientific research
    b. Experts are modeled, then the steps they use are put into a program
    c. Through creative games

One the other side of this paper write an essay telling me about you in 100-300 words.

Unit 2: Circle of Excellence

Name	
number	

Match the vocabulary to the meaning.

1		optimal	A	condition of being
2		ideosyncratic	B	important, original or basic
3		state	C	Most favorable, the best or greatest
4		re-access	D	To renew access to return to something again
5		stance	E	something, often a metal device attached to a boat or ship, that serves to hold something firmly in place
6		anchor	F	position or posture
7		fundamental	G	things you have as a supply or source of support
8		create	H	Unique to the person, an individualize characteristic
9		unique	I	The only one or being without a like
10		resources	J	Make, bring into existance

Circle of Excellence Speech

Pre	Imagine you putting your circle of excellence in front of you. You stand on it and smile at the audience
Name	
What event did you put in your Circle of Excellence?	
Closing statement	
Finish	Look for 1-2 seconds at the audience then pick up your name card with a smile.

Unit 3: Stress

Name	
number	

Match the vocabulary to the meaning.

1		constrain	A	not having enough of something such as money
2		poverty	B	to copy something
3		program	C	An exaggerated and Irrational fear
4		periphery	D	An outline, plan or system to be followed to reach a goal
5		mirror neurons	E	Specialized nerve cells that cause imitation and empathy
6		model	F	Understanding what another person is feeling or thinking
7		stress	G	Pressure and or tension that constrains
8		future pacing	H	To hold back, limit, restrict or stop
9		empathy	I	Imagining something that you will do in the future
10		phobia	J	Outward bounds or borders

Tell one person you would model and why. Make this short only one or two sentences.

_____

_____

Presentation: Break down a simple task into smaller steps. You might try tying a shoe or putting on a shirt. Plan on presenting to the class or to your group. Your presentation should be 1-3 minutes.

Unit 4: Well-formed Outcomes

Name	
number	

Match the vocabulary to the meaning.

1		criteria	A	To start, especially to begin something important.
2		outcome	B	Practical and reasonable, seeking what is achievable or possible, based on known facts
3		buy in	C	to succeed in doing or gaining something, usually with effort
4		innovation	D	Precise, the one exactly
5		ecological	E	a word formed from the initials or other parts of several words, e.g. "NATO," from the initial letters of "North Atlantic Treaty Organization"
6		initiate	F	Fit naturally in the environment
7		realistic	G	Goal to be achieved
8		achievable	H	process of inventing or introducing something new
9		specific	I	accepted standard used to judge something by
10		acronym	J	To take part or have a share in something

Quiz: Make a well-formed goal for the school year. (see sample on the next page.)

11	Positively stated	The mind works in one direction, lead it to the positive.	
12	Sensory based	What will you see, hear and feel when you get your outcome?	
13	Initiated and maintained by yourself	You can start it yourself and keep the goal going to completion	
14	Maintain positive present state	Will it work in all areas of your life	
15	Ecological	What will you lose or gain when you achieve your positive outcome	

16. Make this a well formed outcome: **I do not want to get behind in my class work during the Autumn Festival. (Or use whatever festival is coming soon.)**

Unit 5: TOTE

name	
number	

Assignments: Using the well-formed outcome you came up with last week, create your own TOTE model by chunking down the steps. Remember to come up with a reward for the exit.

1. Test: What is your well-formed outcome?
2. Operate: What are some steps to getting this outcome? List four.

3. Test: What is your test for your goal?
Hear?
See?
Feel?
4. Exit: What will you do if you get your goal? (reward)
5. What can you do if you do not get your goal?

1		routine	A	A figure of speech that does not mean literally what it says
2		dream	B	Something you hope and wish for
3		visualize	C	goal you make a firm decision to do In the USA people often make this at the beginning of a new year
4		practice	D	Do over and over to get better
5		rubber meets the road	E	the point in a process where there are challenges, issues, or problems
6		idiom	F	Picture things in your head
7		goal	G	Something you want to get or achieve
8		achieve	H	things that you usually do each day
9		operate	I	To get your goal
10		resolution	J	To do or to work

Unit 6: NLLA Assignment 1

name	
number	

There are four pages for this assignment. I usually do it over two or three weeks.

start	When you do this with someone else, take a minute to say "hi," and to help each other be as ease. This is called establishing rapport and we will learn more about it in a later lesson. This is a good time for you to do the Six Second Stress- buster together and take out your Circles of Excellence. Find out the area you will explore.
Rapport	
Environment	Where are you now, where is your environment?
Behavior	What are your actions in that environment that will support you?
Capabilities	What skills and inner resources do you need in this environment to support your behaviors?
Beliefs and Values	What do you believe about yourself? I believe_____
	What do you value?
Identity	Who are you?
Purpose	For whom or for what will you serve in the greater field? Who will you serve that is greater than you? (family, country, organization, world)

Unit 6: NLLA Assignment 2

Please remember to save your study guides papers. Your final will be taken from these guides and you will have them to study.

Identify the levels each worker is working at in the poem "Six Stone Workers."

level	Six Stone Workers.
	The first said, I'm putting in my time until the day is over."
	The second," I am hitting a rock."
	The third. "I am crafting a brick."
	The fourth, "I am earning a living and putting the bread on the table."
	The 5th said, "I am a master craftsman building a cathedral." (large church)
	The 6th said, "I am creating a space where people come to get closer to God."

Gregory Bateson recited this poem, and then asked, "What is the difference that makes the difference?"

Your answer

Cloze Sentence

It's not how much you __1__ that makes people look up to __2__, it's who you __3__.--- Elvis Presley

1	
2	
3	
What NLLA level is this?	

Word bank	you
Use only 3 words	be
	make
	are

Unit 6 Study Guide: NLLA Assignment 2

Match these idioms, slang phrases and quotes to their meanings

1		Tip of the iceberg	A	opened up to you are greater opportunities and you have the skills and capabilities to access those
2		Feeling Groovy	B	Always forgetting things
3		Makes you tick	C	how something works
4		'elle va birn dans sap eau'	D	Make up or create a new word or phrase
5		On the same vein	E	detects well
6		get a handle on	F	Staying on the same subject
7		hang out	G	to spend time at a place, usually relaxing
8		piece of cake	H	Understand something more fully and deeply
9		kicks in	I	starts
10		scatter brained	J	You can only see a little bit of the whole
11		The world is your oyster", or	K	Clear clean, nothing on it
12		good nose	L	Something that is easy to do
13		bird dogs	M	Start something
14		blank slate	N	when he looks for something he keeps going until he finds it
15		trip me/us/them up	O	Staying on a related subject, not changing the subject, but looking at more or it.
16		coined	P	Understand something more deeply and fully
17		In the muscle	Q	Slow down progress
18		dive in	R	Comfortable in your skin (French)
19		on a similar vein	S	Feeling good, congruent, at one with oneself
20		On the same note	T	Learning that involves more than the brain, it is experiential.

Choose three of the above idioms, quotes or slang sayings and write a sentence for each one.

1)
2)
3)

Unit 7: Somatic Mind

name	
number	

Match the vocabulary to the meaning.

1		Independent	A	Thinking brain
2		Enteric	B	Stomach
3		Migrate	C	To act alone
4		Tummy	D	The gut
5		Impacted (medical term)	E	Heart and gut brain
6		Repository	F	Hang down
7		Somatic brain	G	Storage place
8		Dangle	H	Being conscious at some level of impulses one or more of your senses sending a message to your brain
9		Perceptual awareness	I	Move
10		Neocortex	J	Unable to move the bowels and defecate

Logical Level Alignment exercise (Which statement matches each level)

Environment – behavior – capability – beliefs and values – identity - purpose

	I sneeze when catching a cold
	I believe that Shanghai is a good place to become healthy
	Living in New York makes me feel sick
	I am sick
	I am able to keep myself healthy by drinking enough water
	I am a person who can help other people be healthy

What differences did you feel or detect in your body when: One sentence, please.

You slouched?
You sat up straight and tall?
Bend over and touch your knees?

Unit 8: Eye Accessing Cues

name	
number	

Assignment:

Complete the Eye Movements Exploration Game with at least two other people and have one person complete it with you if you did not do it in class. Please do it in Chinese if you are Chinese, Korean if you are Korean, Japanese if you are Japanese and so on. It then becomes an exercise in translation, too.

Quiz:
1. How do the eyes connect with the brain?
a) Right eye to right brain, left to left.
b) There is no important connection between eyes and brain
c) Right eye to left brain, left to right.
d) Right eye to left optic nerve and left to right optic nerve.

2. What does it mean to be "normally organized?"
a) A person normally gets his work done in an organized manner.
b) A person whose eyes follow the same accessing cues as most right hander's do.
c) A Basque person who follows an "exception to the rule" pattern.
d) A left handed person with mirror image organization.

3. What are the attributes of the left brain? (More than one answer)
a) dominate
b) logical
c) artistic
d) verbal

4. Where does a kinesthetic oriented person tend to look most frequently?
a) Down and to the right.
b) Up and to the left.
c) Down and to the left
d) Laterally left.

5. When you ask a normally organized person "What is your favorite picture? " Why might s/he look down and to the right?
a) The person is listening to his inner voice tell him.
b) The person is looking for the picture in his visual remembered area.
c) The person is checking to find out which one feels right.
d) The person is wondering if he has a favorite picture.

6. You ask Mary what color her new bike is. She looks up and to the right. How is she organized?
a) Normally organized
b) Mirror organized
c) Exception to the rule
d) Synesthesia

Eye Movements Activity

This is also an activity in translating. Translate it into the person you are asking's native language.

#			
1. Vc	Imagine your teacher (boss or a friend) with purple hair.		
2. Vr	Picture your 1st hour teacher, or a coworker.		
3. Ac	Imagine your favorite movie star calling your name.		
4. Vc	Imagine a purple plane in a red sky.		
5. Vr	What is the color of your backpack, purse or wallet?		
6. Ar	Imagine your favorite song.		
7. Ac	Imagine Mickey Mouse or Angry Bird (or another cartoon character) singing "Happy Birthday to You."		
8. Ad	Tell yourself inside your mind that you did a good job.		
9. K	Imagine a ball in your hands.		
10. K	How cold is an ice cube in your hand?		

11. Ad	Ask yourself "What do I want to do tomorrow?" Hear yourself answer in your head.	.	
12. Ar	Imagine you are hearing your favorite song		
13. Ac	Imagine hearing a dog's bark coming from a bird's mouth		
14. K	What does it feel like to stroke a piece of fine velvet?		v

Unit 9: Representation Systems

name	
number	

1.	What is your primary representation system?	
2.	What is one thing you can do to learn better?	

Modalities EXPLORATION

1.	Pick something you are thankful for.	
2.	Picture it in your mind. Now make the picture brighter. What happens	
3.	Now make the picture grey. What happens?	
4.	Put a frame around the picture. What happens?	
5.	Now make the picture all in tones of red? What happens?	

MODALITIES PRESENTATION FOR NEXT WEEK (sample below)

1.	Ground and center	
2	Pick something you are thankful (grateful) for.	
2.	Share one visual characteristic	
3.	Share one auditory characteristic	
4.	Share one kinesthetic characteristic	
5.	Have a closing statement	
6	Reconnect with the audience	

True and False

1		You should teach a child only in his or her preferred modality.
2		Submodalities can enhance a dream or goal.
3		Students who like to study where it is quiet are visual.
4		Children who need a special blanket or stuffed animal to sleep well are often kinesthetic.
5		People who are kinesthetic watch your body as you talk.
6		Students who are auditory like lots of diagrams and pictures.
7		Students who are visual make a picture of the word they are to spell in their mind.

Identify your Primary Representation System

	VAK		
1			You enjoy touching and handling things.
2			You were a good speller in school.
3			You enjoy listening to audio books.
4			You love to read.
5			Spoken directions confuse you. You want a map or diagram.
6			You often turn on a little background music when you work.
7			You enjoy getting with a group and discussing things more than reading about it.
8			You use color pens and pencils and colored paper for handouts and notes.
9			You enjoy writing and journaling.
10			You tend to talk to yourself when you work.
11			You like to do things with your hands.
12			You are into athletics, dance, sports, and/or working out.
13			You could spend many happy hours doing jigsaw puzzles.
14			You tend to tap a pencil, jiggle your foot or otherwise have a lot of nervous energy.
15			You remember jokes, stories and conversations.
16			You are a collector.
17			If you need to really understand something you will often read it out loud.
18			You find maps easy to use and you understand them.

19			You like to doodle or draw pictures.
20			When you read you like to follow along with your finger or a marker.
21			You enjoy games, role playing and simulation activities.
22			You use rhymes and jingles to remember things.
23			Much of your understanding of a conversation comes from reading body language and facial expressions.
24			You have a natural sense of direction and can locate places easily.
25			You almost always take notes at lectures.
26			If someone tells you what to do, you understand quickly.
27			You follow written directions well.
28			You talk rapidly and use your hands a lot when you speak.
29			To understand how things work you like to take them apart and then put them together again.
30			You enjoy talking with others on the phone.

1-K	2-V	3-A	4-V	5-V	6-A	7-A	8-V	9-A	10-A
11-K	12-K	13-V	14-K	15-A	16-V	17-A	18-V	19-K	20-A
21-V	22-A	23-K	24-V	25-V	26-A	27-V	28-K	29-K	30-A

Unit 10: Sub-modalities and Mapping Across

name	
number	

Mapping Across Sub-modalities Work Sheet

resourceful state					stuck state				
Visual					Visual				
bright				dim	bright				Dim
colorful				Black/white	colorful				Black/white
close				far	close				Far
clear				hazy	clear				Hazy
large				small	large				Small
in				out	in				Out
flat				3-D	flat				3-D
Auditory					Auditory				
loud				soft	loud				soft
high				low	high				low
left				right	left				right
fast				slow	fast				slow
close				far	close				far
words				tones	words				tones
clear				muffled	clear				muffled
Kinesthetic					Kinesthetic				
strong				weak	strong				weak
large				small	large				small
heavy				light	heavy				light
smooth				rough	smooth				rough
constant				jolting	constant				jolting
hot				cold	hot				cold
intense				gentle	intense				gentle

Change and what you noted when you mapped across
Change you noted that did not make a change in the

Unit 11: Rapport and BAGEL

name	
number	

Match the vocabulary to the meaning.

1		rapport	A	Get along well together
2		unique	B	pass, transfer or give to
3		convey	C	When people share a good understanding of each other.
4		Hit it off	D	Husband or wife
5		spouse	E	different from anyone else
6		a couple	F	Makes things more equal
7		sounding board	G	An English bread
8		specs	H	Slang term for specific details
9		evens out the playing field	I	A person who listens to you as you tell your problems so you can work them out on your own
10		bagel	J	Two or three

Match the best answers.

11	I cannot see what to do next?	A	I am hearing that you have a problem. How can we make it sound more harmonious?
12	It just does not sound right.	B	I sense that you do not yet know how to heal. Let's see what we can do to help you feel better.
13	I just feel stuck, doctor, I cannot get well.	C	A good book is like a feast!
14	It smells fishy to me	D	You are so right, it stinks. Something is wrong here.
15	This book tastes like a candy bar!	E	Maybe I can help you get a clearer picture of what you might want to do.

Match the best answers.   (Some may be used more than one time)

16		Matching	A	Your client stands with his right foot forward, you put your left foot forward.
17		Mirroring	B	You match your friend's tone of voice then calm yours a bit.
18		Pacing	C	You and your friend are walking down the street. You walk the same as she does
19		Leading	D	Your patient breathes fast and you breathe faster also.
20		(one is used twice)	E	Your audience that you will present to will be dressed casually so you choose casual clothing also.

Write a short reflection on the eye exercises. It is in the reading.
_____
_____

Unit 12: Extemporaneous and COACH State

name	
number	

Match the vocabulary to the meaning.

1		spur of the moment	A	Greek words that mean to arrange or put the body in order
2		eloquent	B	The number 1 fear of most people
3		extemporaneous	C	Something that you are attracted to or what to move towards
4		COACH	D	Acronym for Centered, open, attending with awareness, connected, holding
5		CRASH	E	Constant and steadfast
6		somatic syntax	F	Acronym for Contracted or shrunk inward, reactive, analysis-paralysis, separating, and hurt/hateful.
7		public speaking	G	To take a learning from one situation and be able to use it in many situations.
8.		attractor	H	vivid, moving, persuasive or powerful
9		stability	I	spontaneous, improvised, or impromptu
10		generalize	J	idiom meaning no time to prepare

1. Create a sentence using spur of the moment about a time when you acted on the spur of the moment.

2. Create a sentence telling about one of your biggest fears.

3. Create a sentence about something you have learned that now you use the knowledge across settings.

4. When you did the COACH state what is one thing you did that strengthened it?

Unit 13: Paralanguage A

name	
number	

Match the vocabulary to the meaning.

50 points

1		Paralanguage	A	A symbol of glyph that looks like this*
2		nonverbal	B	Stress or intensity given a word or syllable
3		accent	C	Do not understand what is being said as if it were some foreign language. It is meaningless, incomprehensible
4		ASL	D	Variations of pitch
5		asterisk	E	Without the use of spoken words
6		emoticon	F	A visual representation is far more descriptive than words.
7		intonation	G	Nonverbal elements of communication. They modify the meaning and convey emotion.
8		Make or break	H	A little thing that will cause complete success or utter failure
9		a picture is worth a thousand words	I	American Sign Language, the 4th most common language in the USA
10		It's all Greek to me	J	Textual portrayal of a writer's mood or facial expression

Create a **1-4** word phrase for each emoticon. (common emoticons from the WEB)

		Too much Thanksgiving! (Do not write this: my stomach hurts and I do not feel well. I had so much turkey and gravy, potatoes, beans, cranberry sauce, sweet potatoes, punch, stuffing and everything else. I just ate too much for Thanksgiving.)
1		
2		
3		
4		
5		

Unit 13: Paralanguage B

name	
number	

Match the English sentence with the meaning putting stress on the bolded word or symbol.

1		**Josh** won't give Alyssa an apple?	A	Just one apple?
2		Josh **won't** give Alyssa an apple?	B	He won't or maybe he can't. Is there a problem?
3		Josh won't **give** Alyssa an apple?	C	Will she need to take it or grab it, or is he selfish and wants the apple all to himself?
4		Josh won't give **Alyssa** an apple?	D	So what if Josh doesn't give her an apple. Who cares?
5		Josh won't give Alyssa **an** apple?	E	Oh my, that is awful!
6		Josh won't give Alyssa an **apple**?	F	Was it an apple or maybe it was an orange or a banana or something else?
7		Josh won't give Alyssa an apple**?**	G	Was is Josh or was it someone else?
8		Josh won't give Alyssa an apple**!**	H	Was it Alyssa or was it someone else?
9		Josh won't give Alyssa an apple**.**	I	What do you mean, why wouldn't he?

Choose an English show of any sort, and watch it for five minutes just watching for the paralanguage. Watch it at least 3 times. The first time watch it with no sound. The second time just listen but do not watch, and the third time watch all together. Put your reflections down here. It is best if you put your reflections down as you do each one rather than waiting until the end.

No sound
No picture
Both picture and sound

Unit 14: Perceptual Positions

	name	
	number	

Match the vocabulary to the meaning.

1		objective	A	understand through the use of your senses
2		subjective	B	to perceive or understand clearly
3		perceive	C	To be aware of by means of the senses
4		dissociate	D	To connect or join. In NLP we often connect the complete sensory experience into an issue to explore the perceptual positions of others
5		associate	E	having actual existence uninfluenced by personal prejudices
6		perceptual	F	existing in the mind, persons feelings, beliefs, perspective, or desires
7		clarity	G	Versatile, able to look at an issue from many different views.
8		flexibility	H	Detached from the issue
9		explorer	I	A person who goes to different places to learn more, investigates unknown regions
10		Other position	J	separate

Match the meaning to the perceptual position?

1		1st position	A	Someone close to the explorer who knows the issue and the person
2		2nd position	B	Someone who perceives the issue, you the explorer, and the person who is close to you
3		3rd position	C	A position that is out of the issue but can see the issue, you
4		4th position	D	Yourself, how you experience the world. The explorer

Match the words to the perceptual position?

1		1st position	A	They them, their
2		2nd position	B	Me, I
3		3rd position	C	You, yours, ours
4		4th position		One is used twice

Choose an object and describe it objectively and subjectively.

objective	
subjective	

Unit 15: Psychogeography A

name	
number	

Match the vocabulary to the meaning.

1		walk in the shoes of another	A	Sensitive, and caring
2		high horse	B	(Idiom) To think you are important, to act arrogant or haughty
3		confrontational	C	Where people are physically in a relationship
4		psychogeography	D	An idiom for taking second position and experiencing what another person experiences
5		spatial sorting	E	Meeting face to face feeling an eagerness to fight
6		empathetic	F	Physical sorting out parts to explore and physically moving or changing the geography with each part.

Look at the psychogeography of these people. Can you tell the relationships they are in? (These are from Microsoft clip art)

Close friends Or confrontational	Acquaintances	Non-confrontational position	Looking together, united	Mentor or teacher
A	B	C	D	E

(Can be used more than one time)(Some can have more than one answer)

Write a sentence about someone you know who is empathetic.

Your Assignment: Answer the question: "Tell me about Yourself. " Write out your answer and read it out loud. Time yourself. It should take about 1 minute. You will present in class. You may not read your notes, you will hand them in. You will be graded on time as well as the usual factors.

This may be very valuable to you in the future so take your time and come up with a good introduction.

Unit 15: Psychogeography B

name	
number	

Match the idioms, slang and vocabulary to the meaning.

1		*simmer	A	Put aside for the time being
2		*back burner	B	Get rid of something, put it completely away from you
3		*blow it	C	Just a little better
4		*ditch it	D	Spoil your chance at achieving or getting something
5		*blows my mind	E	Something I never imagined or something unexpected.
6		*Chatty Cathy	F	Refresh one's memory
7		*newbie	G	A person who talks and talks
8		*pet peeve	H	To be in a state of gentle ferment while ideas come up
9		*brush up	I	Something that irritates you
10		*one step up	J	A person who is new to something, slang

Choose any one of the (starred) idioms above and write a sentence for it.

Who would you like to hire with when you graduate? List two different options.
If you are retired, who would you like to interview, dream big.

1)
2)

Choose one of the two options and tell why in one well written paragraph.
20 points

Unit 16: Contrastive Analysis

name	
number	

Match the vocabulary to the meaning.

1		difference that makes the difference	A	keep working to the end
2		Cup of tea	B	tired
3		Go with the flow	C	something you enjoy doing and that is easy for you
4		Down in the dumps	D	easy to start with everything going well
5		get off to a flying start	E	the important thing that causes the change to occur
6		hang in there	F	came smoothly and was easy to do
7		hit the hay	G	Sad or discouraged
8		sweet chick	H	go to bed
9		Bright light	I	Nice girl that guys like
10		wiped out	J	A person who is outstanding, who shines

Do your own contrastive Analysis

Do your homework well:

B	body posture	
A	accessing cues	
G	gestures	
E	eye movements	
L	language patterns	

Stuck in a homework rut:

B	body posture	
A	accessing cues	
G	gestures	
E	eye movements	
L	language patterns	

Think about your experience. What is the difference that makes the difference for you?

Unit 17: Presuppositions

name	
number	

Match the vocabulary to the meaning.

1		presupposition	A	A statement we suppose or accept to be true
2		couple	B	Native to and originating in a particular region
3		nudge	C	Preparing for a future event that may or may not happen. (occur)
4		Get the ball rolling	D	Gentle push
5		indigenous	E	Start
6		just in case	F	Idiom, meaning 2-3 items or things

7. Georgia is tired and has a paper to do. She can just go to the internet and copy one on the topic she is assigned. She could change a few words to make it sound more like she did it. She does it and gets an A on the paper.

What is her map of the world? (circle)

A.	It is never ok to plagiarize someone else's work
B.	It is important to get enough sleep to stay healthy

8. Hans lived in Germany during WWII and often starved. Now he lives in the USA but he still remembers starving. His wife Gail always takes the food off the table as soon as he has his plate full so he does not eat too much food. (true story)

What is his positive intention?

A.	Food is an important resource and we should eat all of our food.
B.	It is important to eat all the food you can because you do not know when you will not have food.

9. Josh and his wife Tiffany want to go out on a date together. Dates are so romantic. Then grandma calls and says she is too tired to watch the children. They decide to take the children with them and go to the park for a walk.

Which presupposition is being used?

| |
| |

10. Tell about a time when you found that the map was not the territory.

| |
| |
| |
| |
| |
| |

Unit 18: Anchors and Pentagon of Excellence

name	
number	

Match the vocabulary to the meaning.

1		anchor	A	State of being, the quality of having existence
2		pentagon	B	Something that holds something else in place
3		shake it off	C	A five sided polygon.
4		state	D	Idiom for a filthy, derogatory sexual sign
5		dirty	E	Imagine yourself stepping into the future using the NLP program.
6		Ok or OK	F	Okay, acceptable
7		future pace	G	Created carefully.
8.		crafted	H	An NLP term for breaking state
9		Pavlov	I	Idiom for getting something done so it is no longer something you have to worry about.
10		Off your back		Russian physiologist who lived from 1849-1936

Create your own NLP Pentagon of Excellence

You may be asked to tell about any one of these in class.

Color and etc.	
Time when you were excellent	
Time when you were excellent	
Time when you were excellent	
Words you heard someone say when you were excellent	

Unit 19: Meta Model Traps A

name	
number	

Match the vocabulary to the meaning.

1		distortion	A	We put a lot of information together mentally
2		vent	B	Lump things together and delete unnecessary details
3		internal dialogue	C	Distort information that comes in
4		reframe	D	To look at something in a different way
5		trap	E	An amount, to gather together all the bits of a problem into one amount
6		chunk	F	Someone to talk to
7		generalization	G	To talk about a problem and get it off your chest, to let go of stress
8.		deletion	H	self-talk
9.		escape	I	Get away from
10.		sounding board	J	A thing that catches and stops something

Underline the trap words in each sentence. Above it write another word or words
That could reframe the trap to a more positive one.

1. You can't do the job.
2. You shouldn't get this right.
3. It is impossible to rake all these leaves.
4. You must do this now.
5. You couldn't shovel all this snow.
6. You are impossible.
7. I am unclear how to make the Chinese food.
8. I am unsure how to make the "R" sound.
9. You make me to do the dishes.
10. We must get our homework done tonight.

Unit 19: Meta Model Traps B

name	
number	

Match the vocabulary to the meaning.

1		Don't understand	A	A small part is controlling the whole of something
2		Drop in the bucket	B	Confused and bewildered
3		Surface structure	C	Testimony
4		Deep structure	D	Murky, obscure, totally unclear
5		Tail wagging the dog	E	To be very, very boring.
6		Clear as mud	F	Tediously long in speaking or writing, wearisome
7		Clear as day	G	What we see and hear on the surface
8		Die of boredom	H	The way you represent the world internally in your body and mind
9		Long-winded	I	A small part of the whole
10		Work it to death	J	Obvious and easy to see or understand
11		extrapolate	K	To twist a report or story to one's advantage
12		meld	L	To infer something from something that is already known
13		deposition	M	Adding so much detail and going over something so much that the original loses its meaning
14		(different) spin on	N	Join in a popular activity so you can share in the success
15		Jumped on the bandwagon	O	combine with something else

Choose five of the words and idioms above and use each of them in a sentence.

1.
2.
3.
4.
5.

Unit 19: Meta Model Traps C

name	
number	

Put the words in the correct categories.

Language Trap	
Model operators of necessity	
Modal operators of possibility	
Universal Qualifiers	
You make me	

Word bank	It causes me	always	Can't	Impossible
must	Have to	everyone	Won't	They make me

For each of these language traps write a sentence using the trap and an escape. See the sample for help.

Language Trap	
Sample You make me	
Trap	They make me so mad I could just spit cotton. (this is an idiom meaning you are very angry)
Escape	How can they make you angry, could you choose not to be angry and would that better help you deal with the problem?
Model operators of necessity	
Trap	
Escape	
Modal operators of possibility	
Trap	
Escape	
Universal Qualifiers	
Trap	
Escape	
You make me	
Trap	
Escape	

Unit 20: SCORE A

		name	
		number	

Match the vocabulary to the meaning.

1		Solutions	A	the person who guides the explorer
2		SCORE	B	an NLP program to find solutions to problems
3		Problem	C	Where will you be when the problem is solved, what happens after you get your goal.
4		Symptom	D	the person who is doing the program and exploring options to solve the problem
5		cause	E	the difference from where you are to where you want to be
6		outcome	F	what causes the problem, things that stop you from getting your goal
7		resources	G	What you need to solve the problem, your operators
8.		exit or effect	H	Where you want to be, your goal
9.		explorer	I	Answers to problems
10.		guide	J	Where you are when you want to be somewhere else
11.		spacial	K	clumsy
12.		two left feet	L	Do what comes naturally.
13.		go with the flow	M	something that gets you to the outcome
14.		emerge	N	come to the surface
15.		installation of a strategy	O	do a program over and over to get it in the neurology
16.		driver	P	of or pertaining to space

Find a short news article to present to the class. Write 2 closed and two open ended questions to ask your team mates. Put the questions below.

17	closed	
18	closed	
19	open	
20	open	

Unit 20: SCORE B

name	
number	

The SCORE could be used to write a talk. Imagine you are working for a research company developing a new product. Write a few ideas that could be made into a talk to present to talk investors into investing in your research. If you want to do another topic consult with your teacher.

Steps	A word or two about what you might talk about
Cause	
Symptom	
Resources	
Outcome	
Effect	

Which do you like best, the SCORE or the Dancing SCORE? Why?

Unit 21: Meta Model

name	
number	

Write a challenge question for each of these Meta Model examples.

Have fun creating your answers with things that you are interested in.

Sample Deletions	This is a good time to start.
What is it that you plan to start?	
Glad you asked, we are going to go to Wuhan Province this summer and now is a good time to start planning while we are on spring break and do not need to worry about our studies.	
Deletions	We will do a big project.
Q-	
A-	
Unspecified referential Index (URI)	People are always helping me get around in China.
Q-	
A-	
Lost Performative	We should not eat candy.
Q-	
A-	
Unspecified Verbs	The boys exercised.
Q-	
A-	
Nominalizations	Our new team leader is calling out for justice!
Q-	
A-	
Presuppositions	All Chinese students are bright therefore there is no cheating going on.
Q-	
A-	
Mind Reading	I know you are excited.
Q-	
A-	
cause/effect	When you get in that car I always worry.
Q-	
A-	
Complex Equivalent	They can't be interested. They didn't respond to my letter.
Q-	
A-	

Unit 22: Disney Creativity Strategy

	name	
	number	

Match the vocabulary to the meaning.

1		Legend in his own time	A	Not practical for real life
2		Flight of fancy	B	Not good, sour
3		Storyboarding	C	To look at the whole thing, 3 or 4th perceptual position
4		creative juices are flowing	D	Get serious about something
5		Out of this world	E	Very excessive
6		Spring board	F	Extraordinary, beyond belief, better than the best
7		symmetrical	G	A group that is not united will not accomplish the goal, they will fall apart.
8.		lemon	H	someone who is famous while yet alive
9.		a house divided against itself cannot stand	I	A creative process where animators draw out the goal then break it down into pieces and then break the pieces up yet again
10.		Fly as high as a kite	J	time when a person or group is feeling very creative
11.		Gets down to brass tacks	K	Think big thoughts, dream big dreams
12		See the big picture	L	You already have it good and now you are getting something more.
13.		Icing on the cake	M	A beginning to jump you into new ideas, start
14.		Over the top	N	Balanced, equal on both sides

On the dream you did, write down a few words about each step. Remember just one dream.

Dreamer	
Critic	
Realist	

Unit 23: Metaphors

name	
number	

Match the vocabulary to the meaning.

1		metaphor	A	The message you want to give or deliver
2		more than one light	B	Simply a figure of speech that compares two unlike things
3		point	C	To think of something in more than one way. A butterfly and education
4		tie it back	D	The value of the money paid
5		money's worth	E	Bring the thought back to the original idea or thought

Choose any one of the pictures above and use it as a metaphor. For example: life is like a race, carry your brief case and always be prepared for the next client and you will win the race. (Pictures from Microsoft Clip Art.) Do two.

1)

2)

Unit 24: Conflict Resolution

name	
number	

Match the vocabulary and idioms to the meaning.

1		Caught between a rock and a hard spot	A	Idiom for being in conflict with another
2		compromise	B	Set an issue aside for a time
3		alternatives	C	Easy to detect or see
4		It takes two to tango	D	A state of being perplexed and uncertain
5		Be of two minds	E	The act of opposing or resisting, to be in conflict
6		opposition	F	No real desired choices
7		quandary	G	Each side of a conflict gives a little and takes a little
8		obvious	H	Different choices or courses of action
9		shelf it	I	It needs be that there are two people with different ideas in opposition to have a conflict
10		Be at odds with each other	j	Idiom for internal conflict

Choose a conflict to resolve. Write your notes here. Do not write in complete sentences, just write quick phrases to help you remember.

	Problem on left hand	Problem on right hand
Imagine each as a person and describe the		
Environment		
Behavior		
Capabilities		
Beliefs and Values		
Identity		
Purpose		
Positive Intention		
Positive intention of the positive intention		

Find the level at which they reach some mutual agreement and circle it.

Unit 25: Swish Pattern

name	
number	

Match the vocabulary and idioms to the meaning.

1		Compulsion	A	A process where order happens caused by local interactions between the parts of an initially disordered system.
2		obsession	B	Being habitually occupied with or involved in something.
3		Self-organization theory	C	A strong, usually irresistible impulse to do something
4		Behavioral psychology	D	An area of psychology that combines elements of philosophy, methodology, and theory
5		die for	E	Slang word for pimples that occur when a face breaks out
6		Zits	F	Really like something
7		Addiction	G	Richly appealing to the senses or the mind.
8		Crave	H	An idea, image, desire or feeling that dominates ones thoughts or feelings
9		Luster	I	Softly reflected light, a sheen
10		Luscious	J	To want something very much

Choose any two of the words above and write a well-written sentence using the word correctly but not defining the word.

1.
2.

Compare and Contrast. Do the Swish Pattern and write a short reflection. Note three submodalities you enhanced and changed. (you can do more.) There is a submodalities worksheet on the next page.

Cue Image	
Desired Image	
Submodality	
Submodality	

Submodality	
Reflection	

Submodalities work sheet

Cue Image					Desired Image				
Visual					Visual				
bright				dim	bright				dim
colorful				Black/white	colorful				Black/white
close				far	close				far
clear				hazy	clear				hazy
large				small	large				small
associated				dissociated	in				out
flat				3-D	flat				3-D
still				moving	still				moving
framed				panoramic	framed				panoramic
Auditory					Auditory				
loud				soft	loud				soft
high				low	high				low
left				right	left				right
fast				slow	fast				slow
close				far	close				far
words				Tone/sounds	words				Tones/sounds
clear				muffled	clear				muffled
near				far	near				far
constant				intermittent	constant				intermittent
mono				stereo	mono				stereo
rhythm				free	rhythm				free
Kinesthetic					Kinesthetic				
strong				weak	strong				weak
large				small	large				small
heavy				light	heavy				light
smooth				rough	smooth				rough
constant				jolting	constant				jolting
hot				cold	hot				cold
intense				gentle	intense				gentle
still				moving	still				moving
constant				intermittent	constant				intermittent
emotions				Flat line	emotions				Flat line

Unit 26: V-K Dissociation

name	
number	

Match the vocabulary and idioms to the meaning.

1		therapeutic	A	Something that happens, an event or incident
2		synthesis	B	To say or view something in a different way, often clearer or better
3		reframe	C	The effect an event on a person (or thing)
4		impact	D	To become unstable, to upset the stability of something
5		manipulate	E	Combination of parts to form a whole
6		occurrence	F	Providing or assisting in the treatment of disease and/or a cure
7		destabilize	G	a word that stands for a sound, an onomatopoeia,
8		life's real	H	To move, arrange operate or control often in a skillful manner
9		warts and all	I	With all defects and imperfections seen, not idealized
10		chi-click	J	Actual and happening, not a dream or an illusion

1. Create a sentence using one of the two idioms.

2. Create a sentence using one of the vocabulary words.

3. Write about a time that was impacting to you that you will work with or did work with.

4. Write about what happened when you did the V-K Dissociation Program.

Unit 27: Xavier's Strategy

name	
number	

1		triage	A	Getting something you were not expecting
2		silo	B	Suitable and appropriate name, it fits the thing named
3		aptly named	C	*Cliché* (overused expression) for a very large disaster.
4		essence	D	Remain happy or joyful in a difficult situation
5		dispatch	E	A usually tall cylindrical structure, often found next to a barn, in which grain and silage are stored
6		recipe for disaster	F	To sort or rank things in terms of importance or priority
7		disaster of epic proportion	G	A mixture of people and events that could only possibly result in trouble
8		cognitively impaired	H	A condition where the brain does not function as fully as a normal brain does. Causes include genetics, accident or illness.
9		secondary gain	I	To relegate to a specific destination or send on specific business
10		Keep the chin up	J	The most important part or aspect of something, the core

Xavier's Strategy

Think of something you would like to organize and use the strategy.

The thing you will explore:

Choose three main topics and then chunk down the items or needs into the correct silos.

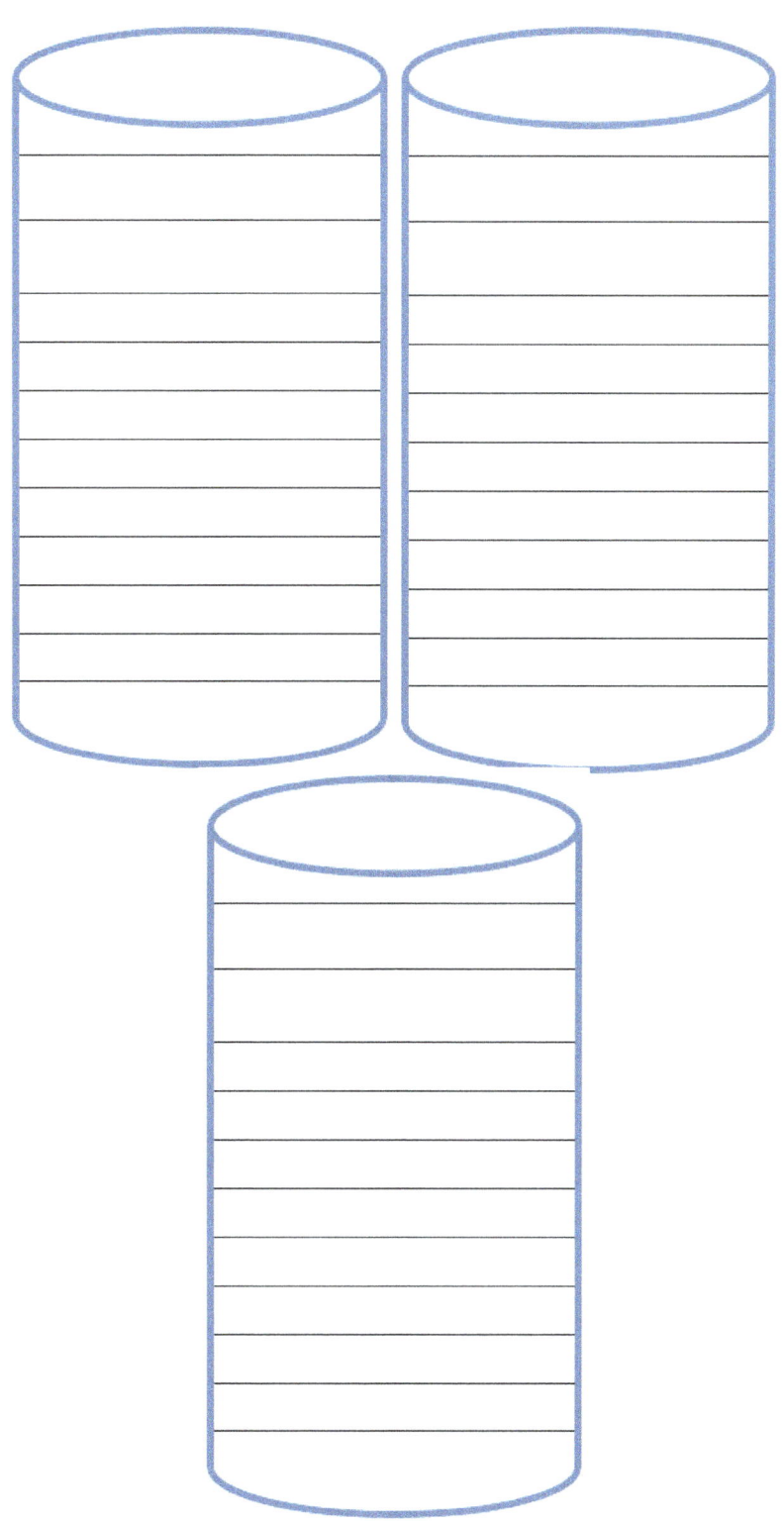

Unit 28: Reframe

name	
number	

Match the vocabulary to the meaning. Idioms are starred.

1		Top of the world*	A	Not judge someone harshly understanding that people see the world in different ways
2		Devastated	B	Easily get a top grade on an exam or easily do well when confronted with a challenge or test in life
3		Sink into despair*	C	Idiom for something that will cause very serious problems, especially to the world as you know it now
4		end of the world*	D	A clique meaning an upcoming problem appears to be of magnified importance
5		dance up a storm*	E	Bring to total ruin
6		Cut some slack*	F	Idiom meaning to lose all feeling of hope
7		Loom large*	G	In a boring lifestyle or pattern of behavior that never changes
8.		Ace the test*	H	Idiom meaning to do something with a lot of energy
9		egg him on*	I	Idiom meaning to encourage or urge someone to continue doing something, usually something unwise
10		Stuck in a rut*	J	Idiom for everything is happy and wonderful

Below are some words that often have a negative connotation. Find some synonyms that will reframe the words into a positive light.

Hard (work)	Money (rich)	nasty

Boring	necessary	hasty

difficult	plod	obsessed

Enjoy the challenge of enhancing your vocabulary by exploring positive connotations that will expand your English vocabulary and even help you help others.

Unit 29: Six Step Reframe

name	
number	

Match the vocabulary to the meaning.

1		stiff drink	A	Acting as if insane or crazy, as if they are not fully present in their mind
2		Crazy as a loon	B	The expressive side of one's imagination, and a prelude to creative thought (this idiom also has a sexual meaning. Use it carefully to make sure you mean what you say.
3		out of their mind	C	Interrupt with a comment
4		piped up	D	An unconscious or involuntary body movement made in response to a thought or idea rather than to sensory input
5		darn level best	E	To make better, to improve
6		bats in his belfry	F	Potent or strong drink, having a strong physiological effect
7		ideomotor	G	Negotiate
8.		bargain	H	Trying as hard as it can with what is available
9		ameliorate	I	To be eccentric or a little crazy, much as the erratic flying of bats
10		creative juices are flowing	J	Acting as if insane, much as a loon bird does

Do the Six-Step Reframe

1.	Relax and enter your quiet, contemplative state of mind. Focus your attention on your problem or symptom. Write down the problem or symptom.	
2.	Establish communication with your symptom. Pay particular attention to words, images and feelings. Tell how you communicated and what your cognitive mind learned.	
3.	Ask the positive intention or purpose of the symptom. Write it down.	
4.	Go to your creative part and ask it to find three or more other choices to satisfy the positive intention but having no negative consequences. List the choices.	
5.	Have the part that creates the problem or symptom review the choices and accept them. If not acceptable repeat the process. If not accepted write down the further choices that you came up with.	
6.	Ask other parts if they agree to the choices. If there are any objects address them repeating the cycle until all parts are in agreement. If you can, write what the results were for you.	

This process was originally created by Grinder and Bandler with Judith DeLozier as a result of their work with Milton Erickson and Virginia Satir.

Unit 30: Intervision

name	
number	

Match the vocabulary and idioms to the meaning.

1		innovators	A	Idiom meaning stopped, unable to move, turned to stone
2		strategy	B	Way of seeing things that is individual and like no one else
3		synergy	C	New and not like anything formerly used, unique
4		Intervision	D	A quandary, perplexing
5		supervision	E	One person has the answers and helps others find them
6		perspective	F	The opposite of supervision. No one person is in charge, all work together, the team is equal, all is mutually visible
7		novel	G	The sum of the whole is greater than the parts
8		intervisor	H	Person who is helping advise in this inter-related group
9		petrified	I	The science or art of using all the tools available to execute the plan
10		dilemma	J	Vvisionaries, people who are changing the world

Draw here the problem and the solution. Remember this is a group activity. This is to be a drawing not a word explanation. The strategy is done in two parts. Do the first part, listen to the others in your group and share your explanation. Then proceed as a group to the second pat where you draw your solution.

Problem	Solution